EDITED BY

STEVE DUCK
JULIA T. WOOD

CONFRONTING RELATIONSHIP CHALLENGES

UNDERSTANDING RELATIONSHIP PROCESSES SERIES
VOLUME 5

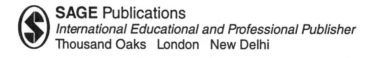

SAGE Publications
International Educational and Professional Publisher
Thousand Oaks   London   New Delhi

For information address:

 SAGE Publications, Inc.
2455 Teller Road
Thousand Oaks, California 91320

SAGE Publications Ltd.
6 Bonhill Street
London EC2A 4PU
United Kingdom

SAGE Publications India Pvt. Ltd.
M-32 Market
Greater Kailash I
New Delhi 110 048 India

Printed in the United States of America

Library of Congress Cataloging-in-Publication Data

Main entry under title:

Confronting relationship challenges / edited by Steve Duck and Julia T. Wood.
     p.   cm. — (Understanding relationship processes series ; 5)
   Includes bibliographical references and indexes.
   ISBN 0-8039-5648-7 (cl). — ISBN 0-8039-5649-5 (pb)
   1. Interpersonal relations. 2. Interpersonal conflict.   I. Duck,
Steve. II. Wood, Julia T. III. Series.
HM132.U54   1993 vol. 5
302—dc20   94-23540

95 96 97 98 99 10 9 8 7 6 5 4 3 2 1

Production Editor: Yvonne Könneker
Ventura Typesetter: Janelle LeMaster

CONFRONTING RELATIONSHIP CHALLENGES

UNDERSTANDING RELATIONSHIP PROCESSES

Series Editor
Steve Duck, *University of Iowa*

This series of books on the theme **Understanding Relationship Processes** provides a coherent and progressive review of current thinking in the field. Uniquely organized around the notion of relational competence, the six volumes constitute a contemporary, multidisciplinary handbook of relationship research for advanced students and professionals in psychology, sociology, communication, family studies, and education.

Volumes in the Series

1. INDIVIDUALS IN RELATIONSHIPS

2. LEARNING ABOUT RELATIONSHIPS

3. SOCIAL CONTEXT AND RELATIONSHIPS

4. DYNAMICS OF RELATIONSHIPS

5. CONFRONTING RELATIONSHIP CHALLENGES

6. UNDER-STUDIED RELATIONSHIPS

Contents

Series Preface

This short series, Understanding Relationship Processes, responds to recent calls for attention to processes in relationships. A close look at the nature of processes in relationships will reveal that, over and above the importance of change, temporality, and an orientation to the future, there lies beneath most process thinking on relationships the implicit notion of competent use of knowledge across time. For example, this assumption is true of many elements of the work on relationships, such as the (competent) transition to marriage, (skilled) conflict management, (appropriate) self-disclosure, and (orderly) organization or (satisfactory) maintenance of relationships diachronically. The assumption also is contained in any discussion of intimacy assessment or creation of "a couple" (by which authors evaluate, usually implicitly, the degrees of intimacy or progress that are adequate, allowable, suitable, or competent) and is latent in discussions of relationship breakdown where researchers treat breakdown as failure or incompetence, contrasted with skill or competence.

Such competence is evident in, and constrained by, a variety of influences on behavior. In focusing on some of these topics, this series moves conceptually outward; that is, the series began with the contributions of individuals—and their developmental experiences—to relationships and moved toward social context and interpersonal interaction. Individuals bring into relationships their individual characteristics and factors that reflect their point in the life cycle and their developmental achievements. Individuals are influenced by the social settings (situational, cultural, linguistic, and societal) in which relationships take place; they are constrained and influenced by the structural, transactional, behavioral, and communicative contexts of their relationships; and they sometimes conduct relationships in dysfunctional environments or disrupted emotional contexts. The series takes these contextual themes in sequence and deals with the latest research and thinking to address these topics.

Accordingly, each volume focuses on a particular context or arena for relationship activity. The volumes of the series are as follows:

Individuals in Relationships. Volume 1 deals particularly with the ways in which internal or intrapersonal context is provided by structures of the mind or of knowledge that are prerequisite to success in relationships; however, rather than focusing on such things as if they were the end of the story, the chapters place such knowledge styles and structures in context by referring frequently to *behavioral* effects of such structures.

Learning About Relationships. Volume 2 covers especially the skills and experiences in childhood that lay the groundwork for competence as a properly functioning relater in adult life; the volume emphasizes the wide range of social sources from which development of competence is derived and the richness of the social sources from which developing minds acquire their sense of relationship competence.

Social Context and Relationships. Volume 3 focuses especially on the social structural constraints within which relationships are located and the ways in which the two partners must negotiate and deal with the dialectical and interior pressures that are created by such contexts.

Dynamics of Relationships. Volume 4 deals with the dyadic management of relational conduct in the context provided by the earlier volumes and explores the issues of competent relational management that are created by the transactions of relating—not the factors that influence or prepare the ground for relationships, but the actual *doing* of them.

Confronting Relationship Challenges (Steve Duck & Julia T. Wood, coeditors). Volume 5 turns the series toward the difficult side of relationships and away from any implication that relationships are only good and delightful. Relationship processes encompass "binds" as well as "bonds" (in Wiseman's [1986] elegant play on words), and both must be included in an understanding of relationship processes.

Under-Studied Relationships: Off the Beaten Track (Julia T. Wood & Steve Duck, coeditors). Volume 6 recognizes and begins to rectify existing scholarship's tendency to focus on only particular types of relationships and particular issues in relationships, and thus to ignore or underacknowledge the range of real-world relationships and the myriad processes they entail. A full understanding of relationship processes must include consideration of theoretically inconvenient and/or socially disfavored instances as well as instances (or phenomena) whose value and importance traditionally have been acknowledged in research.

STEVE DUCK

8

Volume Preface

The first two volumes in this series, **Understanding Relationship Processes**, outline the contribution of individual knowledge to the conduct of relationships, whether from the point of view of cognitive structure or of the learning that takes place in childhood. The next two volumes explore the relational contexts provided by, respectively, various external, nonindividual, and nondyadic influences, and by interior, dynamic, transactional processes. Volume 3, *Social Context and Relationships,* focuses on contexts provided by various social, cultural, structural, and network processes. Volume 4, *Dynamics of Relationships,* focuses on the sense in which specific relational behaviors are located in *sequences* and in partners' continual accommodations to one another.

The present book, *Confronting Relationship Challenges,* Volume 5 in the series, moves us toward a different set of issues— that is, what can go wrong with relationships or what can make them troublesome. The consistent attention to values, benefits, and joys of relationships, coupled with scant attention to problems, challenges, and costs of relationships, has cultivated a body of scholarship that could be interpreted as suggesting relationships are unreservedly good things. Writers have indicated the benefits and blessings of relationships, the fact that they are close and supportive, and the evidence showing that we all regard them as central to our lives and happiness. However, that pleasantness has another aspect. That which can be pleasing can also deny pleasure; that which can be supportive can fail to provide support; that which can generate happiness can also prompt pain and, indeed, suffering.

The contributors to the present volume consider some of the ways in which relationships provide us with challenges. Not all aspects of relationships are good, even when the relationships are close, and some require considerable skills of management and tolerance. Relationships involve shame and anger as well as joy and love, acts of betrayal or letting down as well as displays of commitment. In addition to challenges within relationships, everyday irritations from outside relationships can also seep in to tarnish our connections with other people. And within relationships themselves there are dynamics that can create tension, resentment, and disappointment from time to time.

As well as looking at such aspects of relationships, the chapters in the present volume make the subtler point that relationships themselves are not simple positive/negative, black/white, good/bad, competent/challenging things. Many relationship experiences are an oxymoronic mixture of elements (love/hate, for example, or the sweet sorrows of parting). An obvious example is the fact that pain as well as growth can result from conflict. Furthermore, several aspects of relating are not self-evidently positive or negative, but may appear in the light of later occurrences to have been mixed blessings or perhaps the reverse of what participants first interpreted (or understood) them to be. Finally, retrospection may select and selectively edit different aspects of relational events as characteristic of those events, so that positivity is transformed into negativity, and vice versa.

This volume and this series thus challenge any appearance that relationships consist of single interactions devoid of contexts, unitary experiences devoid of nuance and reformulation, or developments that are not transformative of meaning. Relationships are more than mere sequences of behavior or cumulations of individual acts; they gain their existence from the meanings of such sequences and cumulations—and the human processes of creating and sharing meaning are both complex and continuous (Duck, 1994a). In investing activities and communication with dynamic continuity, partners in relationships create a context within which to comprehend their connectedness to one another and to confront the challenges it brings.

In Chapter 1, Duck and Wood assert the importance of exploring both rough and smooth contexts of relationships and of considering how partners manage the two elements together to produce a sense of the relationship's character. Unpleasant relational experiences are important for the development of sound *theories* that should be able to account for negative relational experiences, recognizing them as common human experiences that are as fully part of relationships as are positive experiences. The combination of positive and negative experiences creates the wholeness that most people experience in their relationships.

Retzinger opens Chapter 2 by noting that quarrels are common in personal relationships. She then explores the role of anger and shame in the conduct of everyday relationships. Taking the view that conflict is a response to a lapse in the social bond and the emergence and handling of shame and anger, Retzinger seeks to fulfill the mission of the present volume by focusing on these processes that underlie conflict in personal relationships. She argues that when persons interact in conflict there are exchanges of meaning. Meaning is intricately tied to the bond between the individuals, the manner in which they communicate, and the emotions expressed and exchanged. As a result, some kinds of interaction may be more prone to conflict than others. Retzinger argues that if the role of emotions and meaning in conflict can be described, we may have a better understanding of how relationships are built, maintained, damaged, and repaired.

In Chapter 3, Wiseman and Duck deal with a common relationship that receives virtually no research attention, that of enemies. Just as people have friends, they have enemies, antagonists, and opponents who try to make their lives more difficult and who interfere with their attainment of goals. Enemies are not merely conceptual abstractions, but persons who actively interfere with the processes of social life. They represent a particularly important and interesting relationship challenge for ordinary folks and also offer students of social relations some important theoretical challenges. Enemyship is a distinctive type of relationship that most existing theories of relationships are quite unable to explain. Furthermore, the analysis suggests that, far from being simple opposites, friendship and enemyship have a certain number of important similarities; however, they also have some distinctly different dynamics. For example, whereas mutual acknowledgment is a sine qua non of friendship, a feature of enemyship in many cases is its unacknowledged character—and *that* needs management.

Coleman and Ganong focus in Chapter 4 on the challenge of reconfiguring a "family" after divorce. Pointing out that the traditional model of "the family" overlooks a number of possible alternative structures that have recently come to prominence, the authors consider the comparisons between revision of parents' and children's roles in a family and between the processes that occur when two adults reconceptualize themselves and their roles after divorce. Coleman and Ganong indicate that the emotional challenges of reconfiguring a family are compounded by various institutional insensitivities that add to the difficulties of reconfigured families. This leads them to recommend that scholars develop models that contribute to the more complete institutionalization of postdivorce reconfigured families.

In Chapter 5, Wright and Wright assert that it would be most useful to shift the currently dominant focus on the relational challenges represented by codependency as a personality syndrome to codependent relating as a process that emerges and persists within a particular kind of personal relationship. They point out that a process view is implicit, if not explicit, in most present-day approaches to codependency treatment. These approaches emphasize the necessity of the codependent's altering her or his pattern of relating to the "dependent" in order for any personal or relational change to occur. One implication of the proposed model is that codependent relating is not likely to surface apart from an appropriate "mix" of personal and situational influences. Those influences include the self-attributes of not one, but two individuals, whom we label as a "codependent" and a "dependent." Wright and Wright thus offer an exciting new—relational—way to conceptualize the codependency challenge.

In Chapter 6, West explores the particularly dark challenge of relationship violence through the lens of an ideological analysis. Taking the view that ideology is built into the way in which we all conduct our relationships and also shapes the contexts and partners' options within those contexts (compare Volume 3 of this series, *Social Context and Relationships*), West presents the case that an ideology of "normal" family structure and the relative power of men and women pervades the ways in which violence in relationships is treated. Presenting evidence that various cultural institutions are ideologically invested in supporting a family structure in which some relational partners are seen as the "property" of other people, West indicates how such contexts affect those persons who are the victims of violence in relationships.

Bowen and Michal-Johnson consider in Chapter 7 one of the most pressing social challenges of the present age: HIV/AIDS. They examine three specific high-risk relational situations that militate against individuals' protecting themselves against HIV/AIDS: alcohol abuse, drug abuse, and relationship violence. Their treatment of each of these contexts is consistent with this series's focus on processes, as they specifically concentrate on the personal and interpersonal processes that increase or decrease the HIV risk of sexual activity. Just as this particular volume challenges many of the assumptions that underlie traditional understandings of relationship goals and behaviors, Bowen and Michal-Johnson ask us to consider how HIV risk challenges traditional assumptions about relationship processes.

In Chapter 8, Lyons and Meade develop an analogy between the remodeling of a home and the changes that take place in a relationship when one of the involved persons develops a serious chronic illness. They ask what relational adaptations are necessary to accommodate to the physical problems and what challenges the partners particularly face in coping with such adaptations. Lyons and Meade offer an intriguing interpretation of some of these changes in terms of dialectical theory and stress the paradoxical unity of competing forces in the relationship that are brought about by the illness and its management.

In the final chapter, Harvey, Barnes, Carlson, and Haig discuss the impact of memories on the process of grieving and the effects of bereavement as these experiences affect the survivors of the deaths of loved ones and how those deaths have affected them over a period of time. The authors discuss the idea of being "held captive" by memory, as both a positive and a challenging experience for the survivor. Because such memories constitute an important context for the continued life of the surviving person, the memories construct and shape not only feelings about the dead loved one but also the survivor's experience of everyday life. Another topic of the analysis is how habits connected to interaction with dead loved ones also may exert continued power over the bereaved person.

Together, the chapters in the present volume add considerable depth of perspective to our understanding of relationship processes by indicating the dynamic crucible in which amalgamation of the everyday-life routines and forces of communicative, psychological, sociological, and developmental influences takes place. They thus follow up on the argument implicit in the third and fourth volumes of this series, that relationships have many sides that are lived by the participants in contexts, not merely "outcomes" produced by cognitive states or relational history. Relationships are constructed and forged by real human beings facing everyday dilemmas and dynamically wrestling to construct meaningful interpretations of themselves, each other, and their relationships as all evolve and interact in continually changing contexts.

STEVE DUCK
JULIA T. WOOD

1

For Better, for Worse, for Richer, for Poorer: The Rough and the Smooth of Relationships

Steve Duck

Julia T. Wood

The present series is devoted to the exploration of processes of relationships, which is a subject that proclaims the central importance of the continuities and contexts of particular features of relationships to our understanding of how relationships work and how they fail. Over the course of time, relationships are associated with both happy and unhappy feelings and sometimes with bittersweet moments where the two blend. Also, partners presumably experience variability in each other's (and their own) feelings and behavior across time. In short, relationships hardly ever turn out to be the monotonic enterprises that labels such as *friendship, marriage,* and *love* all too easily suggest. In the processes of everyday living, even close partners encounter challenges and travails, hit

1

flat spots, have relational "bad hair days," and generally mix the rough with the smooth in ways wisely foreseen by the writers of traditional wedding vows. The present chapter and this book series assert the importance of exploring both rough and smooth contexts of relationships and especially the value of considering ways in which partners manage the two elements together to produce a sense of their relationship's character.

The observation that ordinary folk regard "relationships" as central to happiness (Klinger, 1977) has too long obscured the fact that relationships are also sources of frustration and challenge. Even people who read the relationship literature know that processes of relationship dissolution dog ordinary experience (Duck, 1982; Orbuch, 1992), that violence occurs in intimate relationships (Christopher, Owens, & Stecker, 1993; Deal & Wampler, 1986; West, 1993), and that friends and lovers can be mean, petty, vindictive, and cruel to one another. Well before many of us were born, the lyrics of popular songs bemoaned the dark side of relationships, one in particular noting, "You always hurt the one you love."

Despite the obviousness of pain and challenge in relationships, for every 50 research studies on love, there might be only a single analysis of hate (Shoenewolf, 1991); for every 75 on caring, there may be only 1 on neglect (La Gaipa, 1990); for every 100 studies of attachment, we find a single study of revenge (Emmons, 1992); and for every 1,000 on attraction, there might be only a handful on repulsion or the "pangs o' despised love" that Shakespeare eloquently identified 400 years ago (Hindy, Schwartz, & Brodksy, 1989).

In this chapter we will discuss some of these "darker sides" of relating that present continual challenges to relaters, yet have so far been largely overlooked by both research and theory. The remaining chapters in the present volume identify specific challenges, some of them common (management of shame and anger), some of them less common yet still familiar (grief, the reconfiguration of family structure after divorce, enemies), and others more remote from most lives but still realities (sexual aggression and violence, high-risk sex, physical handicaps). We focus in the present chapter on a range of less-than-pleasant relational experiences in personal relationships. We believe not only that such experiences stand in need of fuller exploration per se, but, more important, that study of them is important for the development of sound *theories* of relationships and relating. To this end we propose a preliminary model that offers criteria for differentiating among relationship challenges that are worthy of study in future attempts to develop relational theory.

Theories should be able to account for negative relational experiences not by regarding them as special or unusual cases, but by recognizing them as common human experiences that are as fully part of relationships as are positive experiences. It is the combination of positive and negative experiences—and the definition and management of the one in the context of the other—that creates the wholeness that most people experience in their relationships. Furthermore, labels such as *positive* and *negative* are too often simplistic and misleading. Many "positive" relational elements have implications that may be "negative" (e.g., family love involves obligations both real and "felt"; Stein, 1993), and some processes traditionally regarded as "negative" may have "positive" outcomes (as some conflicts may actually result in relationship development and growth; Lloyd & Cate, 1985) or may be interpreted by partners as salutary for their relationship (e.g., conflicts can lead to the assertion of individuality, generation of respect for another's strongly held views, or clarification of boundaries of relational roles; Wood, Dendy, Dordek, Germany, & Varallo, 1994).

Thus we not only challenge the tendency to overlook negativity as an integral part of relationship life, we also are skeptical about the tendency to see negativity and positivity as clear and unequivocally opposite. Rather, we suspect that "good" and "bad" relational experiences are sometimes a matter of personal definition and personal meaning, but always intertwined, sometimes seamlessly, in the broader human enterprise of making sense of experience (Duck, 1994a, 1994c). In this chapter we therefore concurrently place the "dark side" in the context of the overall process of relating, depict the two as inherently connected rather than as distinct parts or types of relationships, and question how labels of darkness or negativity are imposed.

The Janus Character of Relating

It has been known for centuries that any particular emotion is seldom isolated from other emotions. Most feelings are shadowed by contrasting or qualifying ones. The most obvious example is the popularized "love/hate" relationship, but there are less dramatic examples also. For instance, one of the six love styles defined by Hendrick and Hendrick (1986) is *mania,* a kind of love that involves not only passion and devotion but negative feelings—jealousy, anxiety, dependency, possessiveness. If this be love, then it is something of a paradox, but so too are other styles of love. For instance, *agape* involves self-sacrifice, *eros* involves loss of control, and the life energy of *ludus* is uncertainty. Several languages recognize that although love is a positive emotion, it also involves disturbance of control of bodily functions (as in lovesickness, *Liebeskummer,* or the *crime passionel*). Our own language, too, is rich with metaphors that convey images of such loss or the consumption of self by the emotion: head over heels in love, falling in love, irresistible attraction, or consumed by passion, for instance (for further discussion of the role of metaphors in the framing of emotional experience, see Duck, 1994a; Kovecses, 1991). Thus even love, perhaps the most positively regarded of relational emotions, carries a large backpack of less positively regarded challenges that are nevertheless part of its character and inherent to the experience of loving.

Taking this observation further, Baxter (1993) and Rawlins (1992) have argued that relationships, in terms of both emotional structure and everyday practices, are subject to dialectical forces that challenge participants. For instance, there are a number of internal challenges that influence the management of self in personal relationships, such as connection/autonomy (the need to sustain independence along with interdependence in a relationship) or predictability/novelty (the need to enliven experience with novel stimulation yet also sustain a level of predictability and comforting certainty about the relationship). Researchers have also noted the thrust of the openness/closedness dialectic that faces a person with challenges to balance candor and discretion about personal feelings and experience. Baxter (1993) further discusses the ways in which such internal dialectics manifest an "external" counterpart, which calls on partners in a relationship to manage tensions between their relationship and the context in which they and it are immersed. For example, partners are free to construct an eccentrically personalized form of relationship in many respects, but still do not have absolute freedom from social constraints, norms, judgments, and consequences.

Baxter's point, similar to our own, is that dialectics are embodied in and managed through the actual interactions between people. In other words, dialectics and other relationship phenomena are practical challenges, not individual experiences that persons have, and partners continually handle them in the course of everyday life over extended series of interactions. To have an enemy is not merely to know that one is challenged in the abstract but to deal with the fact in one's everyday thoughts and activities, to unpick rumors and negative stories, to counteract ploys of the enemy, and to handle the enemy well in situations where it matters that one do so. Likewise, relational challenges of all sorts are practical and palpable experiences that are played out in complex contexts shaped by large historical and cultural influences as well as by relational history and the projected future and also by present activities and goals. Conflicts—what they mean and how they are enacted—in a personal relationship are shaped by the rest of the relationship and by its usual assumption of continuity. That is, a conflict not only has to be managed in the present but also may reflect what has gone before and may carry implications for the shape and conduct of the relationship for days, months, or even years ahead.

Ordinary Relationships
as Two-Faced Beasts

That the dark side of relationships has been undertheorized is regrettable. It has resulted in a lack that stands in need of correction (Cupach & Spitzberg, 1994; Duck, 1994c). Relationships are complex experiences in which grief and joy, pleasure and pain, enjoyment and irritation, ease and discomfort, satisfaction and frustration are recurrent and paired elements. However, this is perhaps balanced by a key point to be made in this chapter: *Life is like that*. Life experiences, including relationships and relational partners, entail not only contrasts but also uncertainty, as has been previously noted (Berger & Bradac, 1982). Furthermore, they are *variable* experiences (Duck, 1994a). To separate these effervescent variabilities, contingencies, and complexities neatly into positive and negative categories is to fall prey to the human tendency to look for labels that give meaning to (and also simplify) the seething untidiness of ordinary life.

Uncertainty and Variability as Emblematic of Relationships

An insufficiently acknowledged point about relational and other experience is the ongoingness that saturates them. Ongoingness translates to a sense of incompleteness that has led some to describe relationships as "unfinished business" (Bennett, in press; Duck, 1990; Shotter, 1992; Wood, 1995a, 1995b). The important implication of such a view is that relationship participants do not (yet) know the outcome of particular (inter)actions or the full consequences of individual actions. Such (inter)actions are embedded in longer-term sequences and patterns of relationship behavior to which any present action may pertain in convoluted and unforeseeable ways. For example, a present action or situation is not isolated from other mental contexts; it can refresh memories of past activity or excite expectation of goal fulfillment and the likely achievement of objectives (Edwards, Potter, & Middleton, 1992). Alternatively, present experience might be contoured by memories of previous hurts or triumphs of the sort that are all too easily lost when the meaning of relationship actions is ascribed exclusively to present observable exchanges (Duck, 1994a; Wood, 1995b). Hence some relational challenges do not surface as such at the time, because their consequences are not appreciated until later. By contrast, other challenges are immediately thrown down by apparently small behaviors because of their unforeseen impact on a partner's perceptions of larger relationship structures (e.g., a particular remark could create suspicion or threaten the relationship's future in the partner's eyes; for instance, a slightly flirtatious remark to a third party may be seen as infidelity by a partner who has experienced "straying" in the past) (see Radecki-Bush, Bush, & Jennings, 1988; Radecki-Bush, Farrell, & Bush, 1993).

This essential unknowability of outcomes is a feature of relating to which researchers have so far given too little attention (Billig, 1987; Duck, 1990, 1994a). Researchers have too often validated hypotheses through self-reported restricted-choice responses that strip away the uncertainty of outcomes. Furthermore, retrospective reports reinforce the *illusion* of certainty because they are accounts made *after* (at least some) consequences are known, though those consequences may not have been foreseen at the time of the experience. It is the inability to recognize all implications *as* we act that marks relational processes. The experienced reality is in fact that uncertainty clouds and contextualizes the *meaning* of relationship exchanges, interactions, and experiences. Thus for researchers to claim to be able to identify *the* meaning of particular acts is at best unwise unless those researchers have made strenuous efforts to contextualize the acts in the participants' own experience of the ongoingness of their unfinished relational business (Duck, 1994a). By stripping away such contexts, researchers also strip away much of the meaning of challenging human experience in unfolding relationships.

However, much research on relationships (as well as on social activity in general) also strips away a related aspect of everyday life experience: the multiplicity of elements and choices that confront people behaving in the real world. As Billig (1987) and Edwards and Potter (1992) have proposed, much of life is experienced as puzzlingly multisided possibilities that current simplified and stripped-down models of social behavior do not represent or include. Such processes entail numerous contingencies and alternative possibilities among which persons must choose. Whereas a look backward allows individuals to offer explanations of how they made up their minds or solved problems, or how past events "actually" unfolded, many events are opaque and intricate at the time they are being experienced. As we proposed earlier, the same observation is true of relationships. It is in the process of looking back over the history of relationships and projecting into the future that we are most able to designate the clear paths and turning points that much research has unearthed (Miell, 1984, 1987; Surra, 1987).

The research direction that we propose recognizes that people's lives are more complicated and less transparent than they have been represented to be in many studies. In these lives, real people are embroiled in an interpersonal milieu of a blooming, buzzing confusion of multiple and not always consistent contexts, signals, understandings, needs, values, goals, and emotions that present them with challenges for interpretation and action. The ambiguity that laces relational activity, as well as other activity, highlights the critical importance of human beings' efforts to make sense of experience (Duck, 1994a). As Hopper (1993) notes, "Beneath the intelligibility of social life lies a messy reality full of . . . discrepant and conflicting stimuli" (p. 810). Therefore, he argues, persons use "rhetorical devices that [impose] a sense of order onto situations that [are] otherwise fraught with ambiguous and contradictory events, emotions, and inclinations toward behavior" (p. 801).

From this point of view, persons make sense of their experience in serial fashion: That is, they attribute meaning to "events" each time they describe or contemplate those events, and they may construct such meaning differently on different occasions or for different audiences (Duck, 1994a). Thus the accounts that individuals give for other people's behaviors or for relational processes may legitimately vary across time as these persons reflect upon their circumstances (Harvey, Weber, & Orbuch, 1990). Indeed, we have known for some time in the personal relationships field that accounts given by partners after breakup are often different from the accounts they give when their relationships are going well (Weber, 1983). In unsophisticated accounts, one partner simply does not recall the positive aspects of the other partner at breakup; they are replaced by negative characteristics that dominate description. In sophisticated accounts, the elements to which a partner previously gave positive contours are now given negative ones: The steady, reliable date becomes the unimaginatively boring ex-fiancé; the strong, forceful friend becomes the selfish, uncompromising ex-friend; and the attentive, caring lover becomes the smothering "ex" (Felmlee, in press).

Such transformations in experience indicate to us the fallacy of regarding relational processes as inherently negative or positive in quality, or of separating the whole of relational activity into "challenges" and "not challenges" too breezily. This effort to find meaning is a constant of life (Duck, 1994a, 1994c)—and incidentally a constant of the lives of researchers concerned with relationships—that is based on the desire to categorize and qualify experiences that are otherwise uncertain, contingent, and ambiguous, and therefore chaotic, unmanageable, and always interesting.

A Model of Relational Challenges

In an effort to encourage vigorous study of challenging relational processes, we propose a preliminary model that attempts to represent and distinguish among sundry sorts of challenges. Although our working model focuses on relationship challenges, we regard these as part of, and interactive with, the whole of relational experience, as the foregoing points emphasize. Relational challenges do not usually arise full grown out of nowhere; rather, they have histories of previous littleness and are related to other relational phenomena. Typically, a "problem" is brought into existence by one person's negative interpretation of the other's behavior, an interpretation that is open to dispute.

That said, we make two clear dimensional distinctions about relationship challenges. One dimension is atypical/prototypical. Some challenges are typical of (social understanding of) particu-

		Prototypical	Atypical
		Difficulty	**Impairing**
Underlying Feelings Toward the Other Person Are Good	Positive Regard	obligation binds duties	teasing silent treatment conflict
		Inherently Negative Relations	**Spoiling**
Underlying Feelings Toward the Other Person Are Bad	Negative Regard	bullies-victims enemies	betrayal revenge

Figure 1.1. A Model of Four Types of Relational Challenge
SOURCE: This model is a substantially modified version of a figure that first appeared in Duck (1994c).
NOTE: As noted in the text, this figure contains no detailed account of the temporal context of these dimensions, but obviously challenges may be either brief or enduring, intermittent or constant, temporary or long lasting. In each case a part of the meaning of the challenge is assumed by its temporal extensiveness.

lar forms of relationships and result from the prototypical structure of these relationships, such as bullying or the duties that go with friendship. Others represent atypical departures from normalized relationship conduct, as when persons unexpectedly betray relationships, let partners down, or get into sporadic conflicts. The second dimension (positive regard/ negative regard) focuses on the overall feelings of participants toward one another, whether good or bad. Some relationships present challenges notwithstanding the goodwill of partners toward one another (such as the obligations and duties of close personal relationships or the teasing and needling that occasionally irritate a loved partner); others are founded on the ill will of one person for the other, as in enemyship or revenge (see Figure 1.1).

The figure contains no detailed account of the temporal context of these other dimensions, but obviously challenges may be either brief or enduring, single instances or patterned behaviors, intermittent or constant, temporary or long lasting. For instance, a brief quarrel is psychologically different from chronic abuse, a single affair may be forgiven more easily than a string of infidelities, occasional bad moods may have different consequences from those of habitual drunkenness, and the temporary stresses caused by a child's brief illness are going to have different relational consequences from those that result from a diagnosis of multiple sclerosis. In each case a part of the meaning of the challenge is assumed by its temporal extensiveness. With this proviso, we now elaborate the model and demonstrate its heuristic potential by sketching kinds of challenges that fit within each of the main quadrants.

Inherent Binds Prototypical in Relationships Marked by Positive Regard

There are hassles and complexities in every "close" relationship from time to time, some of which are particularly powerful instantiations of challenges. Whenever two human beings, each with needs, preferences, priorities, and so on, exist in relation to one another it is perhaps more remarkable when things work out than when they do not.

It has long been recognized that voluntary relationships, although by definition entered into with good intent and positive regard for the other person, nonetheless become sources of obligation and duty. Wiseman (1986) notes that friendship is not organized around particular tasks but is instead planted in stable intimacy as an end in itself, and yet is a fragile relationship subject to the vicissitudes of life more than other relationships on which institutionalized social pressures exert an adherent influence. Friendship's well-intentioned voluntariness is at once a strength and a weakness.

This paradox is extended by Wiseman's further demonstration that the emotional intimacy of friendship provides a number of structural binds, or "banked resources," on which each person can call in times of need. Although such a bank must not be overused, it must not be refused, either. Thus one challenge of relationships is to handle the balance of freedom and commitment created by the complex expectations that inhere in the relationship.

In the field of research on social support, this point had been developed extensively. For instance, Stein (1993) notes that the closeness of family membership brings with it a number of actual and perceived obligations that require a person to assume responsibilities of care for family members during times of illness or disability (see Lyons & Meade, Chapter 8, this volume). The pleasures of companionship and membership in a family system are tempered by responsibilities to provide service and support in times of emergency or difficulty, just as the traditional marriage ceremony requires couples to accept responsibilities in times of sickness as well as benefits in times of health. Furthermore, the extent to which individual family members are expected by others and themselves to take care of one another is influenced by cultural factors beyond the interior dynamics of the relationships themselves. Cultural constructions of sex roles, for example, assign caregiving to women more than to men (Okin, 1989; Wood, 1994).

Likewise, marriage entails restrictions on personal freedom, such as the giving up of sexual dalliances—at least publicly. Certain other relational roles impose time-management constraints (e.g., parent-child relationships). Thus to enter the role of parent is to accept challenges to one's timetable, to one's other commitments, and to one's freedom of action. The new role brings with it a set of pleasures, yet it is also accompanied by extra demands that temper and contextualize the benefits. The same is true of friendships and all other personal relationships that are voluntarily entered into with goodwill. The closeness (or intimacy) of a relationship is in part assessed by the extent to which it obliges one simultaneously to carry out duties of care and support in times of "for worse" and to enjoy times of "for better."

Inherent Challenges Prototypical in Relationships Marked by Negative Regard

Unique expectations and challenges inhere in relationships defined by participants' negative regard and intent. In relationships such as enemyship (Wiseman, 1989; see also Wiseman &

Duck, Chapter 3, this volume) or *Feindschaft* (Harré, 1977), the relationship is not one that has inherent benefits to offset obligations; rather, it is a relationship experienced as, and expected to be, primarily negative. Harré (1977) observes that there is a range of negative behaviors that most societies record as permissible, understandable, acceptable, or even appropriate between persons who are enemies. Harré further notes that both loving and hostile relationships do not result primarily from predisposing conditions, but instead are mutual relational achievements based on the management of almost ritual elements of social interaction in which style is an important part of the process. Harré's insight reminds us that enmity is not a static abstraction but an ongoing process or a social accomplishment that is engendered by practices, not by feelings or thoughts alone.

In some cases, one meets the structural relationship challenge by ignoring or avoiding an enemy and having nothing to do with the person. However, there are other cases where frequency of interaction with enemies or rivals is unavoidable—noxious neighbors, dour deans, contentious colleagues, awful administrators, and revolting relatives, for instance. In such cases, one is faced with the task of managing interaction that one cannot escape, and the challenge becomes a practical one, not only of facework but also of network management, building alliances, and anticipating and defeating the machinations of a sapping enemy.

Goffman (1963) notes that degradation ceremonies take place in social settings as part of facework, and that a "proper flow" of hostile acts can be analyzed in terms of general principles of self-presentation and responses to face-destroying ploys. Harré (1977) raises the interesting question of how a person signals disassociation from another, and the management of hostility and enemyship can be regarded as an extension of this issue. Compared with the familiar "tie signs" that indicate togetherness as a social "with," in Goffman's terms, how, asks Harré, does one indicate that one rejects and is *not* with someone else? Equally intriguing is the matter of conversational style in hostile relationships. Planalp and colleagues have iden-

tified alternative ways in which acquaintances and friends structure their conversations to convey different degrees of relationship (see, e.g., Planalp, 1993; Planalp & Benson, 1992; Planalp
& Garvin-Doxas, 1994). If the general principles of their analysis—that degree of relationship can be determined from conversation—can be extended to all forms of prototypical affectivity,
then researchers should be able to discover rules and rituals by
which enemies, rivals, and antagonists stylize their discourse to
embody and define different forms of relationship.

Smith, Bowers, Binney, and Cowie (1993) have demonstrated
that, in the case of children who are bullies and victims, such
disassociations are based on the participants' interpretations of
behaviors. Aggressive children in their study tended to infer
hostile intent from ambiguous behavioral cues and then to react
by selecting aggressive dissociative response options. Thus they
seemed to "read hostility into existence." It remains for relationship researchers to discover whether such tendencies in
adults are the basis for hectoring and animosity in life beyond
playground bullying.

Challenges Impairing
Relationships Marked by Positive Regard

Relationships in which persons see themselves as structurally
opposed to one another are distinct from ones in which temporary and/or minor irritations of greater or lesser consequence
occur in relationships that are generally comfortable and sound.

Baxter (1992) reports that playfulness is an important element of most well-functioning relationships. Playfulness is most
often construed as jointly constructed game playing or fun, but
there can be occasions when only one person sees the joke and
the other becomes annoyed or feels humiliated and/or ridiculed.
If the annoyed partner misperceives the other's intent and the
other reacts insensitively, then the playfulness can quickly turn
to, or be experienced as, needling or vicious teasing, taking its
definition and meaning from the interpretation and reaction
that is given to it (Harris & Sadeghi, 1987). Teasing, another
underresearched element of relationships in everyday life, is

distinguished by its unique blend of aggression, humor, and ambiguity (Shapiro, Baumeister, & Kessler, 1991), a blend that sometimes gets out of kilter, at least in some participants' views. Important to the definitional determination of a tease is the recipient's interpretation of the teaser's intent and the recipient's resources and inclinations for handling it. If teasing is interpreted as maliciously intended, then it is experienced as hostile and painful even if the teaser intends it as benign and friendly. Like playfulness, therefore, what is intended as teasing may be experienced as needling if it is perceived as such.

Harré (1977) has explored "needlings" as ritualized activities that might irritate a partner or instead become the basis for playful teasing that sustains a relationship. He suggests that needling depends on the use of strategic ambiguity. A remark that could be taken as innocent might alternatively be regarded as a spiked barb, or, if it is taken as a spiked barb, the speaker can deny the presence of malice and contend that the remark was in fact innocent. In this sense, what counts as needling seems to depend on the character of the author and the recipient, as well as the history of a relationship. When good intent is displayed or inferred, the challenge to the relationship is negligible.

Spoiling Relationships

On the other hand, continuous and/or unambiguous needling, such as snubs and put-downs, are instances of relationship hassles that stem from bad intention and the deliberate attempt to make life troublesome for another person. They are a counterpoint to those instances of momentary conflict that arise in otherwise gratifying relationships. The last class of relationship challenges concerns the spoiling of a previously satisfying relationship, but in keeping with our general position here, we believe that the management of such issues is in fact a special case of the general rules of behavior governing maintenance of relationships.

There are no predetermined or universal consequences of inflicting relationship damage, or even a priori clarity concerning what counts as damage. An act of betrayal may lead to the peremptory ending of one relationship and yet to enhancement of another in which the discussion of underlying causes is used to improve the relationship. In keeping with our previous argument, and as argued by Mead (1934), we note that outcomes depend largely on the meaning negotiated in interaction between the persons involved rather than those attributed by outside observers. Relational effects of action depend on the way in which a challenge is construed and handled between partners, including the way in which, individually and collaboratively, they link it to or dissociate it from the overall relationship. Thus a betrayal designated as a one-time aberration from the "normal relationship" may pose a less serious threat to relational continuity than one defined as part of an ongoing and odious pattern.

Jones and Burdette (1994), for example, define interpersonal betrayal as a failure to maintain a central element in relationships, namely, the trust or expectations on which it is based. Betrayal is especially harmful because it calls into question the essentially private culture of the relationship (Baxter, 1987; Wood, 1982) and, by implication, the identity of both partners in relation to one another. It is a fact of the normal conduct of relationships, however, that as the partners become more intimate, they also become more vulnerable. Kelvin (1977) notes that in the process of allowing others to become more intimate with us, we make ourselves simultaneously and unavoidably vulnerable to harm connected with the information we have dispensed. Any information we have disclosed to others in the course of becoming intimate may, if relational circumstances change, be turned into weapons that may be used against us. This is one reason a sense of betrayal in a relationship is more significant than simple rejection that takes place before a relationship has begun. Because it occurs in a functioning relationship with a history and in the context of expectations of continuity, it normally presents one of the most serious relationship challenges and also threatens the victim's sense of self as constructed in the relationship.

The consequences of seeing oneself as having been betrayed present a challenge not only in terms of management of self but also in terms of management of the network. La Gaipa (1982) shows that a concomitant of spoiled relationships is the need to manage the rumor mill that develops in a person's network after a relationship's trouble becomes public knowledge. Yet it is also true that interpreting the offense to the network in a way that accepts, forgives, or accounts for the lapse of trust can also help to strengthen and continue the relationship by nourishing the social ties that support it (Duck, 1982; Rusbult & Buunk, 1993). Although a betrayed partner may feel regret and disappointment, there is no inevitability to the outcome of betrayal.

Indeed, in discussing the consequences of trouble in relationships, Rusbult (1987) suggests that a person facing such difficulties can take one of four courses of action: *exit* (i.e., leave the relationship literally or psychologically), *voice* (i.e., stay in the relationship and address the problem), *loyalty* (i.e., put a brave face on the situation and just carry on), or *neglect* (i.e., deny the problem, be unresponsive to a partner's efforts to give voice). This model indicates that the partners in a floundering relationship confront a range of options from which the most meaningful one is presumably selected or the one selected is defined as best. In like manner, Rusbult and Buunk (1993) indicate that the maintenance of relationships in the face of difficulty depends in part on the way in which partners choose to handle the situation, whether through a willingness to accommodate, the derogation of desirability of alternatives, or a willingness to sacrifice one's own interests for a greater relational good. Such an analysis underscores the fact that normal maintenance of relationships sometimes requires the handling of special challenges as well as routine attention to the relationship's health (Canary & Stafford, 1994). Thus maintenance of relationships is an ongoing and normal challenge rather than something apart from relational life in general. Both challenges and their management are fundamentally sense-making processes (Duck, 1994b).

However, in keeping with our argument about the uncertainty of classifying behavior as inherently positive or negative

or as having inherently determinable consequences, we note
that "betrayal" is a classic case. Although it is easier to recognize
the pain and damage suffered by a person who is betrayed than
to see the repercussions for one who betrays, there may nonetheless be challenges unique to the role of betrayer. For a person
realizing with shame the full extent of the consequences of a
thoughtless act there may be recrimination, self-loathing, guilt,
and awareness of his or her own dark side, capacity for wrong-
doing, and selfishness. Betrayers sometimes claim that they
want their relationships to continue, or that they did not intend
the consequences that now appear very likely. Among other
things, they must confront their central role in jeopardizing a
relationship, which is not a challenge faced by the "innocent
party." In short, there are a number of issues involved in the
role of betrayer that need clarification and understanding if we
seek to understand betrayal as a fully rounded relationship
challenge that, like all relational phenomena, involves and
affects all participants.

Management of
Relationship Challenges

Although in the foregoing we have focused on interior challenges, a contextual tension also confronts relationships. The
ways in which societies move and develop are important as
background for the conduct of relationships (Simmel, 1950),
and this presents problems simultaneously to persons in relationships and to researchers who study them. Not only do the
new forms of relating made possible by societal and technologi-
cal change alter the conduct of intimacy (e.g., relationships
conducted over electronic systems [Lea & Spears, in press] or
the changes to courtship brought about by the availability of the
automobile [Bailey, 1988; Rothman, 1984] or the telephone
[Sarch, 1993]), but partners face new challenges in stabilizing,
maintaining, and conducting relationships in the face of ever-
changing social conditions. People develop expectations and
ways of relating at Time X and under Conditions Y in light of

societal expectations and norms (McCall, 1982). Thus a couple with a perfectly happy marriage in the 1790s would look very out of place amid definitions of marital happiness in the 1990s, and the passionate, physically expressed friendships between women in the 1800s would be labeled lesbian today. Indeed, the evidence suggests that although such changes do occur and may be quite substantial, they are also rather slow to occur. For example, Prusank, Duran, and DeLillo (1993) indicate that changes in the representation of relationships in popular magazines have been somewhat deliberate (a slow trend that others see as beginning to move more quickly in recent years). In the past there has been a move from a belief that communication is an unalloyed boon (late 1960s), to a focus on open expression of one's own needs in relationships (late 1970s), to a view that places one's own needs in the context of the other person's (late 1980s). Such mediated backgrounds for the judgment of "success" or "failure" of one's own relationships presumably affect a person's judgment of the conduct and value of his or her own relationships.

To some extent, we are all doomed to be situated in our own construals of our personal and social histories as well as in the cultural contexts in which we happen to be placed, and particularly those against which we crafted initial relationships, goals, and values. Although much research is currently devoted to the notion that experiences in early life set the tone for the nature and style of relationships in later life (Bartholomew, 1993; Hazan & Shaver, 1987; Miller, 1993), we cannot overlook the fact that the conduct of relationships may also be "set" by the early interactions in the relationship and by the social context in which the relationship takes place (as, for example, fear of AIDS has recently altered some of the ways in which sexual behavior is conducted in relationships—see Bowen & Michal-Johnson, Chapter 7, this volume). When the times change and, with them, the conditions, constraints, and options for relationships, individuals' expectations may not adjust immediately. Thus some of the issues addressed in this volume arise not from inherent characteristics of particular types of relationships, but from tensions consonant with expectations cultivated in one era and constraints, opportunities, necessities, and developments characteristic of another.

Conclusion

Two facts concern us most at this point. First, researchers' quest for order and explanation has perhaps simplified or overlooked the complexities and evolving character of everyday life as a crucible for relationship experiences and retrospections. Second, in dealing with variable experiences, individuals (including researchers) are faced with real practical contingencies that affect behavior and must be reconciled with expectations, in a manner consistent with relational culture and tradition. An irritated spouse, a disgruntled romantic partner, a frustrated child, or a humiliated friend is not simply an individual having a cognition in one's presence; he or she also represents a social predicament that one has to handle. Furthermore, responses to challenges are not simply a present predicament, but a process temporally situated in the ongoing stream of behavior. As such, responses to challenges reflect and reshape individual relationship histories and carry repercussions not only for particular relationships but more generally for partners' relationships with other people. The everyday variabilities, their management, and their consequences are, moreover, eternally continuous challenges for relationship lives. The harbored resentment, the remembered snub, the perceived injustice, the blocked achievement, the bungled sexual encounter, the forgotten anniversary are not without consequences for the partners' attitudes toward, and anticipations of, immediate and future interactions with one another and others.

In addition to presenting challenges to partners themselves, relationships also present theoretical and methodological challenges to researchers in this field. Many of the principles offered to explain "close relationships" seem not to be self-evidently applicable to the relationship forms discussed in the present volume. Nor indeed are many of the methods used to study conventional subjects (i.e., college sophomores) necessarily applicable or appropriate to these kinds of relationships. Theories based on the currently overstudied subjects in the currently fashionable paradigms offer partial and limited insight into the complexities of social and personal relationships in "real life." As researchers enter the more mysterious world of everyday life and everyday human relationships, so we are likely to document what common sense might lead us to suspect: that most relationships have both good and bad elements and that neither of these is either self-evidently labeled or independent of the other.

Clearly, not all pain leads to the ending of relationships, and much of it is both normal and potentially constructive. People do stay in relationships that cause them frustration, pain, and disgruntlement. In the normal lives that personal relationship researchers seek to understand, individuals deal all the time with relationship challenges that, far from being unusual issues requiring specialized theoretical treatment, are in fact normal and inherent aspects of relationships.

Thus it is time for researchers to pick up the gauntlet that such everyday relationship challenges themselves present to our theories. We have claimed that relationship challenges (a) arise from socially constructed relationship structures and the individuals involved, (b) are more or less continual processes of relational life all through the course of a relationship, and (c) have to be understood as existing and being managed in all relationships, whether these are marked by regard that is generally positive or negative. In short, to be adequate, theories of relationships must become as complex, and as processual and as heterogeneous, as the phenomena they seek to represent. Daily hassles and trivial challenges, as well as more consequential ones, should be understood within theoretical frameworks that recognize that they are normal parts of most human relationships and that they, like all relational processes, are interwoven with multiple other individual, interpersonal, and cultural phenomena.

Shame and Anger in Personal Relationships

Suzanne M. Retzinger

Quarrels are common in personal relationships. Kelley et al. (1983) view relationships as conflictful to the extent that conflict occurs frequently, intensely, and/or for long periods of time. The failure to deal with conflict may be the single most powerful force in dampening marital satisfaction (Cuber & Harroff, 1965), if not the most prominent cause of marital failure (Mace, 1976). Despite the prevalence of conflict and emotions such as anger and shame in normal relationships, researchers have paid little attention to these emotions and the challenges they pose to partners. Whereas some conflicts are intense and may escalate into serious struggles even at the slightest provocation, ending in verbal and emotional abuse, violence, and/or separation, others come and go without leaving much of a mark on relationships. Conflict may also bring people closer together, as Simmel (1955) notes. If dealt with productively, conflict can lead to greater levels of intimacy.

In part, then, the challenge of conflicts is to comprehend their likely consequences. In this chapter I explore this particular relationship challenge by viewing conflict as a response to a lapse in the bond between persons that can lead to shame and the humiliation of one or the other partner. Taking the view that conflict is a response to a lapse in the social bond and the emergence and handling of shame and anger, I seek to fulfill my mission as a contributor to the present volume by focusing on the processes that underlie conflict in personal relationships.

Little is known about why some conflicts are destructive and others bring people closer together, but central to the challenge of conflict is the nature of the relationship itself. Emotions and the state of the bond appear to play important roles in protracted and escalating conflict (Retzinger, 1991; Scheff & Retzinger, 1991). The bond involves "strategies with which parties navigate . . . their relationship" in interaction (Baxter & Simon, 1993, p. 225), on both emotional and cognitive levels. When persons interact in conflict there are exchanges of meaning. Meaning is intricately tied to the bond between the persons, the manner in which they communicate, and the emotions expressed and exchanged. Some kinds of interaction may be more prone to conflict than others. If we can describe the role of emotions in conflict, we may have a better understanding of how relationships are built, maintained, damaged, and repaired.

Because the roles of emotions and bonds in conflict have not been a central focus in research, there is much to be learned about studying them as they occur in interaction. I begin to redress these absences by focusing here on two emotions, shame and anger, and how these surface in interaction. I explore not only the nature of shame and anger, and why they are so often linked, but the kinds of behaviors they elicit and their connection with the social bond.

This chapter is divided into five interrelated sections. In the first, I discuss some of the problems connected with exploring conflict in relationships as well as some of the major sociological perspectives on conflict. The second section deals with a particular component of conflict: alienation. Alienation can involve either too much closeness or too much separateness. In the third section I examine emotional reactions to alienation within a social bond perspective, and in the fourth I explore in depth the emotions that emerge most frequently during alienation and conflict. The fifth section is devoted to discussion of the major ways in which emotional "contagion" occurs between interactants. I conclude with a summary of the chapter and discussion of some implications for further investigation of conflict.

Conflict in Theory

In terms of conflict in personal relationships, much of the focus has been on distinguishing satisfied or functional couples from dissatisfied or dysfunctional ones. The most consistent pattern found has been that dissatisfied couples express more negative emotion than do satisfied ones, with a greater reciprocity of negative emotion (Gottman, 1979; Jacobson, 1977; Margolin & Wampold, 1981; Markman, 1981; Noller, 1984; Notarius & Markman, 1981; Patterson, 1982; Sillars & Weisberg, 1987). Sequential analyses have indicated that when one spouse expresses negative emotion, the other reciprocates in kind more often in dissatisfied marriages than in satisfied ones (Gottman, 1979). They have not, however, explained the process through which these sequences perpetuate themselves.

Whereas most studies have dealt with general categories of negative and positive emotions, Gottman and Levenson (1986) have coded specific emotions. These researchers classify "anger, contempt, sadness, fear and their blends" as negative emotions (p. 42). Observing specific emotions can be revealing, but it can also be problematic. The most obvious danger is that one may confuse emotion and behavior. Behavior can indicate that a certain emotion is occurring, but behavior and emotion are not synonymous. For example, in their analysis Gottman and Levenson include "whining" as a "negative affect," along with anger, contempt, sadness, and fear. Although these last four are emotions, whining is a behavior; Labov and Fanshel (1977) suggest that whining is a manifestation of an underlying emotion that they call "helpless anger."

Another behavior that is often confused with emotion is aggression. Aggression is most often associated with anger and shame, but it is not equivalent to either of these. Aggression is a behavior, whereas anger and shame are emotions, often experienced as painful. Anger sometimes leads to aggression, but often it does not, as Campbell (1993) has observed. Confounding behavior and emotion can lead to serious theoretical as well as methodological problems, which in turn can lead to inaccurate results. The crucial issue is the reliable inference of emotion from behavioral indicators (for one such system, see Retzinger, 1991).

A second serious but less obvious problem with marital research involves the use of a simple dichotomy: positive/negative. Dichotomizing emotions involves a value judgment that may obscure the functions of emotions such as anger, fear, and grief in close relationships, emotions that are frequently labeled negative. The implication is that in a good relationship the "negative" is reduced and the "positive" increased. Little has been mentioned about the *function* of anger in personal conflict; it is too often assumed to be intrinsically dysfunctional. As I will show in the present chapter, anger is not necessarily dysfunctional. Anger in fact can serve valuable purposes in relationships, as becomes clear when its role in relationship processes is considered in context.

Conflict About Conflict

Many sociologists and psychologists, working from different perspectives, have focused on conflict. Although they generally agree that conflict is inevitable, they do not always agree about its function, holding varying views on whether conflict is functional or dysfunctional. Coser (1956), Marx (1844/1964), Sumner (1906), and Simmel (1955) do not regard conflict as inherently destructive, and note that it has positive functions. Simmel (1955) asserts that conflict "resolves divergent dualisms; it is a way of achieving some kind of unity" (p. 13). Simmel, like Marx, views certain types of conflict as adaptive.

Coser (1956) also argues that under certain conditions conflict can be functional. He suggests that conflict is the root of personal and social change. It stimulates interest and curiosity, prevents stagnation, and builds group cohesion; it represents a medium through which problems can be aired. According to Coser, conflict is dysfunctional when it is rigid and/or when "insufficient toleration . . . permits hostilities to accumulate" (p. 157). Boulding (1962) agrees that tragic consequences resulting from conflict are dependent on the *rigidity of the system* and not the conflict itself. Both Coser and Boulding posit that the more intolerance there is and the more hostility that is repressed, the more dangerous the ultimate conflict.

Whereas some view conflict as serving the function of readjustment, social change, and cohesion, others, such as Parsons (1949) and Rosenstock and Kutner (1967), view conflict as inherently dysfunctional. In Parsons's (1949) view, conflict is endemic; it is itself a disease or sickness in a system. Like Parsons, Rosenstock and Kutner (1967) view conflict in itself as destructive, causing rigidification and withdrawal of the parties involved.

Deutsch (1969) makes a distinction between destructive and constructive conflict. He agrees with Simmel and Coser about conflict's positive functions, but says that "destructive conflict is characterized by the tendency to expand and to escalate. . . . such conflict often becomes independent of its initiating causes and is likely to continue long after these have become irrelevant or have been forgotten" (p. 11). Things move from bad to worse: Tactics become extreme, the number of issues increases, and motives become adversarial.

Conflict does not always resolve differences, unify persons or groups, or result in constructive change; sometimes it is destructive, erodes relationships, and ends in violence. A quarrel may clear up unexpressed misunderstandings and lead to greater intimacy, but it may also produce bitterness and estrangement. Not all conflict strengthens solidarity in communities, groups, or relationships. When further alienation rather than greater unity occurs, conflict can be destructive.

As with conflict, it may be more useful to view anger, grief, and fear as painful, rather than as negative or dysfunctional, or to ask about the function of the emotion in relationships. Freud (1926/1959), for instance, has proposed that anxiety is a crisis response that serves a signal function, internally warning that something is wrong. Bowlby (1973) views anger in much the same way. He suggests that anger is an attempt to reestablish a bond and to keep a loved one from leaving; he notes that anger can be functional or dysfunctional, depending on whether the behavior it motivates reestablishes or damages a bond. If anger serves to strengthen a relationship, it is functional; dysfunctional anger destroys a relationship.

Bowlby notes that the outcome of anger for the relationship determines whether that anger is functional or dysfunctional, but he does not specify the processes unique to these different outcomes. Understanding the dynamics of conflict, as well as how people deal with conflict, has a great deal to do with the effects of conflict on relationships.

Conflict and Alienation

The social bond is an important element to be considered in relation to conflict. A further clue to the nature of conflict is found in Simmel's (1955) assertion that conflict follows separation, rather than separation being a result of conflict. Simmel describes a sequential process, noting that hatred is caused by hurtful feelings generated by rejection. This sums up the most fundamental aspects of conflict. In this chapter I will attempt to make these processes more explicit.

Other researchers have also viewed conflict in light of the social bond. J. Coleman (1957) has found patterns in the initiation of dispute that imply the importance of the social bond; he notes that when there is enough contact but no bonds to protect people, conflict escalates. In his book on the topic published almost 40 years ago, Coleman suggests that future studies of conflict should investigate the strength of attachments between persons and to community affairs. Kreisberg (1973) has noted that adversaries in conflict tend to become increasingly isolated from each other; communication barriers increase, anger increases, and perceptions of the other side become increasingly inhuman. Patterson (1982) also mentions that social isolation makes conflict escalation more likely.

Pruitt and Rubin (1986) note two types of bonds, which they call "group membership" and "dependency," indicating bonds that are, respectively, too strong and too weak. "False cohesiveness" may give the appearance of group membership (Longley & Pruitt, 1980); conformity may be an attempt at belonging— the bond is weak. According to Pruitt and Rubin, those with weak bonds are at risk of escalation of alienation, as are those who seem to have too much dependency; the more dependent persons are on others, the more prone to alienation they become.

Following Bowen (1978), Scheff (1990) argues that alienation takes two forms: isolation and engulfment. Somewhere between these two extremes is connection, or solidarity. Being too close, or not allowing another autonomy, is just as alienating as isolating oneself in a relationship. If relationships are either too distant emotionally (isolated) or too close (engulfed), strong emotional and behavioral problems are generated. Alienation seems to be an important factor in conflict. People have intense emotional responses to alienation (whether engulfment or isolation) from those they care about. I view alienation as the inability to regulate the distance between togetherness and separateness.

In all relationships there is tension between togetherness and separateness; this tension appears to be a fundamental dilemma, and may or may not result in alienation. The phenomenon appears under various rubrics: communion/agency (Bakan, 1966), connection/autonomy (Baxter, 1988), approach/withdrawal (Bowlby, 1963), altruism/anomie (Durkheim, 1851/1966), intimacy/isolation (Erikson, 1963), interdependence/autonomy (Fitzpatrick, 1988), solidarity/alienation (Marx, 1844/1964), disengaged/enmeshed (Minuchin, 1974), enmeshment/separateness (Olson, 1986), and approach/avoidance (Rubin, 1983). A relatedness perspective with two dimensions is not new, but has been much neglected; the cyclical pattern of relationships has been pointed out for decades by family systems theorists (Bowen, 1978; Minuchin, 1974) as well as others.

Baxter (1988) views all relationships as dialectical, with connection/autonomy being a major tension: "The contradiction is so central to the essence of relationships . . . that it can be regarded as the principal contradiction" (p. 259). She sees this dimension as a paradox, in that too much of either dimension can destroy either autonomy or the relationship.

In itself, separateness/togetherness does not present a problem. Each person needs both autonomy and connection with others. A problem may arise when one person is unable to move between the two and becomes alienated. The way a couple handle conflict may be, in large part, dependent on how they handle this dimension of their relationship. Fitzpatrick's (1988) typology of marriages is based on this concept: "traditional" couples favor connection, whereas "separates" and "independents" favor autonomy. Some mixtures may be ripe for conflict, such as a match between a "traditional" man and a "separate" woman.

Being in a rigid state of either isolation or engulfment involves alienation—having fragile bonds with others. Although it might appear that engulfment is a secure bond, no secure bond can exist without complete functioning of self. Understanding distance is crucial to the understanding of conflict; the source of conflict often lies in alienation between persons.

The self works as a control system that helps sustain a person's relationship to important others between certain limits of distance and accessibility. The interrelationship between the individual and relationship process is complex, involving closeness and distance, approach and withdrawal, attraction and repulsion. In engulfed relationships, persons may be so concerned with fitting together that they are unable to see each other as separate people; there is a kind of "pseudomutuality" (Fitzpatrick, 1988). Marriages that are chronically engulfed have strong influence on the partners, pressing for togetherness; any form of uniqueness (e.g., individual thoughts and feelings) is experienced as betrayal or disloyalty—abandonment. Each person functions in emotional reactivity to the other. In relationships where one partner is chronically engulfed, complaints might take on the tone, "I'm being suffocated by the relationship" or "Give me some breathing space" (Raush, Barry, Hertel, & Swain, 1974; Rubin, 1983).

Isolation is the other extreme on this spectrum. There may be complete "cutoff" (Bowen, 1978), where one person isolates him- or herself from the other in an attempt to escape engulfment. When spouses are extremely alienated from each other, they may exhibit "pseudohostility" to hide their need for intimacy (Fitzpatrick, 1988, p. 67), or a partner might complain, "He doesn't pay enough attention to me." In relationships where both partners feel engulfed or isolated, or where one partner feels engulfed and the other isolated, the partners are alienated.

In his family typology, Olson (1986; Olson, Lavee, & Cubbin, 1988) demonstrates the emotional difficulties generated by extreme types. In his research, he found that families prone to crisis were rated either low in cohesion (isolated) or high in cohesion (engulfed). Families with either type of alienation—emotional isolation or engulfment—had problems of emotional reactivity (anxiety, anger, and guilt). To cope with these feelings, persons may deny the need for either togetherness or separateness, which further alienates them from others. Olson found that chronically alienated families had high levels of problems with their children.

Alienation, then, can be detected in ideation of separation, differences in power positions, language of disconnection, use of triangles and other nonleveling responses (indirect communication), lack of acknowledgment or response, withdrawal, lack of eye contact and other hiding behaviors, de-selfing (giving up the self for the relationship—self-alienation), and threats of abandonment (Retzinger, 1991).

Researchers in diverse disciplines have discussed conflict and alienation and have indicated the importance of the social bond. They have also mentioned dominant underlying variables such as emotions of anger, fear, and wounded pride, but they have never constructed a bridge to connect these variables. Although emotions result from escalated tactics, it is not clear how or why these tactics occur. Prior explanations have been black boxes; alienation gives a clue to the nature of conflict, as do manner and the emotions that are expressed and exchanged between persons.

Social Emotions and the Bond

Human beings seem to have an innate propensity for sociability (James, 1910). We live in groups and are dependent on our bonds with others. The human animal, unlike any other creature, has a very long period of dependency on its caregivers. Early in life, humans are unable to flee or to fight. Although the emotions of rage and fear are oriented to the survival of the organism (stimulating fight and flight preparedness), the human infant is primarily organized to clutch and cling; if early relationships were dependent on fight or flight, infant mortality rates would be quite high. Another group of emotions seem to have developed to ensure species survival; these are geared toward bonds that tie us emotionally to our fellow humans.

Social emotions are distinguished by the fact that they are about survival of *relationships*. Shame appears to be the most social of all human emotions. It has been said to be the emotion "second to none" in its importance in human relationships (McDougall, 1908). Unlike other families of emotion, a major characteristic of shame is the self in its relationship to other persons; it always involves a self-other process. Shame is not concerned with the organism as an isolated entity, but with relationships between persons, the regard of others—preservation of solidarity. Shame guards the boundaries of privacy and intimacy (Schneider, 1977; Wurmser, 1981) crucial to the functioning of relationships.

Shame and pride play crucial roles in relationships. Shame signals a threat to the bond—either too much or too little distance or respect. Pride signals a secure bond. The emotional system helps maintain a person's relationship to important others, pushing toward restoring the bond (Bowlby, 1988; Lewis, 1985). Building and maintenance of bonds is signaled by pride; reparation is signaled by complex patterns, and can involve constructive conflict.

Shame is a powerful human mechanism, a normal and necessary part of a well-functioning society. Goffman (1967) points out that embarrassment (shame) is not a "regrettable deviation from a normal state. . . . [I]t is not an irrational impulse breaking through socially prescribed behavior but a part of this orderly behavior itself" (pp. 97, 110). Shame is an essential part of the ritual order. Each human being is acutely aware of self in relation to others. Shame is a mechanism used to monitor the self in social context. People usually avoid behavior that causes self or others shame and attempt to repair interactions that have become threatened or damaged (Goffman, 1967).

At every moment, the bonds between people are being built, maintained, damaged, or repaired; if a relationship is not being built, maintained, or repaired, it is being damaged by default (Neuhauser, 1988). Persons are alienated, connected, or some combination of these. Although the state of the bond is virtually invisible and is difficult to detect directly, manner and emotions continuously reveal it.

Emotions are part of the self-governing system; they operate as homeostatic mechanisms that help regulate the distances between people. Bowlby (1973) terms this process *environmental homeostasis*. Anger prepares the organism to fight and at the same time serves a communicative function (because of its accompanying facial and bodily gestures), warning others so that readjustments can be made on both sides. Shame signals threat or damage to the bond—telling us we are too close to or distant from the other for comfort and well-being.

Emotions can help preserve the status quo (Scheff, 1988) as well as serve as catalysts for social change. Emotions serve the social order by restoring balance. Emotions indicate to the individual whether he or she is receiving adequate respect. When a person receives an improper amount of respect, either too much or too little, strong emotions can ensue.

In groundbreaking work, Lewis has identified two states of shame that were virtually invisible to researchers before her: "overt, undifferentiated" shame and "bypassed" (covert) shame. Overt shame is the familiar type, marked by bodily arousal (blushing, sweating, rapid heartbeat, and so on) and feelings of discomfort—this is the type of shame that *feels* ashamed. Bypassed shame is a low-visibility state that is difficult to detect. It occurs in thought processes and ideation of the self in relation to others, rather than in bodily arousal. Bypassed shame can have a dramatic effect on relationships.

Shame is actually a family of emotions with certain characteristics. The nature of shame, as noted earlier, is such that it always involves the self in relationship to others, even if only in the imagination (as when one imagines that oneself is being viewed negatively). This genus includes many variations, from social discomfort and mild embarrassment to intense forms such as humiliation or mortification, including embarrassment, dishonor, disgrace, chagrin, and mortification (Lewis, 1971; Schneider, 1977; Wurmser, 1981). Characteristics for identifying shame states include the variants, vocabulary, stimulus or source, position of self in the field, conscious content, experience, appearance, and defenses against shame.

There are hundreds of ways of disguising the shame experience through vernacular language. This may be one reason relationship researchers have failed to attend sufficiently to the role of shame in conflict, and in relationships in general. Lewis (1971) notes that certain words continually reoccur in contexts of shame, and that these are accompanied by the use of certain gestures: *uncomfortable, insecure, uneasy, tense, blank, confused, small, worthless, inadequate, stupid, foolish, silly, weird, helpless, unable, weak, curious, funny, idiotic, restless, stunned, alone, disconnected, alienated, split, impotent, low self-esteem,* and so on (Gottschalk, Winget, & Gleser, 1969). Each of these words (as well as numerous others) belongs to an experience with common characteristics, mainly the self in its relation to another, with at least the imagination *of how we think we look in others' eyes.* The vocabulary for describing shame states is vast compared with the vernacular language used to describe anger, guilt, fear, or grief. This is a clue to the prevalence of shame.

The source of shame is a perceived injury to self where self is the object of the injury. The injury may be imagined, real, or a combination of the two. Stimuli can take very subtle forms, involving only slight gestures (e.g., a nose wrinkle, speech cadence slightly off) or blatant, overt forms. On the overt side, the self may feel childish, paralyzed, helpless, passive, and so on, whereas the other appears powerful and active. The person may blush, tear, or have other unpleasant bodily arousal. Overt shame is highly visible. In a shame state the self functions poorly as agent, whereas the other appears intact. Both self and other are focal in awareness.

The other in these situations is perceived as the source of the injury and appears in some way as alienated from self. The other may be viewed as less caring about the relationship than the self. The other is focal in awareness and may appear to be laughing, ridiculing, powerful, active, in control, unjust, hostile, or unresponsive.

Bypassed shame is seen mainly in conscious content, which includes many varieties of thought about the deficiency of self; the self remains focal in awareness. Thoughts may take the form of what one *should* have said, or what one *might* have said, or may include the replaying of earlier scenes over and over in mind. Shame can be manifest in rapid speech as well as thought. Comparisons between self and other in which the self comes out appearing inferior in some way—less beautiful, intelligent, strong, and so on—are frequent; or the shamed person may simply wonder if he or she is sufficient. Persons in a covert shame state might simply function poorly as agent or perceiver; their thoughts, speech, and perception may be obsessive. Thoughts of the person in a shame state might be divided between imaging the self and imaging the other. Imaging the self involves thoughts about self-identity and whether self has been discredited.

The position of the self in relationship to the other is what is important in distinguishing the shame experience from other experiences; in this way shame comments on the state of the bond. Self-other involvement suggests the ubiquity of shame.

A link between shame and anger can be found in Cooley's (1902/1970) work. Cooley found the most common form of hostility to be rooted in social self-feeling. He focuses on the importance of the social bond: "We live in the minds of others," we feel *pride* when we are noticed favorably, and *shame* when our bonds are threatened (p. 208). Others have observed the co-occurrence of anger with other emotions involved in social self-feeling, such as shame and humiliation (Kohut, 1971; Lansky, 1987; Lewis, 1971, 1976; Retzinger, 1985, 1987, 1989; Scheff, 1987).

Shame-Rage Affinity

It is common knowledge that conflict often involves some amount of anger, but only a few studies have made explicit the prominence of shame and its role in both conflict and physical violence. The work of Katz (1988), Lansky (1987), Lewis (1971), Retzinger (1991), Scheff (1987), and Scheff and Retzinger (1991) suggests that emotions, particularly shame and humiliation, are central to conflict.

Lansky (1987) has shown that in spousal abuse, the perpetrator usually feels shamed by the victim's manner, however subtle; the violence he or she engages in can be seen as a form of self-defense against a perceived or imagined attack on a self that is overly dependent. Through case studies, Katz (1988) has shown the quick development of rage. For example, he notes that although a particular argument may have been about paying the bills, the resultant killing was not really about who would pay the bills. Underlying the external topics are *moral implications* and *humiliation*. In my own work, I have shown that conflict escalation involves sequences that move from alienation through *shame* to *anger* to *disrespect* within and between couples (Retzinger, 1991). Scheff (1987) has explored the prominence of the shame process in a quarrel between a therapist and client over a slight by the therapist. The shame and anger in

Hitler's appeal has also been addressed (Scheff & Retzinger, 1991).

In my earlier work on resentment, I observed that whenever persons described a situation that caused them to feel angry, shame was also prominent (Retzinger, 1985, 1987, 1991). In that research, I recorded rapidly alternating sequences from shame to rage, using videotapes and printed photographs. In *5-second time spans,* sequences went from shame, to anger, to shame, and back again.

Lewis (1971, 1981) in particular has discussed the prevalence of shame whenever anger occurs. Using hundreds of transcribed interviews, she traced sequences of evoked emotion back to the moment when anger first appeared and found that shame, caused by real or perceived rejection, had preceded the anger. Lewis suggests that shame and anger have a powerful affinity: If shame is evoked, anger is quick to follow. It seems that when a bond is threatened, an array of painful emotions are triggered, anger being only the most obvious.

The sequence of shame-anger tends to be self-perpetuating. Each provokes the other, owing to the special quality of the affective communication in shame-rage. It involves a "self-to-other message about how rageful the self feels at its *inferior* place 'in the eyes' of the other" (Lewis, 1981, p. 190). Anger is evoked when one person perceives that the other does not value her or him, which elicits a state of shame over the devaluation. But when shame is evoked and not acknowledged, sequences from shame to anger can occur because shame is often experienced as an attack coming from the other. "So long as shame is experienced, it is the 'other' who is experienced as the source of hostility. Hostility against the rejecting 'other' is almost always simultaneously evoked. But it is humiliated fury, or shame-rage" (Lewis, 1976, p. 193). In this way, shame and anger seem to have an affinity, though anger may be the only feeling recognized.

Unacknowledged shame acts as both an inhibitor and a generator of anger, often rendering a person impotent to express anger and simultaneously generating further anger, which is likely to emerge as demeaning or hostile criticism, blame, insult, withdrawal, or violence. Shame-rage sequences may explain Peterson's (1979) finding that, among the couples he studied, satisfied couples fought anger through to resolution, whereas among dissatisfied couples anger ended in sequences of aggression and withdrawal. Aggression arises from anger; withdrawal characterizes shame and shame-rage sequences.

A characteristic response in shame is to hide; when shame arises, one finds it easier to project the problem onto the partner than to acknowledge one's own shame. This may explain why it is so easy to blame or criticize the other, and why some quarrels seem endless. Because of the virtual invisibility of shame and its painfulness, it is easy to deny one's own feelings, passing responsibility on to the other in the form of blame. This may result in endless tit-for-tat conflict.

Within this framework, anger can be viewed much as Bowlby (1988) envisions it—as a reaction against a real or perceived injury, and a means by which people attempt (though often not effectively) to remain connected to those they care about. Anger can also be viewed as a defense utilized to protect oneself from feelings of shame. Anger can represent an attempt to ward off shame associated with perceived attack and to reestablish the relationship while maintaining face and self-respect.

One challenge, then, in relationships is that when shame is evoked and not acknowledged an impasse occurs on both social and psychological levels. Whereas in his analysis of interaction ritual Goffman (1967) looks at embarrassment between persons in terms of deference, Lewis (1971) looks at the same dynamics in terms of shame. The greater the alienation, the more likely it is that intense conflict will occur. When shame is evoked in person A and is not acknowledged, A perceives this as an attack from person B, becomes angry with B, and may act disrespectfully toward B, which evokes shame in person B, and so on in a cyclical pattern. Scheff (1990) calls this a triple shame-rage spiral. That is, one person has an emotional reaction to his or her own emotion as well as to the other person's, which perpetuates the cycle of conflict between the two; when the persons involved do not acknowledge these dynamics, it becomes difficult for them to extricate themselves from the quarrel.

Self-perpetuating cycles of shame-rage are implied in the work of Saposnek (1983) and Johnston and Campbell (1988) on divorce and conflict; these researchers look at conflict in terms of loss of face. In the present scheme, loss of face is one of many metaphors for damaged bonds. Goffman (1967) has dealt with face-saving extensively. Social behavior is motivated by the desire to maintain social bonds—to stay connected with those we care about, to look good, to present oneself in a favorable light to significant others. All members of all groups attempt to protect and repair their images—to maintain or repair bonds. In line with Goffman's thinking, one of the most common ways to exchange shame between persons is through disrespect.

Manner and Disrespect

What we say is only a part of the communication process. *How* we communicate is at least as important as what we say, sometimes more. Understanding gestures is important for understanding conflict, because gestures generate immediate responsiveness (Blumer, 1936). Gestures (manner) influence how communication is taken; they define the relationship (D. D. Jackson, 1965; Ruesch & Bateson, 1951; Watzlawick, Beavin, & Jackson, 1967).

The manner in which we communicate can have more emotional impact than anything we actually say. Manner carries more implication than words, because it is about the immediate relationship between persons. Although both words and gestures carry emotion, words emphasize *information,* cognitive content, whereas gestural communication emphasizes *feeling* (Archer & Akert, 1977; Mehrabian, 1972). If manner is offensive, even communication on the most trivial topic can lead to escalation of conflict. If manner is respectful, readjustment or change can follow, no matter how weighty the topic. Focusing only on the topic of argument is fruitless. This helps to explain why "talking things out" does not always lead to resolution and why heated arguments can arise over trivial things; the manner in which disputed issues are managed or settled needs to be accounted for.

Goffman (1967) sees deference and demeanor as means of communication that are largely gestural and often quite subtle; people communicate with each other through dress, grooming, posture, movements, and glances, every time they come into one another's presence, with or without awareness. Deference and demeanor go beyond speech in defining relationships. Every word, gesture, facial expression, action, or implication gives some message to the other about social worth (Goffman, 1967).

Through observing manner, each person monitors the amount of respect received; each is acutely sensitive to receiving either too much or too little. The manner of communication informs participants of their roles vis-à-vis the other, status, emotions, immediate intentions, degree of dominance, deference given, and intensity and intimacy of the relationship; it organizes the flow of interaction—that is, when to speak, when to listen, and when to end. It involves posture, gesture, facial expression, voice inflection, sequence, rhythm, cadence of words, and so on. *Manner defines the relationship* by establishing the frame for interaction and providing cues to regulate its progress.

Communicating disparagement or disrespect may play a key role in angry conflict. All social interaction involves obtaining respect to avoid what Goffman (1967) calls embarrassment or loss of face. The implication is that interactants seek to be connected when they care about the other. Some studies suggest that spouses show less consideration (respect) and tact to each other than they show in routine exchanges with others (Birchler, Weiss, & Vincent, 1975; Stuart & Braver, 1973).

Many of the disparaging tactics used in marital quarrels can be seen as attempts to save face at the expense of the other; often they are vengeful. In blaming transactions, the implication is, "I don't want to look (and feel) like I'm wrong (bad, or so on)," and when the bond is weak it is the other rather than the self who is sacrificed. Blaming the other is a clumsy attempt to maintain one's own sense of worth. Anger and rage can be seen as attempts to avoid humiliation (loss of face). It may be more comfortable to use the inadequacies of a spouse as a rationalization than to acknowledge the part played by self, *particularly if the bond is already damaged or threatened.*

Peterson (1979) used couples' written accounts of their daily interactions in an attempt to understand escalation of conflict. The four conditions he describes that perpetuate conflict are *criticism, illegitimate demands, rebuff,* and *cumulative annoyance.* But criticism in itself does not always lead to greater conflict; each of us is subjected to criticism in some form daily. We all have illegitimate demands put on us, and we have all experienced rebuff. Perhaps destructive conflict occurs when one is shamed, does not acknowledge the shame, becomes angry, and expresses this anger in disrespectful behavior.

Summary and Implications

In this chapter I have suggested that angry conflict in relationships involves inadequate or threatened bonds, or alienation (inability to manage closeness and distance adequately); as a result of alienation, shame is evoked, but it is not acknowledged, nor is the bond discussed. Anger follows as a means of avoiding the painful experience of shame, but is expressed disrespectfully, leading to further shame and anger in the other. Continued cyclical loops of shame, disrespect, and anger can lead to erosion of relationships, or, with respectful acknowledgment, anger can lead to productive change.

Disrespect, aggression, and violence arise when intense emotions are present but are not acknowledged or are otherwise not communicated; although emotions and behaviors can be related, they are not synonymous. It is crucial to make a clear distinction between emotions and behavior; for instance, aggression can be harmful, whereas anger is just a feeling. Anger that is not managed productively can lead to aggression.

The integration of theories of conflict, social bonds, and emotion helps to explain protracted conflict. Conflict theorists dealing with macro issues have discussed the importance of the social bond, but recent work on conflict in personal relationships has virtually ignored advances made by these theorists.

Studies of marital conflict are based primarily on atheoretical observations of behavior. Borrowing from several disciplines, I have developed here a theory of social bonds, shame, and conflict. Emotions serve to signal the state of the bond and the need to readjust behavior in relation to the other. Emotions signal to both self and other whether the bond is intact or threatened.

The social emotions are oriented to survival through the preservation of relationships. Shame is not concerned with the organism as an isolated entity, but with relationships between persons, with the self and the self's perception of the regard of others—preservation of solidarity. Shame guards the boundaries of privacy and intimacy (Schneider, 1977; Wurmser, 1981). Although we may be afraid in the presence of certain animals, such as snakes, shame always occurs in the context of interaction between human beings, even if only in the imagination. Shame concerns the functioning of relationships.

As I have mentioned, an individualistic notion of human behavior (with its categorization of emotions into positive and negative) impedes the advancement of knowledge of conflict because of its implicit failure to credit processes and to develop methods for observing processes. The myth of individualism denies inherent bonds with others as well as an emotional system that helps to preserve these bonds. This myth also denies the importance of shame. Rigid individualistic approaches may provide defensive ways of organizing experiences and interpretations of social organization.

One individualistic approach is the perception that some emotions are positive and others are negative. Such confusion can distort interpretation about what is occurring between people. The view that certain emotions are negative may perpetuate interpersonal problems by leading individuals to try to avoid these feelings. It may create problems for researchers as well, in that exploring "negative" aspects of relationships objectively may become difficult, which might lead to misinterpretation of what is occurring in interactions.

Dialectical processes are at work in all relationships. Conflict can be seen as a means of connecting and separating; tension between these two forces can generate change as well as havoc. Shame, like a thermostat, helps to regulate the tension between closeness and distance; shame may be evoked if persons are either too close or too distant. Partners requiring different degrees of closeness and distance may find themselves in the throes of conflict if they do not discuss emotions and bonds. Thus anger and shame play critical roles in both change and stability.

In my own work, I take an integrated approach, viewing emotions in a social light. I see emotions as functioning as internal and external reminders of accessibility and distance between persons. I view anger as a protective measure utilized by the self to protect the self from what shame brings to light—alienation between persons. I view disrespect as a consequence of unacknowledged emotions and a means of perpetuating cycles of emotion within and between partners. In the same line, conflict can be seen as a reaction to inadequate bonds: Conflict is functional to the extent that it repairs bonds; it is dysfunctional to the extent that it creates further alienation. Anger, like conflict, does not have to be viewed as destructive; it can be instructive and positive—reestablishing boundaries, leading to effective problem solving. Under what conditions is it constructive? Constructive processes need to be analyzed as they occur in interaction; a fruitful future research direction might be to compare conflictful interactions in which resolution occurs with those in which conflict escalates.

If we learn to identify and understand potentially humiliating exchanges, we may be better equipped to use strategies that will identify impasse. If shame is acknowledged, perhaps negotiation, readjustment, and change can occur. By identifying shame, we make it possible to get beneath the topic to the basic issue, alienation. By focusing on the presence or absence of specific emotions, such as shame, anger, guilt, and contempt, we may gain greater knowledge of the causes of conflict.

3

Having and Managing Enemies: A Very Challenging Relationship

Jacqueline P. Wiseman

Steve Duck

The present series concerns processes of relationships and deals with matters of long-term importance in relationships rather than the short-term interactions or thoughts of individuals only at the point of initial "attraction" that used to be so prevalent in social psychology. This volume deals with relationships that offer challenges to their participants, leading up to the final volume in the series on relationships that have not been studied very much. These two contexts make the topic of "enemies" a natural one for discussion in this volume, because the relationships of enemies are continuously and pervasively difficult challenges that are not well studied. Attention to enemies is also consistent with the

AUTHORS' NOTE: This chapter is based on a plenary address originally presented by Jacqueline P. Wiseman at the Second Conference of the International Network on Personal Relationships, May 11-15, 1989, University of Iowa, Iowa City. We are particularly grateful for the advice and suggestions of Julia T. Wood concerning the argument of this chapter and some of the research suggestions that it now explicates.

series and volume emphasis on everyday relationship life, because most people at some point in their lives have enemies and must find ways of dealing with these negative relationships.

There has been very little detailed research conducted in the area of personal enemies (in fact, we had to coin the term *enemyship* to give that relationship the same kind of shorthand label that friends use to describe their association). For this reason, we depart from the form used by the other chapter authors in this series. Rather than surveying existing work in a summary fashion, we present exploratory research that provides initial insights into enemyship and that generates ideas and hypotheses for future research on enemies. This chapter is also revealing in the degree of concordance between qualitative sociology and quantitative communication studies that can be noted in citations for research touching on aspects of the enmity relationship. This demonstrates that these two research perspectives —often assumed to be in diametric opposition—can be compatible and complementary.

Enemyship: Introduction and Methods

Enemyship is a kind of relationship in which negative feelings and actions are part and parcel of the ongoing daily nature of the relationship. People have friends, but they also have enemies, antagonists, and opponents who try to make their lives more difficult and to interfere with their attainment of goals. Enemies are not merely conceptual abstractions; they are experienced as real people who interfere with the processes of social life. They represent a particularly important and interesting relationship challenge for ordinary folks and also offer scholars of social relations some important theoretical challenges.

Researchers have shown interest in the ways that people describe and interact with their friends, but less in how they actually manage interactions with them (but see Volume 4 in this series, *Dynamics of Relationships*). By contrast, the question of how people mentally sort out their personal enemies and handle them has received virtually no attention from researchers, even though enemies are common in everyday life.

Short of Machiavelli (1532/1947), who wrote about how to handle enemies, there is very little direct work to guide us here, and even the recent growth of interest in the "dark side" of relationships (Cupach & Spitzberg, 1994; Duck, 1994c) has not covered the topic. There is some previous work on related matters, and Harré's (1977) speculations about *Feindschaft* appear to be some of the first to address the issue directly. There are other sources of indirect inspiration on the topic, such as Goffman's (1959) work on face management and Garfinkel's (1956) considerations of degradation ceremonies. However, historically, sociologists have spoken of conflict and the natural succession of groups as a result of group conflict, but not of the relationships that result from conflict. Likewise, psychologists, clinicians, and communication scholars have tended to overlook such relationships or to focus only on conflict in kin or marital relationships.

In this chapter, therefore, we begin the process of building understanding of enmity as one important form of personal relationship and explore the issues of enemyship *as a relationship*. We investigate the processes through which enemies are identified and managed, but this chapter also represents a first foray into the overall enterprise of making the social and personal aspects of the "enemy relationship" a construct that scholars can explore and try to understand theoretically.

In attempting to map enemy relationship terrain, we explored the comparison of enemyship with friendship. Although we initially instigated this exploration for the purpose of developing understanding of enemyship, the approach resulted in our discovery of how little present approaches to friendship offer any basis for extension to the understanding of enemyship.

Data for the discussion presented below are based closely on the insights reported by Wiseman (1989), who undertook two separate qualitative studies. In the first, she conducted in-depth interviews (1 to 3 hours in length) with 40 men and 40 women, ages 18 to past 80, concerning their definitions of a friend, how they ranked their friends, what they sought in friends, how they made friends, and how they became angry at friends, lost friends, and regained them. She also collected from each respondent a history of three close friendships; additional case histories of problems in friendships were also provided by respondents. The second sample consisted of 30 men and 30 women who were interviewed in depth (again, the interviews were 1 to 3 hours long) on the subject of personal enmity relationships they had experienced. Wiseman attempted to ask the respondents in this sample as many questions as possible paralleling the friendship study. This approach revealed major differences in the generic aspects of friendship and enemyship. The two kinds of relationships are not two ends of the same continuum, nor are they mirror images of each other—at least in the minds of persons who have experienced these relationships. Thus the questionnaire used in the interviews with the second sample pursued the differences between the two kinds of relationships as well. The interview responses of both samples were coded, and the coding was checked for agreement among coders. Responses were then sorted into major categories and a more refined coding was performed for the analysis.

The meanings, interactions, and processes of development of these two diametrically different relationships discussed here are based on respondents' views of both their own place in society and the relationships they described. Thus respondents' selections of indicators of friendship and enmity are tied to their personal histories of interaction with and responses to persons in their social groups and their reactions to them.

Using the material generated in Wiseman's studies and confirming material from other theoretical discussions and substantive studies, we will explore in the rest of this chapter the ways in which people define enemies, how people become enemies or come to see others as enemies, and the social actions people take to remedy enemyships or to deal with enemies in ways that do not change their own self-images by "forcing them to stoop to the enemy's level." However, the detailed examination of the psychological, social, and communicative dynamics of this important feature of enemyship must remain an area for future work. Our initial attempt to understand enemyship situates it in relation to processes that are more fully understood (namely, friendship). As mentioned, by viewing enemies in the context of these more familiar processes and issues, we can clarify what appear to be some of the apparently generic qualities of enmity that distinguish it from the processes underlying friendship.

What Are Enemies?

Perhaps the most significant feature of enemies that emerges from Wiseman's (1989) work is their perceived unannounced nature. It is this aspect of having an enemy that was the most frightening to Wiseman's respondents, because one can do little about a situation when it does not involve open conflict or provide one with opportunities to make one's own case in response. A second feature of enmity is that it is nebulous and enigmatic; it is not a role relationship in the usual sense of having rights and responsibilities in relation to someone in a counter role, as "friendship" classically does. Friendship usually implies equality; enmity often implies a power differential, though the distinction is not absolute. Not all friends see themselves as equals; some describe their friendships as asymmetrical. This is especially true of friendships between younger and older people or between family members who see themselves as friends. The critical distinction seems to be that persons are *conscious of* and *use* power against one another when they are known enemies, and this is subtly different from *having* different degrees of power as a defining feature of the relationship. People also imagine power plays and construct each other as engaging in them when that may not be the conscious intent of the perceived enemy. Just as we construct ourselves and others in any and every relationship, so we do this with enemies— and, of course, it is our construction of the other and of the relationship that is the filter through which we interpret ongoing activities and interactions and through which we design our own actions and responses toward the enemy.

In other respects, enemies are an important "opposite side of the coin" of friendship. Wiseman's respondents described friendship as offering companionship and sharing; as a chance to have someone help understand life; as providing someone to confide in, trust, and rely on; as giving a sense of feeling needed; and as providing happiness at having a positive self-image through the admiration of a friend. Attributed to enemies, on the other hand, were such characteristics as emotional or mental power over the targets of their enmity, the ability to make one feel uncomfortable, and the ability to give one a negative self-image. In contrast to friends, enemies make us feel on guard and vigilant. Beyond such interpersonal power, one's enemies may have (or at least are often perceived to have) broader social powers—they can mobilize other people to dislike one, and can turn even unknown others against one. Enemies are seen as having the power to ruin their targets' reputations through gossip and lies. By exercising such power, an enemy can hurt a person's status or financial position, and can interfere with his or her relationships with other people. Respondents in Wiseman's research reported this to be the case especially in the workplace, and doubly so if the enemy is in a position of authority over his or her target. Enemies can ruin their targets' opportunities for advancement and restrict them to undesirable assignments. Perhaps the most frightening thing is the power that enemies are imputed to have for scheming and using cunning to take advantage of their targets' weaknesses, especially if the current enemies were formerly friends or intimates.

Wiseman's (1986) study of friendship might appear to offer a paradigm for looking at enemies. For instance, inasmuch as her respondents appeared to have in mind types and levels of friendship, one might want to look for assignment to types and levels of enmity. Just as there are friendship careers, there could be parallel careers in enmity relationships, that is, in terms of how enemies are made, neutralized, outwitted, and/or overcome. The data on enmity suggest, however, that, *in the minds of respondents,* enmity is a phenomenon with logic and dynamics of its own, quite different from friendship.

Traits of Friends and Enemies

Initially, we should mention that a small percentage of respondents claimed they had no enemies—or that they left them to God. Those who admitted to having enemies, on the other hand, described them primarily in terms of *malicious actions,* as previously noted. This description by respondents provides one basic dimension on which to differentiate friendship from enemyship, not only in the attributed adjectives themselves, but in their type. In contrast to the above-described sorts of *actions* of enemies, people think of their friends primarily in terms of *enduring/endearing qualities.* For instance, they speak of friends as being decent, loyal, understanding, and caring, as people who will listen to them when they talk. They also speak of friends as persons who will share things with them and accept them for who they are. When they speak of friends' actions, it is in terms of companionship or to illustrate the friends' standing as persons on whom they can rely as resources in times of need or trouble—when things get rough.

Personal qualities are infrequently noted or mentioned in the descriptions of enemies; instead, reference to actions or anticipated actions is frequent. Of course, this distinction is not so simple in practice, because many people report on actions of their friends (spending time together, sharing activities) and on qualities of their enemies (untrustworthy, malicious, ill intentioned). However, the distinction really rests on a matter of degree, not on a simple positive/negative dichotomy (as Duck & Wood argue in Chapter 1 of this volume). Individuals offer predominantly action-based accounts of enemies and predominantly quality-based accounts of friends.

Ranking Systems for Friends and Enemies

Hartley and Wiseman (1984) indicate that people not only utter the preceding sorts of general approval for friends, but usually also rank order their friends on a dimension of closeness, from, say, casual acquaintances to best friends. These designations can be pictured as a pyramid, with "best friends" on the top (in the smallest group) and subsequent levels of larger groups of less close friends as one moves down toward the base of the pyramid. It is very instructive first to outline such a system as a way to contextualize and differentiate people's beliefs about enmity in contrast with the things they say about friendship.

As Hartley and Wiseman point out, the following clusters emerge through degree of intimacy and are transsituational, for the most part. On the *top level* are best friends, who are trusted absolutely. Friends at this level share many things about themselves, knowing that they are accepted. Mutual commitment is unquestioned, but the quality of the relationship does not depend on the amount of time spent together. On the *second level* are close friends who share some personal feelings, but not all. There is mutual respect. These friends may or may not be called on in a crisis. The *third level* is made up of special activity and/or special interest friends, friends to do things with (such as sports or political, religious, or educational interests), as well as colleagues. If the parties' interests change, these relationships may not be maintained. On the *fourth level* are slight acquaintances, incipient friends: people who are thrown together, exchange niceties, and have the potential to develop a depth of friendship over time. On the *fifth level* are pseudo-friends or superficial friends; these may make a pretense of being friendly, but they are not to be trusted. People at this level may be called "false friends"; they cannot be moved up to a higher level. (People at this level could, with a harmful act, slide into the enemy category, thus offering a slender connection between these relationships.)

By contrast, when people discuss their enemies, they do not rank them so much as categorize them by areas of activity and intensity of enmity reaction. Certainly, their labels do not lend themselves to an extension of the friendship levels to provide a negative end of a continuum. In fact, respondents say that there are no levels such as are found in friendship. A person either is an enemy or is not. It is an all-or-nothing category. However, enemies are viewed along a number of dichotomies or axes according to the degree of threat they pose and the arena of one's life in which they operate. Thus, although a person either is or is not an enemy, some enemies are more evil and more dangerous and more vicious than others in their attacks. Some enemies are relatively unimportant in terms of their impact on a person and her or his life, whereas others can have major impact.

The primary axis is the *dislike/hate* axis, where a person characterizes his or her enemies as someone the person either merely dislikes or actually hates—sometimes intensely. One might indeed speculate—although we cannot testify to this from the present data—that the degree of power to hurt is the element that determines whether another person is disliked or hated: Someone who has little or no power to affect my life but is my enemy is probably someone I merely dislike. Someone who can and perhaps does really hurt me, I may hate.

The *active/passive* dichotomy concerns whether someone is a known enemy but not currently working against one (yet still is untrustworthy and must be watched) or an active enemy who is currently taking action against one.

The *personal/professional* axis concerns whether enemies are characterized as adversely affecting one's personal and/or social life (stealing lovers, making one lose points with relatives, and so on). On the professional level, enemies are active rivals at work, self-interested competitors. (Parenthetically, we note that despite probing, and the addition of extra questions, about a member of a family becoming an enemy or the existence of enemies based on political differences in the individual realm, Wiseman found enmity to be confined to Freud's important axes—love and work.)

Other, less important, axes may also be mentioned, such as the *close/distant contact* dichotomy. With some enemies, continued close contact is inevitable (this is especially true of enemies in the workplace). People say that in such cases they must often repress the hostility they feel or take extreme action, such as changing jobs. Those who are more geographically separated from or not forced into daily contact with their enemies feel freer to express their dislike.

The *aware/unaware* dichotomy applies to yet another characterization of an enemy. Some people feel that they have unknown enemies out there working against them, just waiting to be discovered. Others feel that they know who their enemies are at all times. In this respect, enemyship and friendship can be clearly distinguished, because friendship is invariably a relationship based on declaration of itself and mutual acknowledgment by its participants. Parenthetically, of course, one may create an enemy by acting toward a person as if that person is already an enemy—treating the person unfairly, for example—such that his or her reactions may build up and turn into enemyship. Lemert (1967) speaks of this circularity of reaction in his discussion of the interactive roots of paranoia. It is therefore possible for someone to create an enemy by acting in a way that the other person interprets as hostile. Yet these actions may not be deliberate. For instance, Burgoon and Koper (1984) have shown that shy persons are seen by strangers (but not by friends) as being hostile rather than shy. Mead (1934) also notes that the response of the other gives to an act the social meaning that it has, and in the case of joint social acts, responses create meaning for the persons involved that are not necessarily the same. For enemyship, however, there remain two other important elements: (a) enemies one does not (yet) know about ("One may smile and smile and be a villain," as Shakespeare observes) and (b) enemies one knows about but whose particular acts, schemes, or words one does not witness or learn about at the time they are done.

Finally, enemyship involves a *time frame*. People do not forget old enemies (some of the enemies recalled by Wiseman's respondents dated back 20 years), but their feelings of hostility can partially fade. More current enmity still engenders hard feelings that are strong and fresh.

These considerations indicate some issues that beg for consideration during the research on enemies that we urge. For instance, the fact that some people feel that enemies are unknown-but-out-there-waiting might be correlated with certain personality qualities and inclinations, such as anything from locus of control to paranoia. Likewise, the belief that we do not cause or create our enemies suggests perceptions of low locus of control and also raises issues for attributional theories.

Emotional Reactions to Friendship and Enmity

The respondents in Wiseman's studies, quite naturally, had feelings about friendship and enemyship that were diametrically different, yet they seemed to share something that might be called "gut reactions." In the presence of friends, respondents said, they experienced almost a natural "high." They felt adventurous, very happy, excited, but at the same time relaxed, comfortable, and able to be themselves; they felt appreciated for themselves. They felt a special sense of communication as well. With their enemies, respondents said, they felt uncomfortable and tense. They also stated that they felt disgusted, negative, and sometimes sarcastic. More often, however, they felt inhibited to the point of being unable to speak. Frequently, they said, they would leave the scene to avoid any confrontation.

In addition, respondents who knew they had enemies were alert to clues that people assessing possible friends did not seem to notice. They claimed that they suspected the development of enemies through intuition, a sixth sense, "bad vibes," or a certain aura about the person. In other words, individuals seem to be more vigilant and conscious in interpreting interaction with "enemies" than with friends. Respondents also claimed that by watching possible enemies and noting how those persons treated them in comparison with others, they were able to ascertain future enmity. Body language and nonverbal clues— such as hostile stares, coldness, and dirty looks—also indicated that persons were enemies. Respondents noticed rejection and failure to be acknowledged or spoken to. In addition, they noted sneering comments or sarcastic tones of voice, which they took as indicators of ill will. (Third persons, of course, also sometimes tipped respondents off. Friends would tell them how their enemies talked about them behind their backs.)

However, we should note that these signs were not taken by respondents as definitive. Rather, they were signals suggesting that vigilant caution should be exercised. The real tip-off of enmity, the factor that gains a person enemy status, is the overt act. Once again, the respondents did not see this as a process to which they made any contribution—even in small amounts. They saw such acts as "just happening," and they felt powerless to do much about defusing or deflecting them. It is perhaps for this reason that the reported indicators of enemyship include surprising intentional emotional hurts, such as "put-downs"; discrediting things the enemy says; showing little regard for one's feelings, or rejecting one; and giving one "the silent treatment." Respondents claimed to be hurt, angry, and fearful—but without any idea of possible recourse. One might speculate—in line with the earlier observations about power—that this sense of helplessness is an important (or even definitive) element of the experience of enmity.

Sex of Enemies

Respondents had friends and enemies of both the same and opposite sexes. However, their discussion of differences in these types of relationships was, quite naturally, colored by the thrust of the relationships. Furthermore, they differentiated between persons as enemies or as rivals who had never been friends or as enemies who were ex-friends to whom they used to be close either platonically or romantically. Clearly, respondents were aware that, regardless of gender issues, friendships can be converted to enemyships, but that this occurs rather more frequently when romantic relationships are dissolved than in other cases. Thus even in speaking of cross-sex friendship or romance they seemed to have one eye on the possible consequences that would be generated if the relationships became enemyships. Friendship, after all, is based in part on the sharing of confidences; romance or love is based on even greater intimacy. Thus aware respondents realized that there are dangers to closeness. A cross-sex friend who later becomes an enemy may take confidential information gained earlier and use it against one by sharing it with other persons with whom one may wish to become romantically involved.

Nevertheless, when speaking of friends, respondents saw advantages and disadvantages to cross-sex friendships because of the erotic attraction component. Enemies look at sexual differences not erotically but emotionally. Between friends, a major advantage to cross-sex friendships was seen to be the opportunity to exchange views considered to be integral to the friends' gender identities, and thus to understand the opposite sex better, something they then could put to use in their sexually oriented relationships. Men often said that they found women friends to be able to listen to their problems better than their male friends, and respondents of both sexes found persons of the other sex fun to be with, without the complications of a sexual relationship.

Other disadvantages of cross-sex friendships mentioned by respondents were the possibility of inevitable physical attraction making one partner uncomfortable if the attraction was not mutual. In addition, there was the danger that the friends' lovers or spouses might become jealous of the relationship. Respondents also spoke of the apparent impossibility of discussing some topics with a person of the opposite sex, and the fear that such a relationship would be misunderstood by others. As Wood (1993b) notes, "Even when cross-sex friends are not sexually involved, an undertone of sexuality often punctuates cross-sex friendship" (p. 190).

When speaking of enemies, respondents considered it more likely for people to have enemies of the same sex than enemies of the opposite sex. The reasons they gave were either applicable to both sexes or focused primarily on the problems they perceived women to have with other women.

In discussing the problems of same-sex enmities, respondents said that people of the same sex are more likely to compete, both in love and on the job. They also saw same-sex persons as competitive in terms of attractiveness, popularity, and personal qualities. In addition, some pointed out that same-sex persons are likely to be thrown together more often than are opposite-sex persons, and thus have a greater chance of becoming enemies.

As we have mentioned, many respondents felt that women were especially prone to becoming enemies of other women— that women compete with each other and are more malicious toward each other, jealous of each other, and have less trust among themselves than do men. They also mentioned a problem

likely to come out of women's so-called openness or receptivity
to the problems of others: that women will open up to each other
more than will men, and in so doing will give advantages to
their enemies. (In this respect, the respondents echo the advice
of a lord of the Court who warned his son, "Always treat your
friends as though they may become your enemies" [Furguson,
1792].) For women, such fear could be aggravated by the
likelihood that female friends—because, in general, they disclose more intimately to one another than do male friends (but
see Dindia, 1994)—have more information that can be used
against each other than do male friends if either set becomes
enemies later.

Men also saw particular dangers in the development of
opposite-sex enmities. They saw women as competing with
them in terms of both competence and efficiency, and for
prestige. They also claimed that women had different ideological values that could lead to distrust between themselves and
the women. Respondents of both sexes also talked about an
automatic distrust of the opposite sex that operates to the
detriment of peaceful relationships between them.

Making Friends/Getting Enemies:
The Accomplishment and the Surprise

Almost every respondent claimed to be surprised that someone had "become" his or her enemy. The enemy was constructed
or signified suddenly by his or her acts. Thus respondents spoke
of enmity as coming about from particular surprisingly hurtful
acts; to put it another way, immediate knowledge of the hostile
act constructed the actor as an enemy.

This startling feature of the respondents' comments about
enemyship—that it seemed to them to come out of nowhere—is
a significant finding concerning this relationship. It means that
for many respondents, the perception that they made no contribution to the development of the enemyship heightened a
poignant sense of injustice for them. Yet one could speculate
that enemyship, like friendship, is likely to develop from se-

quences of interaction between two persons ultimately resulting in alienation. In the case of enemyship, however, these may be acts whose effects on the other person one does not notice—an unintended oversight, a thoughtless remark, a mindless and unnoted comment *taken as* slighting or insulting by the hearer. Given that individuals can never be fully aware of the impact of all of their words and deeds on other minds, the sense of surprise at any enemy's emergence is perhaps a natural one. It would be interesting for future researchers to explore whether people follow general attributional patterns in explaining enemies. The "self-serving bias" would predict that individuals would be more likely to attribute their own acquisition of enemies to external factors and others' acquisition of enemies to internal ones, for example.

Although respondents reported that their enemies suddenly appeared as announced/identified by some overt negative acts, it is more likely, as we have mentioned, that enemies, like friends, develop over time, emerging out of a context and history of interaction or information about people. Thus one value in studying enmity is that we can better understand and control the making—or not making—of enemies by learning how such relationships are cultivated over time and in context.

To develop the analysis here, therefore, let us compare the making of friends and the making of enemies. From respondents' descriptions, there are apparently two major routes to making a friend. On the one hand, if people are thrown together for a period of time and must stay together (such as workers in an office, students in a class, or members of a team or army platoon), they may gradually become fond of one another through continuous shared experiences enhanced by mutual aid. Self-disclosure or revelation can increase over time. Following this, turning points usually occur in the relationship when crises bring reciprocal responses of aid. Such events have cementing effects on the relationship, and it is gradually elevated to a higher stage.

On the other hand, people also speak of "clicking" with others. When people click, they experience almost instant attraction for each other, can talk easily about almost anything, and look forward to time together almost from the first meeting on. Parenthetically, it is these latter friendships—based in part on yet-to-be analyzed adequately "chemistry"—that withstand the tests of time and spatial separation. Persons in such friendships report that after many years apart, they are able to pick up their relationships as though only a day had elapsed since the last contact. This is not so with gradually made friendships. Army "buddies" are a good example of this. Here men in the same platoon develop, over time and through crises, great closeness. Yet according to research on these men years after discharge, they later drift apart, indicating that whatever components brought them together, their friendships could not last without reinforcement.

How Do People Get Enemies?

In striking contrast to the fairly clear ideas Wiseman's respondents had concerning how their various friendships came into being, their ideas of how they made (or got) enemies were almost nonexistent, as previously noted. Furthermore, whereas respondents stressed the interactive aspects of their friendships, they cited single surprising (to them) acts that delineated the emerging presence of enemies: betrayals of trust, being let down, the breaking of agreements or obligations, or being embarrassed or insulted in front of others. They talked about harm done, or about physical attacks, and/or about back stabbing socially or on the job simultaneously with surprise at these occurrences.

A rather substantial proportion of respondents felt that some persons are automatic or "natural" enemies—an idea that is somewhat of a counterpart to "clicking" among friends. These respondents believed that it is inevitable that among certain people there will be personality clashes, competition for scarce resources, differences of philosophies and backgrounds, or opinions that will inevitably lead to hostilities. They also believed—in a somewhat related manner—that there would always be people out there who would be jealous of them or have no respect for them and their abilities. Thus the closest they came to taking any of the interactive blame for the production of enemies was in acknowledging that they may be perceived as threats or competition for the same friends; the same jobs; the same resources, goods, or roles; or the same love objects. They further believed that such enemies often have shortcomings, and that in order to cover them, the enemies use scapegoat tactics and take out their frustration on others.

Despite these notions, there seem to be three originating sources of enemies: cases in which a person who does not really know another takes a dislike to him or her—inexplicably, as far as the object of the dislike is concerned (we will say little more about this type in this chapter, but see Rodin, 1982); cases that evolve in particular situations, such as the workplace, that are seen as caused by "situational factors," such as neighborly nastiness or collegial rivalry; and cases in which former friends and lovers turn against one another.

Setting/Situational Effects
on Making Friends/Enemies

Unfortunately, some of the same settings that promote friendship are seen as possible fertile ground for the making of enemies. For instance, the nature of competition at work or at school for raises, promotions, grades, or friends is attributed as one origin of enemyship. Respondents in Wiseman's studies feared that neighborhoods could also harbor people with whom they would not get along and who would try to do them harm. Jealousy and envy in such settings are perceived to be catalysts for enemyship as well as for status conflict over power. Any setting or situation in which there is increased interaction of people is also thought by some to enhance the possibility of mutual disagreement, personality clashes, and miscommunication that can cause problems. It is in such situations that one also discovers the hidden side of a person, or learns—to one's discomfort—that for no reason one is able to discern and/or is willing to recognize, someone has taken an immediate dislike to one. Thus, although respondents noted the contribution of setting—rather than their own performance in the setting—

there is also an underlying tendency to claim that one is rational
and justified in one's own dislikes, but that one's enemies are
irrational people whose enmity arises from paltry causes or
grounds based on one's own behaviors that are in fact misunderstood or excusable.

Losing and Bruising

Moving up or down in a friendship relationship pyramid is
much more problematic, however, and the difficulties encountered here once again highlight how complex this stratification
system is. First of all, one cannot be moved up in level merely
by intensifying one's lovable traits (one cannot connive a way
to be more trustworthy even if one can try hard to be as nice as
possible and to conceal or remove negative traits), nor does it
seem to help if one tries to acquire new traits known to be
pleasing. Friendship is an *interactive* phenomenon, and as such
it is not simply additive. It grows out of situations and their
handling, which are then filtered through the interpretations of
the other member of the dyad (Duck, 1994a; Mead, 1934).
Each interaction appears to build on the last, except in the
unusual case of friends who click immediately. Inasmuch as
these persons become top-level friends almost instantly, chemistry precedes an inventory of traits and behaviors in their case.
    What moves people into best friend status is the mutuality
and dual reflexivity of close friendships, a feeling that each
senses and fulfills (wherever possible) the other's needs. The
better this is done, the more likely it is that empathic skills—also
important to friendship—will be enhanced. Thus we like our
friends because they can take our roles as well, because they
understand our thought processes and behaviors to an uncom-
mon extent (Duck, 1994a; Hartley & Wiseman, 1984; Mead,
1934). Then we, taking their roles, detect this favorable version
of ourselves as emanating from them, and this reflection makes
it real. As a result, the more positive self moves beyond mere
hopeful presentation to being the alternative person one enjoys
being, at least in the presence of the appreciative friend (Hartley
& Wiseman, 1984). This mutual admiration society of friends

seems to transcend any variation of interests, beliefs and values, or differences in birth and background, and to be a phenomenon largely reflective of interactional processes and identity management.

A move down the friendship pyramid can be caused by the mentioned factors that result in making a friendship falter or that even lead to its abandonment. Wiseman (1986) has noted that persons develop "unwritten contracts" in their minds concerning what they expect friends to do for them or how they expect them to act. These unwritten contracts are never discussed between the members of the dyad. It appears from the data that friends, unlike lovers, would find it gauche or embarrassing to ask one another to promise never to change or always to be fun loving—or whatever traits they find appealing in each other. Parenthetically, although people know what they like in their friends, they rarely know what their friends like in them. Thus they may change or add traits or characteristics without knowing what this might mean to the other person.

Respondents in Wiseman's study reported that the following things would cause them to rethink a close friendship and reduce its centrality in their lives or its intimacy: (a) if the friend changes an important trait or reveals a significant (and negative) new one, and (b) if the friend fails to provide aid in time of need, especially if the respondent had helped the friend a great deal in the past. Respondents reported that although they did not "keep books" on who does what in a friendship, they looked upon their friends as a "bank" from which favors could be withdrawn upon need. Thus failure to lend reasonable sums of money, to offer a room in one's home when needed, or to honor other reasonable requests that, culturally speaking, a person might expect from a friend, can result in one's having one's friendship level reevaluated. The development of competition over scarce resources can cool friendship also. Depending on the seriousness of the trait lost or added, the favor denied, or the fierceness of the competition, a person can be "dropped down a level," dropped as a friend (through a campaign that involves obvious changes in the miniculture of the friendship), or recast as an enemy (this complete transformation seldom happens).

We should note that this sort of loss of status occurs despite the erstwhile friend's presumably retaining all of the *other* positive traits that were originally cited as having made the relationship an attractive friendship. Even friendships that result from clicking are not immune to termination for the reasons just mentioned, although it appears that they have more resilience than those made over long periods of time. What changes is that the *meaning* of positive traits is reevaluated (Felmlee, in press).

Friendship ranking thus does not work like social class scaling. To be moved down the social class scale, one must lose important or emblematic indicators of class ranking and/or assume negative characteristics. More important, both of these processes take time. People cannot change their social class ranking overnight. Even when their circumstances change, they often are able to cling to remnants of their class through maintenance of some of the important criteria of it. On the other hand, a person's rank as a friend can be changed on the basis of a single act, and this can happen quickly. Likewise, a person's maintenance of otherwise attractive traits, characteristics, or behaviors seen to be important in a friend usually does no good once the meaning of these things has become tainted. As in Garfinkel's (1956) conditions of a successful degradation ceremony, one potent incident can change the meaning of a friendship relationship negatively. As Bergmann (1993, p. 129, echoing Garfinkel) notes concerning gossip, the important activity here is that of *abstraction:* Instead of secluding a given act as a particular and isolated error or solecism, or trivializing it as an insignificant token of a friend's feeble humanity, abstraction treats it as a manifestation of a *characteristic* property that symbolizes the whole person as a person. This abstraction essentially decomposes the friend's former (positive) moral identity and recomposes it into another (negative one) by abstractive typing. We should note, parenthetically, that there seems to be no mirror of this outcome in enemyship; for example, one nice act typically will not end enmity. Is friendship a more precarious, more vulnerable, and less stable relationship than enemyship? Do we perhaps form more rigid and impermeable definitions and representations of enemies?

The Mechanics of Breaking Away

When problematic aspects of friendships override the good or dramatic breaches of expectations occur, people often decide to end the relationships. In such cases, they are much more likely to change the culture of their relationships deliberately than to confront the other parties and discuss alternatives among remedies and some kind of de-escalation or termination. (They often talk about the fact that they would prefer to communicate such serious disaffection frankly with their former friends, but cannot summon up the courage to do so.)

When respondents in Wiseman's study were asked how they went about withdrawing from friendships, their answers indicated their awareness of the importance of interpersonal rituals and symbolic acts developed in the course of the friendships for maintaining them. By noticeably reducing this ritual and symbolic aspect of their friendships, they felt they had furnished unmistakable clues to the other persons that all was not well (at the very least) or that all was over. Here are examples of how some of them described the withdrawal of friendship rituals as a symbol of friendship termination:

> I gradually did things with other people. Therefore, I wasn't always around when the other person called, or came by. I did things I knew the other person didn't like to do.

> Basically, I reduced the times I called or asked him to go and do something. I stopped doing the things I usually did around him. I started breaking some of the habits of the friendship.

> I don't phone the person as often as usual. I don't stop by to see them as often. (I used to stop by with no purpose in mind.) I've made myself less available for the things we usually do together. I am starting to become involved with the new people and new activities.

> I try to show that we have less and less in common. When we're together, I try to be less personal, and offer less disclosure about myself. I try to show less enjoyment in the things that he likes and does.

> I start disappointing them in things they expect. The biggest thing I did to the friend I was having problems with was not asking her to be in my wedding. From this, she knew it [the friendship] was over.

> I started picking fights. I started changing my image, so that he knew I wasn't the same person that I used to be.

Sometimes, it is the person who discovers he or she is on a lower-than-expected level of friendship who breaks the friendship.

> I realized that I was the one that considered Dan to be a good friend, and that he probably considered me just an acquaintance or even a nag. I stopped phoning and visiting Dan. Occasionally, I see him and we merely say "Hi," or "How are you?"

Parenthetically, we note once again no reflection of this outcome in enmity. Even if a person avoids an enemy, the enemy's status in the individual's life—the constructed identity of enemy—remains intact. This suggests that friendship, compared with enmity, may be more dependent on interaction.

The outcome of major disappointment in a friendship is dependent on many factors. In some cases it can be gracefully retrieved or repaired (Duck, 1984). The level assigned to the friendship may be changed by one or both parties. The degree of social margin each friend grants the other, as well as how adept each friend is at giving an acceptable account of the misstep, is also important. In many cases, it seems crucial that the originally injured party be willing to take the first conciliatory step. Although maintenance of a friendship is probably more desirable to most persons than its termination, ambivalence is usually the predominant emotion. People teeter back and forth on the desirability of maintaining a relationship after a serious disappointment, indicating they have a problem in letting it go, but also a problem in returning to the status quo—or facing a reassessment of the across-the-board mutuality that they thought they had with the friend. One respondent, a 35-year-old woman, noted:

> I've tried to make myself make up with her. But what kept running through my mind was that a friend would not say those things. I did ask

my son to ask her son if she wanted to come over for dinner. And she did, but it was all very tense. I did go back at Christmas and take a little gift—homemade cake—but I was never comfortable. I realize that she had gotten to me. And I was not going to put that aspect of myself out on the line again.

Structural Aspects of Spoiled Friendships and Enemy Formation

Forgiveness and reconciliation with friends are themselves under-studied phenomena in the field of social and personal relationships, as is the study of relational repair in general (Duck, 1984). One does learn a little about the handling of enemies by looking at repair of friendships, but such repair is not what people do to remedy enemyships, and the data show once again that the two relationships do not mirror one another. We nevertheless begin this section with a brief consideration of how people handle friendship repair and follow it with a section on handling enemyships.

Making Up a Spoiled Friendship

In addition to dropping a friend by changing the climate or completely terminating the relationship, as discussed in the previous section, two other possible approaches exist: (a) understanding and forgiveness by the injured party, and (b) temporary estrangement followed by "making up." The ultimate outcome depends on many factors inherent in the history of the structure and culture of the friendship. For instance, former friends may become enemies—which seems particularly likely if an act of perceived serious betrayal takes place. What a person has invested in a friendship also seems to affect his or her options for action when the friendship is somehow broken.

On the other hand, if the friendship grew from an antecedent relationship, such as that of workmates or relatives, the outcome may be different from that found if the persons were friends only. Interpersonal roles and their unique behavioral expectations can have two origins: (a) Persons in standard role relationships (parent-child, employer-employee, teacher-student) may become emotionally closer and establish a friendship, or (b) friendships can spring up between persons with no proper role relationship other than acquaintanceship. These latter friendships operate at the interpersonal role level almost from the outset and are, as we have mentioned, fragile, because there is no standard role to fall back on when things go wrong. Friendships that develop out of standard roles can frequently (but not invariably) return to that status when feelings are hurt, as discussed earlier. (In fact, when there is a great deal at stake—a marriage, a job—people are pushed in that direction rather than toward total breakup.) A friend who has no other role to which to retreat must either rise above disappointments and anger or "demote" the other person to a level signifying loss of emotional closeness, such as acquaintance (or "false friend"). One 19-year-old male respondent in Wiseman's study provides an example:

> I forgave him, but only superficially. I've held a grudge against him ever since, I guess. I continued the friendship, but it's been more reduced to just a casual friendship now.

Although Wiseman (1986) has shown that people deny keeping track of favors they do for or receive from friends, there is evidence that people do maintain informal "account ledgers" on friends' positive and negative personality traits or qualities that allow them to assess the significance of misbehaviors to their overall relationships. Hollander (1958) refers to the phenomenon of "idiosyncrasy credits" (also known as "deviance credits")—the amount of misbehavioral leeway that one person will grant another. Wiseman (1970) refers to this as a "social margin," and Haapanen (1977) calls it the "benefit of the doubt." All of these concepts refer to the weighing and/or averaging of the positive and negative aspects of relationships, especially at times of crisis. Obviously, persons assume that with close friends they have a great many deviance credits or a sizable social margin on account for them in the "friendship bank"; and friends do, indeed, try to keep it that way. As one male respondent explained it:

> In any relationship, there are ups and downs, there are times when the personalities come in conflict. Just in the matter of natural feelings of people, ah, their feelings are not always mirrored in the other person, their values may not be mirrored in the other person so that is a conflict and it has to be resolved one way or another. In most friendships, conflicts are usually resolved by just a matter of tolerance. You say to yourself, "That person has obviously done this or that for me; they've overlooked a flaw or a fault or something like that, and shouldn't I do the same?"

This observation is entirely consistent with the earlier point —that friends' actions, including their perceived transgressions —are not "facts" but interpretations, and those interpretations are filtered through overall constructions of the other and the relationship. Thus a positive filter that assumes good affect and intent is likely to lead a person to construct a friend's "bad acts" as unimportant mistakes rather than as serious transgressions and thus as not stemming from vicious motives.

If the summation is sufficiently positive, the solecism will be forgiven. When forgiveness of this type is granted, the transgression is treated as an "allowable error." If it is too negative, it will probably not be so treated. Thus one transgression can tip the scales, so to speak, even though it may not seem particularly serious in and of itself, if the person who transgresses does not have sufficient deviance credits or social margin to offset it.

Another important factor in the resolution of a problem between friends is the way the parties involved handle hurtful behavior. The giving of an acceptable account of the transgression can go a long way toward getting it excused. Such explanations are often coupled with apologies. Failure to offer a reasonable account of disappointing or hurtful behavior adds insult to injury. As Scott and Lyman (1968) point out, one of the ways that the normative social fabric is maintained is through the giving of reasons and/or excuses for actions that are seen as nonnormative by others. Parenthetically, the fact that people often know enough to offer accounts (and sometimes prepare them in advance) indicates that friends may have expertise in taking each other's roles, but that such mutual empathy does not guarantee that all situations that arise that impinge on a friend can be resolved to his or her satisfaction.

But where feelings are hurt and alienation of both parties in a friendship has occurred (through either originating or reactive disappointment), who offers accounts and apologies to heal the wounds? Logic would suggest that the first transgressor should make the first such offers. Interestingly, however, the data indicate that it is more often the person originally hurt by the act of a friend who must make the first move and sometimes even do the major apologizing for not forgiving or understanding and allowing the special margin for error that friends allow each other. For instance, in two cases from Wiseman's study—one in which a man sold a friend a car with a bad engine and one in which a person failed to place a promised bet for a friend on a horse that won—both persons who were "let down" by their friends were originally the righteously hurt and angry parties. However, both the friend who sold the car that broke down and the friend who failed to place the bet resumed their friendships after the people they had failed apologized to *them* for their own earlier failure to forgive. Note that in the quote below, the woman whose feelings were hurt by a friend was the first of the two to write a letter in a Christmas card.

This "first-hurt, first-apologize rule" appears to be derived from the idea of friends as banked resources. The friendship bank should contain an adequate supply of understanding and forgiveness for failure to perform or for errors in judgment by one friend that adversely affect the other member of the friendship dyad. Obviously, this is an area in which two unwritten contracts often conflict with each other, as the injured parties proclaim, "A real friend would not do that" or "A real friend would understand why I had to do that." Time must elapse, usually, for the hurt party to bring him- or herself to make the first contact and do such apologizing. One 30-year-old woman said of her situation:

> I let the whole thing drop for a while. She lived in an entirely different social circle than I did and I thought, well, her social activities were so different from mine. And then, after a certain number of years, I thought, well to heck with that, I'll write a letter on a Christmas card. And she contacted me immediately, and from then on there was never any drop-

ping away and she said to me one time, the nicest thing that ever happened
to her was our getting back together again. So I was glad I did that and
didn't just forget her.

What Can Be Done About Enemies?

Obviously, in the case of enemyship, some of the foregoing
practices are de facto unavailable. Restoring someone else's
faith in one is possible only if that person once had such faith.
In the case of enemies, either they did not trust one another or
the trust was so thoroughly undermined when the relationship
broke up that its reconstruction is beyond simple achievement.

Although one might expect that people would develop strategies to overcome their enemies, would form coalitions for
defense, and would engage in confrontations with their enemies, what actually seems to be the case is that most people
practice avoidance of their enemies. A majority of the respondents in Wiseman's study said that they tried to stay out of the
way of their enemies—even going so far as to walk out of a room
if an enemy entered. Whereas they admitted hating or strongly
disliking their enemies, their primary responses to these feelings
were to be stunned or frightened, to feel threatened, and to
think defensively of ways to protect themselves. Some even tried
to think about the possibility of reconciliation and how to
straighten out problems that may have arisen between themselves and their enemies. (Such thoughts were the first glimmer,
by the way, that they may realize that some of the enmity was
of their own doing.)

Surprisingly few respondents thought in terms of counterattack or retaliation. One could speculate that they found it
demeaning to stoop to the level of the enemy, or that they saw
the task as being one of preserving their good images even if
others attempted to debase them. More often, their thoughts
turned to avoidance, disassociation, somehow getting their
enemies out of their lives. If there was an opportunity to
straighten things out, turn matters around, and reestablish
relationships, that was one consideration, but respondents were
more likely to worry about handling the matter so as to main-

tain their self-esteem and reduce, as much as possible, the worry about an enemy. To this end, they often called on friends as support and allies. They attempted to establish credibility among friends, hoping that their friends would respect and believe their version of whatever the problem was, a process that may cement enmity by making it impossible to "talk out differences."

Some respondents turned to friends to help them cope with their enemies. They claimed that the most helpful things friends did for them was to provide moral support and to agree with them about their enemies' faults or assure them that they were not to blame for the problem. Often, these friends claimed to hate or at least dislike the enemies as well. Only a few friends offered advice on reconciliation and/or retaliation, however. A few respondents claimed that they would not discuss the matter of an enemy with friends or that they had tried, but their friends tried to remain neutral, which was a disappointment to them.

A predominant response of all respondents, as noted earlier, was to see enmity unilaterally, for the most part—with themselves as innocent parties—a response that predicted no particularly effective remedy and instead prompted self-pity or nonconstructive rumination. Also, very few respondents offered any coherent or useful means of handling or neutralizing enemies. The ideas that they did offer were rather puny: Some respondents either denied to themselves that they had enemies to worry about or forced themselves to ignore or not think about the situation. Some claimed to present false fronts to their enemies, smiling and "being nice" so as not to alert the enemies to their awareness of the enemies' existence or, at the very least, to avoid giving the enemies the satisfaction of knowing the respondents were disturbed, frightened, or upset about the enemies' actions.

Obviously, making up with an enemy is much more difficult than making up after falling out with a friend. Few of the respondents said that they had even tried, and those who did try reported high rates of failure. Those who did not try gave the following reasons: They really did not want to be friends with the persons, their hate for their enemies was too deep, or they believed that such persons were unlikely to change regardless of what they, the respondents, might say or do. In other words, the predominant reaction was to feed into the sense of helplessness that characterizes enemyship.

Conclusion

In this chapter we have launched the examination of enmity by pointing out certain issues, perceptions, and tendencies reported by respondents in a pilot study of enemies. Although this work does not allow strong conclusions about relationships between enemies, it does highlight several key issues that provide insight into both enmity and the incompleteness of existing theories of relationships. For example, we are intrigued by the fact that friendships are regarded as far more fragile than enemyships, which are treated as remarkably robust and impermeable. Friendships break up, drift apart and change, need maintenance, and can be ruined by chance remarks. Enmity is not nearly so clearly transformable by single acts or vulnerable to patterns of activity affectively inconsistent with its nature (such as a single act of kindness), yet friendship is threatened by single acts of malice. It is also quite clear that enemyships are regarded as more permanently reliable as such than are friendships. Also, even though enemyships can often grow out of persistent friendship disappointments, the two relationships are not opposites or mirrors of each other, in that friendships would be very unlikely to grow from persistent acts of kindness to enemies, because such acts would be likely to generate suspicion about "true motives." Enemyship is a distinctive type of relationship that has its own unique characteristics and interactive career between participants. People explain the existence of enemies and their reaction to them in ways that tell us of their uniqueness both symbolically and emotionally.

We believe that enemyship cannot be explained by most existing theories of relationships. Simple exchange models of relating are inadequate to elucidate the operation and significance of enemies in daily life as well as the processes through which enemies are managed. Furthermore, we have identified a number of intriguing mysteries concerning enemyship as suitable topics for future research: locus of control, perceptions of power, personality correlates of beliefs and attributions about enemies, and the stability of enemyship. Thus we hope that this limited overview, with its comparative data on friendships and enemyships, offers a starting point for more comprehensive studies of the broad spectrum of relationships, and especially of personal enemies.

4

Family Reconfiguring
Following Divorce

Marilyn Coleman

Lawrence H. Ganong

In this chapter, we focus on relationship challenges associated with family reconfiguration following divorce. As in other chapters in this volume, and in this series of volumes, our emphasis will be on *processes* in family reconfiguring. Although we present some material on family structure and demographics, we do so mainly to help clarify the need for more researchers to examine processes, and because most previous work has focused primarily on family structure rather than on family process. The overall frame within which we explore challenges in reconfiguring families is the belief that cultural ideals related to family life exert a strong influence on the ways in which people conduct themselves, evaluate their own situations, and expect to be regarded by others. Because we have conducted most of our research in the United States, we use

American examples, but there is ample evidence that what we describe is not limited to North America (Bernardes, 1993; Levin, 1993).

The Cultural Context of Family Reconfiguring

As longtime observers and researchers of families in the United States, we are struck by the disparity between how people *think* about families and how they actually *live*. On the one hand, families exist in a wide variety of forms, and family processes are even more varied. It is increasingly difficult to make generalizations about how families function because there are so many ways to be a family. On the other hand, the families that Americans *think* about (and idealize) are much more limited. The ideal family continues to be the middle-class, first-marriage nuclear family, with a mother and father and two, sometimes three, children. This family ideal colors perceptions of how families *should* live and seems to interfere with the ability of society to develop other models of healthy family functioning, or even to accept that there are other models of healthy family functioning. As a result, Americans apologize for their families when they differ from the family ideal (one college senior told us, "I know my family is really weird but my Mom has been married twice and my Dad is on his third marriage") or brag if they are able to "pass" as a first-marriage nuclear family (a biological mother in a stepfather family said, "Our neighbors don't know that we are a stepfamily, they think we are just a *normal* family"). There is a sad paradox in the constricted ways Americans think about family, because families in the United States are extremely diverse. Family realities certainly do not match the monochromatic cultural views of what families should be.

Farber (1973) has argued that what he calls the "natural-family" model presupposes not only that the nuclear family is an ideal but that it exists as a universal, necessary entity in nature, an idea that can be traced back to the New England Puritans, who borrowed from English ecclesiastical family law and especially from Old Testament Hebrews. This nuclear family model has come to be associated with a moral, "natural" imperative. Other forms of family life are considered to be immoral or, at best, less moral. These less moral forms of family life tend to carry with them heavy stigma.

No doubt some of the stigma of divorce has been reduced in recent years, but there is still an undercurrent of moral outrage directed toward those who divorce. Although there is less tolerance for the open expression of such views, deeply felt negative attitudes toward those in nonnuclear families are still held by many. At the social level, there is a thin veneer of civility hiding the punitive nature of traditional mores, which suggests that those who do not conform to the family ideal should be disdained. Cultural adherence to this ideology helps explain why policy makers and government bodies can intrude so thoroughly into family life at the time of legal divorce (e.g., deciding the frequency of parent-child contacts, deciding which parent will pay for what needs of children), yet be reluctant to provide ongoing support to divorcing parents and their children. This ideology also contributes to the difficulty of reconfiguring relationships after divorce.

Reconfigured Families as Incomplete Institutions

Cultural adherence to nuclear family ideology led Cherlin (1978) to argue that remarriage is an incomplete institution. Cherlin contends that remarried families following divorce have more difficulties than first-marriage families because they lack institutionalized guidelines and support to help them solve their family problems. He further concludes that the absence of guidelines and norms for role performance, the dearth of culturally established, socially acceptable methods of resolving problems, and the relative absence of institutionalized social support for remarried adults and stepparents contribute to greater stress, inappropriate solutions to problems, and higher divorce rates for remarried families. Cherlin points to the lack of language and legal regulations as illustrations of how remarriages are incompletely institutionalized. We think that Cherlin's claims of incomplete institutionalization are equally applicable to all reconfiguring families following divorce, whether parents remarry or remain single. We will refer to these points later in the chapter as we examine specific relationship challenges, but here we want to elaborate briefly on the impact of societal application of the nuclear family ideology on reconfiguring families.

Lack of Institutionalized Social Support

Social organizations such as schools, youth groups, religious groups, and health care systems are based on policies and procedures designed primarily for nuclear families (Coleman, Ganong, & Henry, 1984a; Ganong, 1993). When families are reconfiguring following divorce, they find minimal support from these formal institutions, and they often encounter barriers. For example, stepparents who are involved in their stepchildren's schooling frequently find that schools make little allowance for the presence of stepparents. Enrollment forms may have places for parents' names only, seniors are given only *two* tickets for their parents to attend graduation ceremonies, and teachers are ill prepared for a child to have three or more adults (biological parents and stepparents) show up on "back to school" night (Coleman, Ganong, & Henry, 1984b). Although nonnuclear families are ostensibly welcome to participate in these social organizations, few organizations attempt to adjust their practices to facilitate these families' participation. For example, youth groups that make parental involvement a requirement for participation, such as 4-H, inadvertently discourage from joining those children who have only one parent available to help them. Those who do join may find themselves not fulfilling club requirements that parents attend all meetings. This subtle social insensitivity serves as a constant reminder to single parents and their children that they are deficient, encourages reconfigured families to act like nuclear families if they want to be accepted, and puts undue pressure on relationships within remarried families to imitate as closely as possible nuclear family relationships. Rather than providing buffers, the customs of social systems that interact with reconfigured families sometimes increase stress on family relationships.

Nonexistence or Ambiguity of Legal Relationships

From a societal perspective, divorce breaks social contracts between society and the family and opens the door for legal intrusion into family affairs that usually are not considered the business of government. Although family laws and policies are ostensibly designed to protect the interests of children, in reality judges adhere to legal decisions based on custom or on their own naive or idiosyncratic beliefs regarding children's development and welfare. Ideology regarding the sanctity of the family applies almost exclusively to nuclear families; once families are "broken," society no longer needs to respect their privacy. For example, custom dictates that physical custody of children (i.e., where the children reside) be awarded to mothers and "visitation rights" with their children and sometimes joint legal custody (i.e., the right to make decisions about the children) be granted to fathers. Nonresidential parents, usually fathers, are required to contribute to child support, and the amount of child support is not supposed to be contingent on frequency or length of visits. Even when legal custody is officially shared, the legal status of nonresidential parents' relationships with their children following divorce is often ambiguous. In fact, parents and children do not often know what their rights are vis-à-vis each other until they violate a law or the divorce agreement, initiating disputes and conflicts between the divorced parents. Judges, attorneys, law enforcement officers, and others may then be called on to make or to enforce decisions about family relationships and behaviors. This may leave parents and children feeling powerless, which can lead to further legal and interpersonal battles as parents attempt to gain a measure of control over themselves and their family relationships.

Stepparents generally have been overlooked in federal and state laws in the United States; they have few legal responsibilities toward their stepchildren, and few rights as well (Chambers, 1990; Fine & Fine, 1992). Although some recent changes in family law indirectly affect the legal relationship between step-parents and stepchildren (e.g., more states are allowing third-party requests for postdivorce custody), there is little consensus regarding needed legal changes, and almost no political pressure on legislatures to alter existing policies and laws (Chambers, 1990). The American Bar Association has established the Standing Committee on the Rights and Responsibilities of Stepparents, which recently drafted a model act (Tenenbaum, 1991), but there is relatively little impetus to push for legal changes regarding stepparents' status.

Clinicians contend that the absence of a legal relationship serves as a barrier to the development of emotionally close stepparent-stepchild bonds (Ganong & Coleman, 1994). For the most part, stepparents' obligations to stepchildren are based on whatever family members want them to be. Although this flexibility can be seen as an advantage, it is likely that for many stepparents the absence of legal ties adds to their feelings of ambiguity and lack of control regarding their relationships with stepchildren.

Relative Absence of Guidelines and Norms for Role Performance and Problem Solving

Perhaps the most important way the nuclear family ideal affects relationship process in reconfigured families is through the absence of cultural norms that serve to guide relational behaviors in those families. Parents who believe there is only one natural, normal way to be a family may find it difficult to identify their roles and responsibilities when their family ceases to fit the culturally prescribed model. For example, in the idealized nuclear family, father is the primary breadwinner. What role is left for him following divorce? Some fathers may reject the continued responsibility of financially supporting their children because they do not equate paying child support with the role of breadwinner. Others may perceive that the family has ended and, as a result, they no longer see a role for themselves with their children (Arendell, 1992; Umberson & Williams, 1993). This may partially explain why some fathers argue that it is not fair for them to have to pay child support. These arguments are generally framed in the language of injustice, tied either to seemingly pragmatic reasons (e.g., the ex-wife works and makes a sufficient wage to pay for the child's needs) or to complaints about the former spouse (e.g., she is frivolous with money, she spends the money on herself rather than on the child). In essence, these fathers are arguing that they are not responsible for one of the primary tasks of fathers under the nuclear family ideology; for them, the divorce dissolves the family, so they are no longer obligated to fulfill father role responsibilities as exercised in the normal context of "family." The prevalence of the nuclear family ideology makes it difficult to recognize and/or create acceptable alternative models for successfully being a family.

The nuclear family ideology also contributes to confusion about roles and responsibilities regarding children after remarriage. According to Visher and Visher (1988), many stepfamilies imitate or attempt to reconstitute the nuclear family model, behavior Goldner (1982) has labeled "the retreat from complexity" (p. 205). Lacking models and established rituals and rules for behaving, stepfamilies try to re-create the nuclear family because it is familiar and simpler to deal with than the reality of stepfamily complexity and ambiguity.

In order for stepfamilies to re-create themselves as nuclear families, they must complete two tasks: (a) Stepparents must assume parental roles, duties, and responsibilities; and (b) the families must redefine themselves so that only those living in the household are considered to be family members. Stepparent adoption is one of the most widely used methods of achieving these objectives: The noncustodial parent gives up or transfers parental rights and responsibilities to the adopting stepparent, the stepparent legally becomes a parent, and the stepfamily "becomes" a nuclear family. For these families, the issue of how family relationships should be performed is less of a problem because the answer is quite clear—they should follow cultural scripts written for first-marriage nuclear families. Keep in mind, however, that more often than not the nonresidential biological parent does not want to relinquish parental rights, and/or the stepparent does not wish to adopt. This means that for the majority of stepfamilies there are many questions about roles and relationships; trying to re-create the nuclear ideal may only add to existing problems.

Marriage Culture, Divorce Culture

If the nuclear family ideal is so influential, why would people even consider divorcing and forming reconfigured families? Apparently, like two weather fronts meeting to create a powerful thunderstorm, the cultural values of individualism and personal control collide with the nuclear family ideology. According to Hackstaff (1993), in the United States a traditional "marriage culture" competes with an emergent "divorce culture," so in spite of the fact that most Americans believe that marriage should be a lifelong commitment (part of the marriage culture/nuclear family ideology; Furstenberg, 1987), they also believe in divorce as a solution to unhappy, unsatisfying marriages (divorce culture/individualism). Although the coexistence of a strong marriage-oriented belief system and a relatively high divorce rate may seem paradoxical, these competing cultural values help explain why marriage and divorce rates in the United States are the highest in the industrialized world: More than 90% of Americans marry (Cate & Lloyd, 1992), but more than half of these marriages end in divorce.

According to Hackstaff (1993), the values of the marriage culture define divorce as "escape (from), a failure entailing loss, a decision of last resort—a desperate, if not selfish choice, a disruption of identity and an upheaval of positional relationships" (pp. 365-366). Hackstaff contrasts the divorce culture as being "a gateway (to), an ordeal permitting growth, an ever-present option, an affirmation of personal identity and a rearrangement of relationships" (p. 366). The marriage culture is based on those traditional responsibilities in marriage that are rooted in religious or social commitments that transcend the couple. The divorce culture, rooted in freely chosen bonds and a tradition of individualism, is based on egalitarian fulfillment and mutual support in marriage. Many doomsayers believe the rise of the divorce culture is *the* major problem in society, and that divorce should be prevented at nearly all costs (Popenoe, 1993). Others have suggested normalizing divorce, arguing that divorce should now be considered a developmental stage in the life cycle (McGoldrick & Carter, 1989).

These two ideologies, the nuclear family ideal/marriage culture and the individualism/divorce culture, serve as the backdrop for an understanding of the relational processes transpiring in reconfiguring families. We hasten to add that we are not suggesting that these ideologies are the only two that are relevant, although we think they are unavoidable for most postdivorce families and are among the most influential.

Family Challenges Postdivorce: The Process of Redefining and Maintaining Relationships

A great deal has been written about the process of marital dissolution (see, e.g., Bohannan, 1971; Duck, 1982; Gottman, 1993; Hagestad & Smyer, 1982; Price & McKenry, 1988) and about the effects of marital dissolution on the well-being of family members (Acock & Demo, 1994; Amato, 1993; Ambert, 1989; Hetherington, Cox, & Cox, 1985) and family relationships (Ahrons & Rodgers, 1987). However, a gradual shift in focus has occurred in recent years, and more attention is being paid to family processes *following* divorce, with an emphasis on understanding *divorce as an ongoing process* that begins well before physical separation and continues for months or even years after the legal decree is finalized (Block, Block, & Gjerde, 1988).

In keeping with this trend and the focus of this volume, we will examine two major categories of challenges facing members of reconfigured families. First, we will examine the processes of *redefining and maintaining relationships* following divorce. Our focus will be on relationships between family members who no longer share a residence. Changes caused by divorce affect all family relationships, but maintaining ties with family members residing in different households represents an especially difficult challenge for reconfiguring families. For example, former spouses have to develop new ways to relate to each other as coparents, and nonresidential parents and children must develop new patterns of relating to each other intermittently and in the absence of the other parent. We will also examine challenges regarding the *development of new family relationships* after divorce. Postdivorce remarriage potentially adds many new family relationships (e.g., parents-in-law, stepgrandparents), some for which there are no labels (e.g., the relationship between a person's former spouse and his or her current spouse), but the focus here will be on adults' relationships with new partners and stepparent-stepchild relationships.

Structural Reconfiguration Postdivorce

Before examining these challenges, we want to digress briefly to discuss the structural diversity of families following divorce. We do this for several reasons: (a) It is likely that reconfiguring processes are affected by structure, (b) most family researchers have focused on structure, (c) a presentation of structural variations helps to illustrate the diversity of reconfigured family forms, and (d) the diversity of structures and the conceptual complexity such diversity entails provide a framework for understanding why family scholars have "retreated from complexity" in their study of postdivorce families.

There are many ways that families with minor children reconfigure structurally after divorce. A common, almost stereotypical, scenario is one in which mothers who have custody of their children head households with little support from their former husbands. According to this scenario, contacts between the former spouses are few, but rancorous; nonresidential fathers gradually lose contact with their children, either through their own lack of interest (the so-called deadbeat dads) or because of the efforts of vengeful wives and their attorneys (as portrayed in many popular films, such as *Mrs. Doubtfire*). Although this family form certainly exists and the pattern of interaction described is common enough (Arendell, 1992), single parenthood is typically a relatively short-term phenomenon; most divorced adults enter into subsequent romantic partnerships.

It should be noted that legal divorce is not the only way for unhappy marriages to end. For some couples, physical separation becomes a permanent state and serves as an alternative to divorce. This is particularly true for African American couples (Morgan, 1988). In an unknown but probably large number of families, adults cohabit with new partners after divorce but do not legally remarry. Although these may be long-term relationships, some divorced adults have a series of shorter-term cohabiting partners. Furthermore, some divorced adults do not legally remarry because they enter homosexual relationships. Considering that 25% of gay men, and plausibly a similar percentage of lesbian women, were at one time in heterosexual marriages (Masters & Johnson, 1979), it is likely that a number of reconfigured families consist of gay or lesbian couples and residential or nonresidential children from previous heterosexual relationships.

In spite of the several variations mentioned here, the most common way Americans reconfigure their lives after divorce continues to be through remarriage. Between two thirds and three fourths of divorced adults remarry, and they do so quickly. The median interval between divorce and remarriage is only 3 years (Glick, 1980), but given that two thirds of all couples cohabit before remarriage (Bumpass & Sweet, 1989), the typical interval from one relationship to another is even shorter.

It can be concluded that families reconfigure in a variety of ways, they reconfigure quickly, and they reconfigure several times. As a result, common postdivorce variations might include living without a partner, cohabiting, breaking up, living without a partner, cohabiting, and remarrying. This pattern, or some version of it, might be repeated several times over the course of a lifetime; well over 10% of remarriages represent at least the third marriage for one or both of the partners (National Center for Health Statistics, 1993). The family histories of these "serial monogamists" and their children are likely to be substantially different from those of postdivorce family members who experience one prior marriage/committed relationship before settling into a second and final committed relationship. Unfortunately, there have been few studies of families who have experienced multiple transitions, so little is known about how they might differ from families who reconfigure only once following divorce (Brody, Newbaum, & Forehand, 1988). At the very least we know these transitions represent many potential changes for both adults and children: residential changes, the addition and loss of new household members, economic changes, and alterations in family identity. These relationship transitions and the resulting structural changes in households and families are often stressful and may have profound effects on both adults and children.

Household Changes Postdivorce

Family life in first-marriage families generally exists within the confines of a single household. As a result, social scientists, policy makers, clinicians, and others often have simplistically assumed that families and households are equivalent groups. Following divorce, however, family dynamics are often played out in two households, a structural change that can have important implications for family functioning. Unfortunately, researchers have been slow to abandon the notion that families and households are equivalent, resulting in divorce being seen as a process of reduction (e.g., the breaking down of the family, the loss of a parent). This reductionist view has contributed to divorce's being described in terms of loss and pathology— "broken home," "single-parent family"—rather than as a process of family reconfiguration and redefinition that includes gains as well as the inevitable losses of routines, roles, and so on.

In attempting to replace the language of loss and pathology that is so often attached to divorce, Ahrons (1980) has coined the term "binuclear family," which implies that the family does not end with divorce but continues in a different form. According to Ahrons, the reorganization of a family through divorce frequently yields maternal and paternal households, with children as the link or nucleus. These two interrelated households, whether each is a one-parent or a cohabiting/remarried household, form one family system. The term *binuclear* represents the structural concept of a family system with two households, irrespective of the importance of each in the child's life experiences. However, it is the *divorce process* that is most significant in shaping subsequent family dynamics and individual adjustment. Therefore, divorce can be viewed as a process of family reconfiguration that may include expansion of the nuclear, one-household family into the binuclear, two-household family, a process that expands interest in the impact of divorce to include questions regarding the ways in which family members redefine and maintain relationships with each other when they no longer live together on a full-time basis. Of particular concern are two binuclear relationships that are known to have important effects on children, adults, and the entire family system: relationships between nonresidential parents and their children, and relationships between former spouses. By focusing on these two types of relationships, we are not suggesting that other family ties are insignificant. On the contrary, there are many meaningful relationships that could be examined, such as those between residential parents and children, between children and grandparents, and between siblings. However, nonresidential parent-child bonds and former spouse relationships are probably the most challenging ongoing family relationships in reconfigured families.

Nonresidential Parent-Child Relationships

We will limit our attention in this chapter to nonresidential father-child relationships because fathers are by far the largest group of nonresidential parents, and divorce seems to particularly interfere with the child-nonresidential father relationship. In fact, Furstenberg, Nord, Peterson, and Zill (1983) found that only 33% of children in the National Survey of Children had monthly contact with their nonresidential fathers; there was little, if any, contact between more than 50% of children and their nonresidential fathers, and among 12- to 16-year-olds, 44% had not seen their nonresidential fathers in the previous 12 months. Close relationships, if they ever existed, had ceased

between huge numbers of children and their fathers, an estrangement that apparently often continues into adulthood
(Rossi & Rossi, 1990). Although not all studies of nonresidential father-child relations find such high percentages of estrangement (Braver, Wolchik, Sandler, & Sheets, 1993; Mott, 1990),
the tendency for divorced fathers to reduce or lose contact with
their children is so widespread that the few models proposed to
study these relationships, and most of the research, attempt to
explain *father noninvolvement* or *father absence* following divorce. Contact between fathers and children, certainly a minimal criterion for maintaining a relationship, has been the most
popular outcome variable in research on nonresidential father-
child relationships. We begin this section with a review of some
of these studies.

Contact between nonresidential fathers and their children
depends on a number of factors. For example, father-child contact following divorce is strongly associated with the presence
of a joint custody arrangement (Bowman & Ahrons, 1985), however, recent estimates are that only 16% of children nationwide
are involved in joint custody situations of any type (Donnelly
& Finkelhor, 1993). Nonresidential father-child contact also
appears to differ somewhat according to the sex of the child.
Seltzer (1991) concludes from an examination of data from the
National Study of Families and Households that absent fathers
stay more involved with daughters postdivorce than with sons,
although the reasons for this disparity are unknown.

Other factors that predict greater nonresidential father-child
contact include the following:

- *Close proximity* (Dudley, 1991; Furstenberg et al., 1983; Zill, 1988):
  Living near to each other facilitates interaction, just as increasing distance
  adds costs such as additional traveling time and greater transportation
  expenses.
- *Short time lapse since divorce or separation* (Donnelly & Finkelhor, 1993;
  Furstenberg et al., 1983; Seltzer, 1991): For a variety of reasons, father-
  child post-divorce contact appears to diminish over time. Some of these
  reasons are related to proximity changes, remarriage, children's growing
  involvement in outside interests, and fathers' increasing feelings of parental
  disenfranchisement.

- *Presence of relatively young children* (Dudley, 1991): Among other reasons, younger children are probably less involved with friends and activities outside the home and thus are more available to spend time with their nonresidential fathers.

- *Higher education and income level of father* (Donnelly & Finkelhor, 1993; Zill, 1988): These fathers may be more aware of the importance of maintaining relationships with their children and better able to afford the time, transportation costs, and housing entailed in visits with their children than are fathers with low education and income levels.

- *Presence of multiple children* (Donnelly & Finkelhor, 1993): Nonresidential fathers who have larger families may stay in contact partly because the mothers cannot manage all the parenting responsibilities on their own. Another hypothesis is that these men may have had large families in the first place because they especially enjoy children and want to spend time with them.

- *Father's desire to help control the destiny of his child* (Braver et al., 1993): Nonresidential parents who do not feel disenfranchised are financially supportive of their children and continue frequent contact even 3 years after filing for divorce.

- *Nonlitigated divorce and custody proceedings* (Elkin, 1987; Koch & Lowery, 1984): Kruk (1993) reports that legal processes often exacerbate parental conflict and even create hostility in families where amicable negotiation may have taken place, although Clingempeel and Repucci (1982) found that family courts and legal procedures vary considerably in the extent to which they encourage or discourage cooperation between divorcing parents.

- *Parents' remaining single after divorce* (Donnelly & Finkelhor, 1993): When either parent remarries, the number of relationships that must be maintained increases exponentially. It may also be true that some nonresidential fathers remarry women who dislike being reminded of their husbands' previous families and therefore actively discourage all contact with their nonresidential children. On the other hand, residential mothers who remarry may want to reestablish nuclear families; they attempt to establish impermeable boundaries around the household and encourage their new spouses to take on parenting roles that isolate the nonresidential fathers. Many are evidently quite successful with these strategies; remarried mothers (compared with divorced single mothers and never-married mothers) report the lowest level of interaction and conflict with nonresidential fathers and the lowest level of nonresidential fathers' interaction with, and influence on, the children (Acock & Demo, 1994).

Although the bulk of research on father-child contact in postdivorce families has focused on structural characteristics, the logistical barriers mentioned above (e.g., physical distance, lack of legal access, finances) are not sufficient to explain the process of how father-child relationships reconfigure after divorce.

A particularly relevant processual model developed by Hagestad and Smyer (1982) contrasts the exits from marital roles and relationships with the entry or the transition into marriage. This model may be extended to the examination of nonresidential father-child involvement in reconfiguring families. Hagestad and Smyer suggest that role changes are experienced as crises when the transitions (a) are unscheduled or off-time, (b) are not controlled by individual choice, (c) occur with little advance warning, (d) entail status loss, and (e) have no cultural rite of passage associated with them. When role transitions are unexpected *and* are not supported by social scripts or normative guidelines, then having a sense of personal control over the experience becomes highly salient in a person's coping with the changes encountered. An individual who feels he or she has a degree of control over the dissolution process can attempt to balance the disequilibrium experienced with such nonnormative (unscheduled) transitions by slowing down the process enough to allow him- or herself time to grieve the loss of the relationship, establish new routines and behaviors, and gather social support. Conversely, someone who experiences the changes as beyond his or her control and who received no prior warning will find transitions related to divorce, an incompletely institutionalized life change, to be enormously stressful.

According to Hagestad and Smyer, the challenges in ending a relationship are related to the dissolution of three kinds of bonds: (a) emotional attachment to the other person, (b) attachment to the role, and (c) routines of everyday living. Of course, the challenges facing nonresidential fathers and children are somewhat different from those for divorcing spouses. For example, in successful adjustment to family reconfiguring, we expect fathers to dissolve emotional attachments to their ex-wives but to maintain emotional attachments to their children. We also expect fathers to retain attachment to the role of father, although there may have to be a redefinition of the role from in-house father to nonresidential father. The routines of everyday living in the previous household need to be replaced by new routines related to fathering, some for when children visit and some for the periods of time when children are not sharing living space with their fathers. We would expect nonresidential fathers and children to meet these challenges and maintain a relationship successfully to the extent that they feel some control over the process.

There is some empirical support for this model. Often the actions of nonresidential fathers represent attempts to gain control: over the process, over other family members, and over themselves. Arendell (1992), in an in-depth study of absent fathers, found that the men in her sample defined their relationships within the context of rights, encompassing beliefs about individualism, choice, control, authority, and the traditional masculine norms of male privilege and power within family life. Conflicts with ex-wives were power struggles centering on child support and visitation. Legal threats regarding custody battles and modifications to child support and access to children were framed by these fathers as strategies designed to gain control over the process, the former spouse, and the children. Refusal to pay child support was described as a response to violated rights and unfair treatment, and absence from the children was used to justify not paying support. Absence was even seen as a method of gaining personal control through emotion management. Fathers who found seeing their children only periodically to be too painful, or those who were fearful of their anger at former spouses, justified absence from their children as a way to distance themselves from situations in which they experienced these intense feelings. The children suffered because these fathers were not successful in detaching themselves emotionally from their ex-spouses. Other studies have found that fathers who gathered some control over the reconfiguring process, either through legally shared custody or through cooperative, supportive relationships with their former spouses, maintained more contact with their children (Ahrons & Miller, 1993; Umberson & Williams, 1993).

The ambiguity of the nonresidential father role may be too uncomfortable for some men, so they withdraw from their children, essentially abandoning the role, rather than continually face situations in which they feel awkward and unsure of how to continue fathering. A recently proposed theory congruent with our adaptation of the Hagestad and Smyer (1982) model suggests that postdivorce father involvement over time is predicted by fathers' identity, commitment to the father role and to their children, the salience of the role, and the support of significant others (e.g., former spouse, current partner) (Ihinger-Tallman, Pasley, & Buehler, 1993). Nonresidential fathers' ability to dissolve some roles, modify others, and maintain a father identity and attachment to their children is not merely a function of intrapersonal or interpersonal factors; there are no institutionalized paths, no models of orderly sequencing of the transition from residential to nonresidential father-child status, and no culturally shared expectations to guide those experiencing the change through the process of reconfiguring. The reconfiguring process appears to be idiosyncratic and individualistic, with few norms and limited cultural sanctions.

Former Spouses' Relationships

For divorced parents with minor children, a major challenge is working out ways to reconfigure their relationship from marital partners to former spouses. Hagestad and Smyer (1982) describe such a challenge as "decathecting," or withdrawing emotional energy from the relationship with the partner and from the role of spouse while continuing to invest emotional energy in the relationship with the children and in the role of coparent. Put another way, the task for the divorcing couple is to maintain a coparental relationship while abandoning a marital relationship. The quality of the ex-spousal relationship is an important factor in determining the success of the relationship between nonresidential parents and their children.

Parental conflict has profound negative effects on children's well-being, regardless of whether parents are married or divorced (Johnston, 1993). In fact, predivorce parental conflict may have a greater influence on children than separation or divorce per se (Block et al., 1988). Nonetheless, most divorcing spouses initially engage in some degree of hostile interaction, which makes the development of at least minimally cooperative, nonconflictual styles of interaction between parents an important part of family reconfiguration. Given the importance of former spouse relationships to children's well-being, it is somewhat surprising that the former spouse relationship has not received more attention from researchers. Most investigators have not recognized the effects of continuities of the relationships between formerly married couples, despite the attention in recent years to divorce as an ongoing process. For couples who have children, these former spouse relationships can continue for years or even decades after their marriages have ended.

As might be expected, there are few models available from which to formulate hypotheses about former spouse ties. As mentioned earlier, the model of the dissolution of marital bonds developed by Hagestad and Smyer (1982) can be modified for this purpose. From this perspective, we would expect the emotional attachment between partners to be "decathected," the attachment to some marital roles dissolved (e.g., sexual partner, confidante), the attachment to other roles modified (e.g., coparents), and the attachment to daily routines dissolved, replaced by new behavioral routines designed to accommodate the task of being coparents while not sharing a residence and typically while not having daily contact.

Emotional Decathecting

The emotions that many divorcing partners experience create obvious barriers to their maintaining successful former spouse relationships. Anger, resentment, and hurt over past marital wrongs are common responses of people who are ending their marriages. Negative feelings toward former partners lead some divorced adults to sever ties completely. Others want to punish former partners through the legal system, by poisoning relationships between children and former spouses and by making continuing interaction as difficult as possible.

There is some evidence that gender differences may contribute to the decathecting process. For example, Hagestad and Smyer (1982) suggest that women monitor interpersonal relationships more closely than do men and thus are aware of relationship problems sooner. However, Hopper (1993) found that "all divorcing people described themselves as having been keenly aware of their marital problems for a long time" (p. 805). Although divorce is almost always a substantial disruption in people's lives, the divorce process does not have uniform psychological and emotional effects; some individuals welcome separation and divorcing because they offer relief from conflict, physical or psychological abuse, and the psychopathological behaviors of certain family members, whereas others face divorce with regrets, sadness, and fear. It is probably fair to suggest that divorce is an all-positive or all-negative process for only a few; most who divorce go through an array of responses, including both relief and regret. We hypothesize that the functioning of close relationships in postdivorce families is related to how individual family members make sense of the divorce (for an excellent study of the rhetoric of motives among divorced adults, see Hopper, 1993). Adults and children who embrace the "divorce culture" (Hackstaff, 1993), who welcome divorce, or who define it as basically a "good thing" for themselves, will be more likely to anticipate postdivorce family life with eagerness, regarding it as a chance for a new start. Those who ascribe to the "marriage culture" and define divorce as basically a bad thing may feel shame and guilt and also may be frightened and very insecure about the future. To date, the relation between the meaning of the divorce experience and subsequent close relationships in families has not been examined extensively by researchers.

Attachment to Roles and Routines

In describing the adaptations of former spouses to changes demanded in their roles and routines, we find it useful to consider the construct of *relational competence*. In Volume 3 of this series, *Social Context and Relationships,* Klein and Milardo (1993) note that relational competence involves three dimensions:

1. *Task definition:* the interpretation of relational problems, such as accounts, attributions, and motives of rhetoric
2. *Behavioral repertoire:* the sets of behaviors that are selected to cope with the problems
3. *Evaluative standards:* the criteria used to assess whether or not the behaviors successfully resolved the problems

These dimensions of relational competence, in Klein and Milardo's view, are not static characteristics of individuals or relationships, but are socially constructed, in part by the individuals in the relationship and in part by their social networks. To this we would add the notion that individuals in relationships *and* their social networks are influenced by the social constructions of relational competence created by the broader cultural context in which they exist.

The obvious point here is that the process of reconfiguring former spouse relationships does not occur in a vacuum; as in other personal relationships, former spouses are affected not only by each other but by third parties. Klein and Milardo use the term *third party* to refer to social network members individually and collectively, and we will extend that concept to include cultural and social institutions, such as religious, legal, and school systems. Third parties influence the development and maintenance of relational competence "by applying their own perspectives and standards to the target relationship, including values, beliefs, experiences, needs, interests, and objectives" (Klein & Milardo, 1993, p. 59).

In the reconfiguration of a spouse relationship into a *former* spouse relationship, a diverse array of third parties exist: the couple's children, the kin of each former spouse, friends and former friends of the couple, the new partners, the kin of the new partners, friends of the new partners, children of the new partners, professionals from the divorce industry (i.e., attorneys, counselors, mediators), coworkers, clergy, support groups, children's teachers, children's friends, and so forth. All of these third par-

ties are likely to have views on some aspect of relational competence. It is likely that these views will reflect a wide range of definitions of the tasks of former spouse relationships, behaviors
needed to solve relational problems, and standards of evaluating
the couple's behavioral attempts to solve the problems.

The input of third parties can have a major effect, because
the nature of former spouse relationships does not have clear,
consensual definitions, although there are widespread expectations that former spouses should dislike each other (Bernard,
1981). Because there are few cultural norms that former spouses
can rely on to guide their interactions as they reconfigure the
relationship (Goetting, 1979, 1980), they may be especially
vulnerable to third-party opinions and suggestions.

The influence of third parties is likely to be directed to one
former partner only rather than to both partners. Because third
parties often take sides, their attempts to influence the relationship are more likely to be based on what they think is in the best
interests of the individual they are supporting and will reflect
awareness of one perspective only rather than recognizing the
existence of multiple perspectives (i.e., both his and hers). For
the most part, third parties will act out of concern for one
former spouse only, although some third parties, such as children of the couple, may be concerned for the well-being of both.
This framework presents us with a context within which to
consider the difficulty former spouses have when attempting to
reconceptualize, redefine, and remodel their relationship.

A number of problems make the establishment of workable,
cooperative former spouse relationships difficult. For example,
the adversarial nature of the legal system discourages cooperative postdivorce processes and relationships and helps to exacerbate hostility between divorcing couples. Even when couples
want to maintain civil postdivorce relationships, they may end
up in conflict as a result of the actions of their attorneys, who
are trained to defend their clients and "win" for them. This
contributes to cultural expectations of hostility and conflict
between former spouses (as depicted often in popular movies,
such as *The War of the Roses*).

Nonetheless, a variety of postdivorce relationships between former spouses are possible. Based on data from a 3-year longitudinal study of divorced parents, Ahrons and Rodgers (1987) have developed a typology of five postdivorce former spouse relationships, which they call Dissolved Duos, Perfect Pals, Cooperative Colleagues, Angry Associates, and Fiery Foes. The most frequent pattern is that of Dissolved Duos. These couples have little, if any, contact postdivorce and resemble the stereotype of single-parent families—the mother typically has been awarded sole physical custody of the children, and the children gradually lose contact with their nonresidential father.

Perfect Pals are couples who parent essentially the same as they did before the divorce. Decision making about the children is shared, holidays and special events are spent together, and the members of the couple often refer to their ex-spouses as their best friends. These reconfigured families are truly binuclear in that the children continue to be the nucleus of the family although there are now two households instead of one. Family processes for these couples postdivorce do not differ drastically from what they were prior to the divorce, at least from the children's view. Perfect Pals commonly remain single postdivorce.

Former spouses who are Cooperative Colleagues get along well but are much less interdependent than Perfect Pals. Cooperative Colleagues are able to separate clearly the spousal role with their ex-partners from the parenting role, a role that they effectively maintain. Although highly unlikely to regard each other as best friends, Cooperative Colleagues are able to plan together and make joint decisions regarding their children. Remarriage of one or both partners does not interfere with their joint-parenting responsibilities.

The fourth type of postdivorce former spouse relationship is that of Angry Associates. These couples have great difficulty cooperating. They are unable to separate spousal and parental roles. The adults remain angry with each other and have difficulty allowing each other to parent the children. They do not readily share information about the children, nor do they make decisions jointly. Among these couples arguments often ensue over visitation, and the former spouses use the children to punish each other. Couples who have previously functioned as Cooperative Colleagues sometimes become Angry Associates when one or the other remarries.

The Fiery Foes are exaggerated versions of the Angry Associates. These couples remain emotionally tied to each other in a hostile way. Each tries to damage the children's relationships with the other parent and each is likely to go back to court to seek changes in custody and child support awards. Not surprisingly, children of Fiery Foes feel caught between their constantly warring parents. The remarriage of either ex-spouse commonly adds another sparring partner to the ongoing battle of the Fiery Foes.

This typology yields a picture of the variety of ways that former spouses create postdivorce patterns of relating. What it does not do is explain clearly the processes by which the couples create these patterns. It is in the interest of both reconfiguring families and society as a whole for researchers to be able to explain how former partners become Cooperative Colleagues, rather than adversaries or strangers. Understanding how new partners are incorporated in supporting roles rather than in the roles of added adversaries against former spouses is also important, and part of establishing new partnerships is the incorporation of new partners in roles with children.

Developing New Relationships
in Reconfigured Families

Just as divorce is a nonnormative, off-time life transition, so is remarriage. For example, middle-aged adults generally do not anticipate being in the market for new partners. The language and customs of dating and courtship are awkward for older adults because they are designed for young, never-married couples. Just as remarriage is culturally off-time for normative life-course expectations, it also can be off-time for family life-course experiences. Adults do not expect suddenly to acquire children to help raise, especially children who may be school age or adolescents, and children do not expect to gain additional adults in "parentlike" positions. Some people who remarry find themselves involved in multiple off-schedule relationships; for example, stepparents who have never had children simultaneously begin marital and child-rearing careers.

Remarried families, unlike first-marriage families, face the task of beginning several relationships simultaneously (e.g., the remarried couple, stepparent-stepchild relationships, stepgrandparent-child relationships, new in-law ties) while redefining and maintaining altered parent-child relationships, former spouse relationships, and relationships with extended kin. Remarried families generally have more people and more relationships than do first-marriage families (Clingempeel, 1981). The more people and the more relationships, the more important it is that there be clear communication among members if the family system is to function smoothly. Therefore, reconfigured families, by virtue of their complexity, place greater demands on their members' problem-solving and communication skills (Nelson & Levant, 1991).

In spite of the difficulties associated with nonnormative or off-time events, however, most adults repartner following divorce, some legally remarrying, some cohabiting, many doing both sequentially. Consequently, a major challenge for members of reconfiguring families is to establish new relationships that are functional and satisfying. Once again, two relationships can be highlighted for their presumably greater importance in predicting the well-being of individual family members and the whole family system: relationships between remarried/cohabiting partners and relationships between stepparents and stepchildren (Ganong & Coleman, 1994).

Remarriage/Cohabiting Partner Relationships

Clinicians often identify a strong couple bond as one of the primary prerequisites of a successful stepfamily, the rationale being that a strong bond between adult partners facilitates the development of positive stepparent-stepchild relationships and serves as a buffer when other family relationships are stressful (Mills, 1984; Visher & Visher, 1988). Even though some view the stepparent-stepchild relationship as the pivotal relationship in postdivorce remarried families (Crosbie-Burnett, 1984; Mills, 1984), there is widespread agreement that couples' relationships are extremely important for the well-being of both the adult partners and other family members.

The attempt to build new relationships in the midst of the complexity of reconfiguring contributes to making remarriage relationship development different from that of first marriages. Not surprisingly, many remarried individuals are caught off guard by the discrepancy between what they expect to find and what they actually encounter in the process of establishing a remarriage relationship (Ganong & Coleman, 1994). We will address two questions related to developing new couple relationships following divorce: Why do divorced adults seek new partners? Once they have begun a partnership, how do they develop a strong couple bond?

Why Do Divorced Adults Seek New Partners?

Perhaps it is not surprising that researchers have found that the previously married have stronger pragmatic than romantic motivations to remarry (Farrell & Markman, 1986; Ganong & Coleman, 1989; Kvanli & Jennings, 1987). Common reasons given for remarriage, in addition to love, include financial security, help in raising children, response to social pressure, response to legal threats regarding the custody of children, relief from loneliness, desire for a frequent sexual partner, pregnancy, wanting to be taken care of, desire for companionship, shared interests, liking the partner, and convenience. These practical reasons for remarriage or repartnering are not necessarily better than romantic motivations. Social pressure to "be normal," seeking relief from financial stress, and even soliciting help in raising children can be unsound bases on which to establish new adult partnerships.

Although men and women give many of the same reasons for remarriage, there are differences in postdivorce courtship behaviors that suggest that their motivations to remarry differ as well. For example, women may be more likely than men to remarry to establish financial security. It is widely known that women and children often suffer severe economic deprivation after divorce (Hoffman & Duncan, 1988). Remarriage or cohabiting can help alleviate such financial pressure by adding an additional income to the household. In fact, finding a new partner is perhaps the surest and most rapid route out of postdivorce poverty (Hill, 1992). That well-educated and financially secure women are less likely than other women to remarry lends support to this hypothesis (Oh, 1986).

Whether for romantic or pragmatic reasons, remarriers generally make relatively quick decisions about future partners. There is little evidence that they prepare for remarriage (Ganong & Coleman, 1989; Hanna & Knaub, 1981) other than by cohabiting (Bumpass, 1990). Living together may be an attempt to assess compatibility and to get to know one another via daily interaction, or it may be a way to avoid the "dating game." The courtship process may be uncomfortable for mature adults with parenting responsibilities; their social scripts for dating may be outmoded, which makes them feel foolish and uncertain about what to do. Although combining two households is seldom easy, for some it may be more appealing than contending with the ambiguities of dating.

Unfortunately, we know even less about the process of courtship prior to remarriage than we do about people's reasons for remarrying. Most research on courtship and most courtship models have been oriented toward young, never-married adults (Cate & Lloyd, 1992). Investigations of remarriage courtship are very limited and, with one exception (Rodgers, 1987), there have been no conceptual frameworks proposed to explain remarriage courtship processes. A pattern found in one longitudinal study began with partial cohabitation (i.e., prospective male partner spends a few nights per week in the mother's household) followed by a brief period of full-time living together prior to remarriage (Montgomery, Anderson, Hetherington, & Clingempeel, 1992). Given the pervasiveness of cohabiting as an alternative or prelude to legal remarriage, it is surprisingly under-studied. Little is known about how the decision to cohabit is made, how children are informed, or what effects cohabiting has on the entire stepfamily system.

How Do Divorced Adults
Develop a Strong Couple Bond?

Developing a new remarriage relationship is particularly challenging when children of prior relationships of one or both adults are present. Children are powerful "third parties"; they can be expected to have a perspective on reconfiguring and remarrying that differs from that of adults, they generally see themselves as allies of their parents, and they may view steppar-ents as intruders into their relationships with their parents. In addition, the bond between parents and children is older and presumably stronger than the new husband-wife relationship. Consequently, parents' loyalties may lie with their children more than with their new spouses. This should not be a problem except when there are conflicts between stepparents and step-children; when that happens, parents may feel caught in the middle. As we will see in the next section, there are ample opportunities for stepparents and stepchildren to have interper-sonal conflicts and disagreements, particularly in the early months and years of remarriage, the time when the couple relationship is still developing and is most fragile. Because the presence of a stepparent often represents a loss of status and power for children and may contribute to unwanted changes in the parent-child relationship (e.g., such as spending less time together), children may be invested in seeing the remarriage fail. A parent's relationship gain may be seen by his or her child as relationship loss. Remarried couples may therefore be faced with trying to develop couple bonds in the presence of third parties who are actively interested in dissolving those bonds.

Former spouses, the extended kin of former spouses, and others also may be interested third parties who comment on the relational competence of the new spouse. We can hypothesize that remarried partners benefit by comparison with prior spouses in cases in which the prior relationship was unhappy and stressful. However, third parties with a vested interest in seeing the remarriage end, or those who are related to the former spouse in some way, may compare the new partner unfavorably and seek to influence the process of repartnering through their negative evaluations of the new partner. Given the lack of normative guidelines and the complexity of remarried families, it is likely that standards for judging relational performance will vary widely, even when third parties are neutral observers. As there are probably few neutral observers of remarriages, however, judgments of relational competence may vary even more extremely. Nonetheless, we can only speculate about the influence of third parties, because there has been limited investigation of how remarriages are influenced by social networks.

Unfortunately, research examining the process of building a couple bond in remarriage has also been quite limited. In an in-depth study of nine pairs of remarried couples, Cissna, Cox, and Bochner (1990) found two interactive, simultaneously occurring tasks to be associated with relationship development in newly formed stepfamilies. The first task is for the remarried couple to establish the solidarity of the marriage in the minds of the stepchildren. Couples do this in two ways: (a) by telling the children that the marriage is the most important relationship to the adults, and (b) by spending time together as a couple planning how to present a unified front to the children. The second task is to establish parental authority, particularly the credibility of the stepparent. To do this, both the biological parent and the child must develop trust in the stepparent's ability to act like a parent, to discipline wisely and fairly, and to establish a warm emotional bond with the child.

Establishing Stepparent-Stepchild Relationships

The stepparent-stepchild relationship is essentially an involuntary one, entered into by both individuals because of their association with a third person, the child's biological parent. This is not to suggest that stepparent-stepchild relationships are inherently conflictual and problematic; in fact, the preponderance of evidence is that most step relationships are positive.

However, even when these relationships are warm, loving, and satisfying, it is important to remember that they were not begun for their own sake. We mention this because it underscores how relatively little control stepparents and stepchildren have in beginning and, to some extent, maintaining a relationship.

The involuntary nature of the beginning of stepparent-stepchild relationships contributes to the sense that this relationship transition may be experienced as a crisis: It is unscheduled; it is not controlled by individual choice; there are no cultural rites of passage to help prepare people for the role; given the typically short courtships for remarriage, stepparent-stepchild relationships often begin with little advance warning; and, because step relationships are stigmatized (Coleman & Ganong, 1987), they represent status loss. If the transition into a step relationship is experienced as a crisis, we would expect stepparents and stepchildren to attempt to exert some personal control over the process of the developing relationship (Hagestad & Smyer, 1982).

Stepchildren have several ways they can potentially exert control. Some engage in rebellious, acting-out behaviors directed against both the stepparent and the parent (e.g., "He can't tell me what to do—he's not my father!"). Some children move out of the household, often choosing to live with the other parent, and some threaten to move out unless things are changed to suit them, in effect blackmailing the resident parent and stepparent to give them more control. Still other children may exert control by withholding affection, respect, and approval from the stepparent. These children may not be openly rebellious, but they gain control by acting as if the stepparent were not there, a behavior we have called the *end table phenomenon* —these stepchildren treat their stepparents with the same care and affection that most people direct toward furniture. In other words, these stepchildren neither abuse nor attend to their stepparents; they simply ignore them.

Although it may go unrecognized, children often gain power following a parent's remarriage. Children may sometimes command the primary loyalty of the parent in disputes with the stepparent. They also can pit their biological parents against each other, particularly in situations in which the parents fight, making the threat to go live with the other parent very salient. The stepparent's feelings of powerlessness, which may cause him or her to retreat from making demands on the child, can also contribute to stepchildren's gaining more control.

How do stepparents attempt to gain a feeling of control over the step relationship? It may be hypothesized that some stepparents use their superior age and strength to force stepchildren to submit to their control. These stepparents may physically abuse children, threaten to kick them out, or actually evict children from the household if they do not obey. However, most stepparents engage in less extreme measures to gain a sense of control. A common pattern reported by clinicians is that stepparents insist on making and enforcing household rules, including rules for disciplining children (Coale-Lewis, 1985; Visher & Visher, 1988). They assume the task of family disciplinarian, spending a lot of time and energy in power struggles with stepchildren over the enforcement of rules. Other stepparents may withdraw emotionally from stepchildren as a strategy of emotion management (Hetherington & Clingempeel, 1992). Many stepparents apparently do not succeed in these efforts; clinicians have identified a sense of powerlessness, hopelessness, and lack of any control in stepparents who live in stepfamilies who are having problems (Coale-Lewis, 1985). These feelings of powerlessness likely result partly from the stepparent's failed attempts to gain control.

Of course, not all strategies for gaining a sense of control are destructive. Families that discuss together the nature of roles and relationships give both stepchildren and stepparents a feeling that they have input into how their relationship is progressing. Clinicians advise stepparents and stepchildren to spend time getting to know each other and having fun together; in essence, they are advised to act as if the relationship were a voluntary one and to develop it as they would any adult-child friendship. Some clinicians advise stepparents to mimic the process of the development of parent-child bonds by first focusing on nurturing the child and developing a feeling of closeness in the relationship before attempting to set rules or trying to discipline stepchildren. Many families do this on their own, without receiving clinical assistance, but for many, if not most, the idea of stepparents and stepchildren taking time and effort early in the relationship to build a bond as friends does not occur to them. Such behavior is not part of their view of what parents and children should be like.

Herein lies another challenge to stepparent-stepchild relationships—defining the relationship. For many members of reconfiguring families, parent-child relationships are the models for stepparents and stepchildren to follow. For many people, stepparents must be replacements for nonresidential parents, for if they are not, what are they?

There are widely agreed-on roles and some general guidelines for mothers and fathers, but there are no clear role expectations for stepparents. Stepparents studied by Whitsett and Land (1992) reported that they were not sure what would be involved in being a stepparent and they also were not sure of their spouses' expectations for them in the stepparenting role. This problem may be especially acute for stepfathers, because the paternal role, in general, is less well defined than the maternal role, causing fathers to look to their wives for parenting clues (Tinsley & Parke, 1987). When this phenomenon occurs in the early stages of stepfamily formation, the wife is apt to push the stepfather to function as if he were the biological father of his stepchildren (Papernow, 1993). This strategy is probably effective only when (a) the nonresidential father and his kin have no contact with children in the remarried family household; (b) the children are young at the time of remarriage so that they do not remember much, if anything, about prior family life; and (c) all stepfamily members want to re-create the nuclear family and agree, implicitly or explicitly, to function as if the step relationships were biological. These hypotheses have yet to be tested, however.

There are several potential problems with a stepparent assuming the role of parent. First, there are nonresidential parents and stepchildren who will reject the stepparent taking this identity, forcing loyalty conflicts, encouraging hostile interactions, and contributing to overall family chaos. Obviously, stepparents are not free to choose identities independent of the desires of other members of the reconfiguring family system. Second, when stepparents assume they will function as parents, they may rush the development of the stepparent-stepchild relationship, acting as if the relationship is a more mature one than it is. As a consequence, stepparents may try to force discipline onto children before they are ready to accept it, and they may push for intimacy and expect feelings of affection and love before children are ready. These assumptions regarding the relationship may trigger children's rebellion as the children attempt to achieve a degree of control over the speed at which the stepparent is pushing the relationship. Third, when stepparents assume the parent role, they are ignoring differences between stepparents and parents. For one, they are ignoring the fact that stepparents and stepchildren lack shared histories of behavioral interactions to fall back on, the close bonds that develop over the child's lifetime.

If stepparents do not identify themselves as parents, then what are their roles in relation to other family members? Beer (1988) calls individuals in step relationships *relative strangers,* an oxymoronic term that concisely conveys the ambiguity of these relationships. Others have defined stepparents as competitors with absent biological parents and with children; heroes who have come to rescue the family from poverty, chaos, or worse; intruders who disrupt established patterns of family life; friends to children; resources; abusers; quasi-kin; parent replacements; and almost anything. In the absence of societal guidelines and agreed-on functions for stepparents' third- (or fourth-) parent status, they as well as biological parents, stepchildren, and "third parties" all contribute to defining stepparents' relational competence. However, each may be using a different set of standards for what the stepparent should be doing.

Stepparents are challenged to take on a "roleless" role, something like that of a mother-in-law or father-in-law. A stepparent, like an in-law, is a family member through circumstance rather than choice. Stepparents and stepchildren are linked through their relationship with the biological parent, and the motivation to form a bond is, at least initially, generated by the urge to please that parent. Given the lack of societal, familial, or even personal guidelines on successful ways to proceed, it is little wonder that the establishment of the step-parent-stepchild relationship is haphazard and idiosyncratic.

Family Reconfiguring: Challenges to Researchers

Perhaps the complexity of the reconfiguring process is to blame for the paucity of process models to describe and explain the challenges of family reconfiguration. Most researchers to date either have been interested primarily in structural and demographic characteristics of postdivorce families or have been oriented toward describing intraindividual or interpersonal problems they perceive to be related to family reconfiguration. In recent years some interesting longitudinal research has been conducted that has focused on processes in family reconfiguration (e.g., by Ahrons; Hetherington & Clingempeel; Kurdek), but these examinations have been largely descriptive and have been based on models designed to explain other relationship processes, if they have been theory based at all.

We think that adapting process models that were originally constructed for other relationship processes is not as fruitful as designing frameworks specifically for the context of relationship development and maintenance in families that are reconfiguring after divorce. For all the similarities between parenting and stepparenting, the process of developing a parent-child relationship is quite different from the process of developing a stepparent-child relationship. Courtship processes among people who have lived more than half of a normal life span and who have school-age or older children are different, we think, from courtship processes among individuals who are twenty-something. Relationship dissolution for married couples who have children is different from the ending of relationships between college sophomores.

In a rephrasing of Duck's (1982) observation on the process of marital dissolution, we contend that reconfiguring is a multidimensional process that is affective, behavioral, and cognitive; it is intraindividual, dyadic, social, and cultural. There are multiple perspectives on reconfiguring families. Parents, children, new partners and their children, members of the social networks of all family members, and societal institutions all have perspectives on how families should reconfigure following divorce. The suggestion that the process of reconfiguring is complex is a major understatement.

Consequently, any model should include elements that examine intraindividual, interpersonal, social network, and cultural factors. At the intrapersonal level, elements such as the following should be included: role identity; relationship commitment; strategies for affect regulation; cognitive constructions related to self, other, and the relationship; idiosyncratic interpretations of cultural beliefs; the assumptive world; relational competence; a sense of control over one's experiences; and feelings for the partner, self, and the relationship. Some of the intrapersonal elements exist at the dyadic level as well (e.g., assumptive world of the relationship, strategies for affect regulation). At the interpersonal level, role reorganization (e.g., changes in the number of roles, changes in role expectations, attachment to the role, salience of the role), changes in routines (e.g., adding new ones, modifying existing ones, giving up some), reorganization of relationships, and interpersonal affect regulation should be included.

At the level of social networks, some of the variables that should be considered are network structure, overlap of members in partners' social networks, the degree of mutual versus individual concern of third parties, the amount and type of support, whether support is from informal or formal sources, and the amount of distress and negative influence placed on partners by the social network. The backdrop to all of these elements is the cultural belief system, the ideologies that influence virtually every aspect of the process of reconfiguring relationships.

In this chapter we have used some models that we think have promise (e.g., Hagestad & Smyer, 1982; Klein & Milardo, 1993), that could be modified and broadened to include more dimensions of the process of reconfiguring. We have mentioned other work that has focused on specific aspects of reconfiguring (e.g., Hopper, 1993) or that has proposed process models for specific postdivorce relationships (e.g., Duck, 1982; Ihinger-Tallman et al., 1993; Rodgers, 1987). There are perhaps other models that have potential as well.

As it stands, even those who try to develop functional reconfigured families are stymied by cultural ideals and interpersonal restraints. The studies that would move us forward are time-consuming and require in-depth and intimate knowledge of reconfigured families on the part of the researchers who conduct them. Unfortunately, such studies are roundly criticized for their lack of generalizability, yet huge demographic studies can never enlighten us about family process. Can we really develop insight into the workings of families as they reconfigure after divorce without talking with members of those families engaged in the struggle? Can we realistically pose new models for postdivorce families without studying those families who feel they have reconfigured successfully, in ways that are supportive of members of the old family as well as the new?

We propose that the myriad families struggling without guidance, bereft of institutional support, facing stigma and sometimes thinly disguised moral outrage, need support, understanding, and help in negotiating the emotionally charged territory of family reorganization. We need to place emphasis on the processes by which reconfigured families experience success. We need to develop models that contribute to the more complete institutionalization of postdivorce reconfigured families. It is time to move on from our "retreat from complexity."

5

Codependency: Personality Syndrome or Relational Process?

Paul H. Wright

Katherine D. Wright

For a volume devoted to relationship challenges within a series devoted to relationship processes, we consider a chapter on codependency to be especially fitting. The concept of codependency is based on the observation (some critics would call it an assumption) that some individuals in close relationships with exploitative, irresponsible, or abusive partners organize their lives around the presumed needs, interests, well-being, and good reputation of those partners at the price of their own social, emotional, and often physical well-being. Because this concept developed within the field of addiction counseling, the exploitative, irresponsible, or abusive partner originally referred to a person addicted to alcohol or drugs, that is, a *dependent*. Therefore, a partner taking excessive responsibility for such a person came to be known as a *codependent*. Eventually, however, counselors noted that individuals often related "codependently" to partners who, although exploitative and abusive, were not chemically dependent. Nevertheless, they retained the term *codependent*.

The concept of codependency is challenging for two reasons. First, it is highly controversial. At one extreme, numerous practitioners and theorists promote the concept not only as a clinically useful diagnostic category, but also as "an emerging new paradigm in the helping professions and in human well-being" (Whitfield, 1991, p. 199). At the other extreme, numerous critics regard the concept of codependency as worthless or, worse yet, demeaning and destructive. They base such judgments on ideological as well as conceptual and empirical grounds. Second, whereas the codependency *concept,* as currently defined and applied, is an easy target for criticism, the relational *phenomenon* to which it refers continues to loom large in relationship difficulties as reflected in many of the problems dealt with by therapists and social agencies. The challenge, then, is to conceptualize and explore codependency in a way that enhances our understanding of the important phenomenon while avoiding the pitfalls highlighted by critics who believe the concept should be totally abandoned.

As a counselor involved in codependency treatment and an academician concentrating on personal relationships, we believe that it would be most useful to shift the currently dominant focus on codependency as a personality syndrome (see, e.g., Spann & Fischer, 1990) to codependent relating as it emerges and persists within a particular kind of personal relationship. Indeed, such a process view characterized earlier thinking that gave rise to the concept of codependency. Moreover, a process view is implicit, if not explicit, in most present-day approaches to codependency treatment. These approaches emphasize the necessity of the codependent's altering her or his pattern of relating to the "dependent" in order for any personal or relational change to occur. Several slogans that are widely circulated among family therapists reflect this emphasis: "Recovery is a process, not an event." "If nothing changes, nothing changes."

"Insanity is doing the same things and expecting different results."

In the pages that follow, we briefly trace the development of codependency thinking from its origins in alcoholism treatment to its current status as a personality syndrome. Following this, we summarize speculation concerning the sources of the "codependent personality" within dysfunctional family systems. We then consider some representative applications, and follow this with a review of the yield from empirical studies. Then, after covering criticisms of the codependency concept, we review our own embryonic research and present a tentative model of codependent relating consistent with that research. One implication of the model is that codependent relating is not likely to surface apart from an appropriate "mix" of personal and situational influences. Those influences include the self-attributes of not one, but two individuals, whom we label *codependent* and *dependent*. In this chapter, except where specified otherwise, we use the term *dependent* to refer broadly (and conveniently) to the "exploitative, irresponsible, or abusive" partner in a codependent-dependent relationship, regardless of whether that partner has an identifiable addiction.

The Concept of Codependency

Origin and Development
of the Codependency Concept

Several counselors have provided extensive accounts of the origin and development of codependency as a clinical concept (see, e.g., Whitfield, 1991, pp. 13-23). Our own assessment of this development is documented in detail elsewhere (Wright & Wright, 1990, 1991). According to our understanding, interest in what we now call codependency originated within the addiction counseling field concomitant with the recognition that alcohol or drug dependency is not an individual matter. The chemically dependent person lives in a network of close relationships with persons who both influence and are influenced by the problems associated with his or her addiction. Initially, the focus was on the "enabling" behaviors of these nonaddicted partners. Such behaviors are usually disguised or indirect, however, as Lewis and McAvoy (1984) observe concerning opiate-addicted families, the enabler may sometimes go so far as to acquire money by illegal means to support the abuser's "habit." This focus underscored the importance of involving family members and significant others in the treatment of alcohol or drug abuse. Counselors eventually noticed, however, that in adapting to the difficulties inherent in such relationships, nonaddicted partners often expressed some or all of a typical range of problematic behaviors, attitudes, and self-perceptions. It was at this point that some of the therapeutic and conceptual concern shifted to the "codependent." Thus initially the term *codependent* referred to nothing more nor less than an individual who adapted in characteristic ways to a particular relational situation, that is, close involvement with an alcohol- or drug-addicted partner.

From this point, it was but a small step to the observation that persons who demonstrate codependent behaviors and attitudes are often from families of origin in which one or both parents were alcohol or drug dependent. This was eventually taken to mean that individuals reared in alcoholic or similarly "dysfunctional" families internalize personality characteristics that lead them to form subservient and self-effacing relationships with irresponsible and exploitative partners. A consensual list of such characteristics, as we have presented it elsewhere, would include the following:

> low self-esteem; frozen feelings and a lack of spontaneity; a need to be needed; a need to be in control, including an urge to change and control others; a willingness to suffer and behave self-sacrificially; an exaggerated need for approval from others; an inability to maintain clear boundaries between self and significant others; fear of abandonment; and excessive reliance on denial. (Wright & Wright, 1991, p. 439)

Thus, in a series of unheralded changes in connotation, the term *codependent* came to refer more often to a personality syndrome than to characteristic ways of responding within a particular kind of relationship.

It is now common for theorists to think of a codependent as a person who, by virtue of his or her personality, behaves in subservient and self-effacing ways not only in close relationships with "dysfunctional" partners, but in virtually all dealings with other people. Spann and Fischer (1990), for example, assume codependency to be "traitlike"; they define it as a "psychosocial condition that is manifested through a dysfunctional pattern of relating to others" (p. 27). In what we regard as the ultimate expression of the personality view, Whitfield (1989) describes codependency as "endemic in ordinary humankind" (p. 21). Recently, Whitfield (1991) has characterized it as "a disease of lost selfhood," defining it broadly as "any suffering or dysfunction that is associated with or results from focusing on the needs and behavior of others" (p. 3).

Along with changes in connotation, the concept of codependency captured the attention of increasing numbers of counselors. Many of these counselors developed their own particular models of codependency, and the literature burgeoned. Whereas most, although not all, of these counselor-theorists view codependency as a personality syndrome, there is wide variability among them concerning specific characteristics included in that syndrome, as well as its scope and limits (for summary comparisons, see Cermak, 1986; Kitchens, 1991; Schaef, 1986). Moreover, their theorizing has been based largely on clinical impressions and selected case studies. Related to this, delineations of the characteristics of codependency have been primarily descriptive rather than clearly conceptual. Thus, taken as a whole, work on the concept of codependency constitutes somewhat of a conceptual and empirical quagmire.

Presumed Origins of the Codependent Personality

A few theorists who deal with codependency are content to address its symptoms as they find them, without speculating about their origins in the individual's experience. A few others find the antecedents of codependency in conditions that are "endemic" in society, such as troubled personal relationships (Whitfield, 1991), power-oriented social structures (Schaef, 1986), and inevitably repressive and shame-based parent-child relations (Bradshaw, 1988). These theorists couch their causal propositions in such vague and all-encompassing terms that it is impossible to disentangle the specific circumstances that are and are not believed to foster a serious level of codependency. By far most codependency theorists, however, agree that children reared in clearly dysfunctional families are at risk for developing codependent characteristics.

For all practical purposes, the exemplar of family dysfunction assumed to breed codependency stems from parental alcoholism. Indeed, for counseling or research purposes, subjects are often identified as codependents simply on the basis of being adult children of an alcoholic parent or parents (see, e.g., Brown, 1988; Lyon & Greenberg, 1991). Most family therapists propose that children may be predisposed toward codependency as a result of other family problems, such as recurrent sexual, physical, or emotional abuse; parental obsessive-compulsive behaviors (e.g., problem gambling); parental mental illness; legalistic and arbitrary family rules; and parental rigidity and emotional repressiveness. However, it is only with respect to parental alcoholism that theorists have delineated in any detail the linkage between family dysfunction and codependency. They have not specified with any precision how or to what degree the same linkage applies to family dysfunction originating in other problems. Therefore, for purposes of simplicity and clarity, we frame our discussion in terms of the alcoholic family.

Among the numerous theorists who have addressed parental alcoholism and codependency, we regard the work of Brown (1988), E. Coleman (1988), and Mendenhall (1989a, 1989b) to be representative. Although these theorists differ in a few details, it is not difficult to formulate a composite picture. In the "typical" dysfunctional family, an alcoholic parent who was once or is sometimes (i.e., when not drinking) a caring source of satisfaction and support for the rest of the family has become or is sometimes (i.e., when drinking) uncaring, selfish, neglectful, and abusive. In pursuit of the perverse gratification provided by alcohol, this parent imposes demands on other family members that are excessive, arbitrary, and often contradictory. In addition, the problem behavior itself stands as a potential source of embarrassment, shame, and perhaps ostracism for family members should it become known beyond the confines of the family. This creates a family situation in which inconsistency is compounded by a chronically high level of stress.

The nondrinking parent typically sees this situation as both temporary and remediable, and vacillates between waiting it out and trying to control and change it. In the course of doing this, he or she employs any number of tactics, including appeasing, accommodating, protecting, and covering for the alcoholic partner and attempting to control that partner's behavior, usually in indirect and manipulative ways. Through both words and behavior, the nonalcoholic parent will pretend to him- or herself and others that nothing really serious is wrong. As a crucial part of this pretense, the nonalcoholic parent will prevent children in the family from acknowledging and responding to the problem—passively, by simply failing to model responsive behavior, and actively, by instructing, persuading, and cajoling others to join him or her in adjusting their behavior to that of the alcoholic parent. The nonalcoholic parent, in short, becomes entrapped in an obsession of his or her own, that is, protecting the alcoholic partner and denying the reality of that partner's detrimental attitudes and behaviors.

Children in alcoholic families suffer deprivation and abuse as a result of the drinking parent's obsession with alcohol. They suffer further deprivation and abuse because of the nondrinking parent's obsession with the alcoholic partner. The nondrinking parent is simply not available to the children for the kinds of nurturance and support characteristic of "normal" families. Worse yet, when specific problems surface, the children may feel that something is very wrong without being able to articulate what it is. The "pretending" parent, acting and speaking as if nothing is wrong, discourages talk and (ipso facto) encourages nontalk centered on the difficulty. This censoring process negates the children's emotional experiences, leading them to conclude that their feelings are not real or, if real, not consequential. Moreover, to the degree that the nonalcoholic parent is successful in convincing the children that it is their responsibility to adjust to the alcoholic, the children will come to see any problems that parent's drinking creates as in some potent but indefinable way "their fault" and thus their responsibility. According to Black (1982), children in such families come to be governed by a set of unspoken rules: Don't trust, don't talk, don't feel. Moreover, in an effort to deal with the stress and inconsistency of the dysfunctional family, different family members adopt specialized "dysfunctional" roles, such as the Chief Enabler, the Family Hero, the Scapegoat, the Lost Child, and the Mascot (Wegscheider, 1981).

Thus children in chronically dysfunctional families adopt a range of codependent behaviors, including family rules and family roles, that become internalized as enduring personality characteristics. These characteristics carry over into their interactions in groups and systems other than the family, and affect all of their close relationships. Both codependency and family dysfunction are "transgenerational" in that individuals reared in dysfunctional families tend to gravitate toward "dysfunctional" partners and to create dysfunctional families of their own (see, especially, Mendenhall, 1989a, 1989b).

Whereas theorists agree that codependency is an outcome originating in adaptive responses to family dysfunction, they sometimes disagree as to whether codependency is the only such outcome. Mendenhall (1989a, 1989b) suggests that it is. He proposes that developing a codependent personality includes internalizing both family rules (à la Black, 1982) and a dysfunctional family role (à la Wegscheider, 1981), regardless of what the specific role might be. Hogg and Frank (1992), on the other hand, contend that dysfunctional family systems may result in either offspring codependency or offspring contradependency. The latter is characterized by strong opposition, not acquiescence, to the family. They propose further that these differing patterns of response will express themselves, in part, in the adoption of different family roles. A codependent is likely to assume either the Enabler or the Family Hero role. In Wegscheider's (1981) terms, the Enabler "protects" the aberrant parent by covering whatever major obligations that parent may have abandoned, and by providing "reasons" for the parent's derelictions. The Family Hero masks or offsets family problems with exemplary conduct and achievements that give the family something to be proud of. A contradependent is likely to assume the Scapegoat role, that is, to "adapt" to the dysfunctional family situation by creating problems of his or her own through obvious forms of "bad" behavior, such as truancy, delinquency, and alcohol/drug abuse. In any case, consensus on the major point remains: A person who develops codependent characteristics does so as a result of having been reared in a dysfunctional family of origin.

A Sampling of Applications

Because the present-day focus on codependency originated in practices within the addiction field, applications of the concept predate the articulation of the concept itself, primarily in the form of family and "significant other" involvement in the treatment of alcoholism. This application continues. Now, however, counseling and support groups are widely available for those significant others apart from the treatment of their alcoholic or otherwise "dysfunctional" partners. Several practitioners have proposed specialized therapies for dealing with the personal and relational problems that go along with the "codependency syndrome" (see, e.g., Kitchens, 1991; Mendenhall, 1989b). Counselors occasionally link such therapies to well-known personality theories. Mitchell (1989), for example, describes a "corrective redevelopment" program based on Erikson's (1963) stages of psychosocial development. Some practitioners have come full circle in advocating codependency treatment for recovering alcoholics and drug addicts. Loughead (1991) argues that codependency is a basic disorder underlying a wide variety of addictions. She insists that codependency counseling is useful, if not crucial, for the prevention of further problems (including relapse) for alcoholics who have attained sobriety through treatment or support group participation.

Recognizing the strong association between parental alcoholism and codependency, counselors have devoted increasing
attention to problems of adult children of alcoholics (ACOAs).
Harman and Withers (1992) recommend that university students requesting counseling for "general" problems be screened
for ACOA status and assigned to specialized therapy groups
dealing with issues unique to that status. Others have been
even more specific in their recommendations, proposing—and
demonstrating—that it is useful in group therapy with ACOAs
to identify and work with the primary roles (e.g., Hero, Scapegoat) the clients developed within their families of origin
(Corazzini, Williams, & Harris, 1987; Harris & MacQuidy,
1991).

Extended applications of the concept of codependency include cautions to helping professionals (e.g., counselors, social
workers, probation officers), who might find their efforts on
behalf of clients subtly sabotaged by enabling behaviors on the
part of the clients' codependent partners or families (M. C.
Walker, 1992). Some theorists propose further that people in
the helping professions themselves often have strong codependent tendencies that may, unless held in check, be detrimental
to the progress of their clients (Fausel, 1988; Schaef, 1986). In
an application to business organizations, Hall (1991) identifies
"dysfunctional managers" as the next human resource challenge. She proposes that managers who were reared in dysfunctional homes are likely to have acquired codependent characteristics that result in guarded, oblique, and rule-bound ways of
supervising and coordinating key personnel. This codependent
"management style" may then seriously disrupt the effective
operation of the entire organization. Porseth (1986) goes so far
as to caution literary critics not to let "codependent tendencies"
cloud their reviews of the work (or lives) of authors known to
be alcoholics (e.g., Hemingway). In a similar vein, Janas (1986)
presents an analysis depicting *M*A*S*H 4077* of television fame
as a dysfunctional system in which some of the permanent
personnel behaved codependently in providing tacit support for
the alcoholism of the unit's "heroes."

The Yield From Empirical Studies

Systematic and reasonably well-controlled studies of code-pendency have begun to appear only recently and are still scarce. In addition to several freestanding studies, we are aware of two programmatic research efforts. In the first of the free-standing studies, Williams, Bissell, and Sullivan (1991) identi-fied a sample of physicians and nurses as codependents on the basis of their self-reported involvement with chemically de-pendent partners. These subjects reported that their codepen-dency had, at times, seriously impaired the quality of service they provided to their patients. Moreover, they recommended with near unanimity that professional health care training in-clude a significant component dealing not only with addictions, but with codependency as well. In a different kind of study, Walfish, Stenmark, Shealy, and Krone (1992) examined Minne-sota Multiphasic Personality Inventory profiles of 73 women who had sought codependency treatment as a result of involve-ment with addicted partners. In spite of considerable heteroge-neity, few of these women produced "benign" profiles, with the modal profile showing clinically significant elevations on six scales. Finally, in a contrived but realistic helping situation, Lyon and Greenberg (1991) found that self-identified daughters of alcoholic parents, in contrast to normal controls, behaved "codependently" by agreeing to donate much larger amounts of time to assist a male experimenter they believed to be abusive and exploitative than to one they believed to be a "nice guy."

Each of the studies described above yielded results broadly supportive of the concept of codependency. None of them, however, utilized assessments of codependency apart from sub-jects' self-reported involvement with alcohol- or drug-abusing partners or parents. The measurement task has been under-taken, however, by two programmatic research efforts of which we are aware. One of these, initiated by Fischer and her associ-ates, adheres to the view that codependency is a personality syndrome. The other, our own research, approaches codepen-dency as a set of characteristic ways of relating to a specific "dysfunctional" partner (Wright & Wright, 1990, 1991). We will review the work of Fischer and her colleagues here and summarize our own in a section presenting an alternative view of codependency.

As we have noted, Fischer and her associates consider codependency to be a traitlike "psychosocial condition that is manifested through a dysfunctional pattern of relating to others" (Spann & Fischer, 1990, p. 27). On the basis of this definition, they developed a self-report technique called the Spann-Fischer Codependency Scale (SFCS: Fischer, Spann, & Crawford, 1991). The SFCS yields a single score combining three individual characteristics: an extreme focus outside of oneself, a lack of open expression of feelings, and attempts to derive a sense of purpose through relationships.

Using the SFCS in a study of parenting styles, Fischer and Crawford (1992) found that both female and male college students who perceived their fathers as authoritarian tended to score high on codependency. In a more extensive study, Fischer, Wampler, Lyness, and Thomas (1992) used the SFCS with a sample of college students in conjunction with measures of alcoholism, risk taking, family dysfunction, and addictions in members of the subjects' families of origin. They found problems in family of origin to be strongly related to both offspring alcoholism and excessive risk taking on the part of subjects scoring low on codependency. For those scoring high, however, the former relationship was greatly reduced and the latter nullified, suggesting that acquiring codependent tendencies (as measured by the SFCS) may have a moderating effect on problems associated with family dysfunction or family addictions (or both). Proposing further that individuals may adapt to family dysfunction by assuming different roles (à la Wegscheider), Fischer et al. suggest a correspondence between codependency and the Hero role and one between noncodependency and the Scapegoat role. This proposition is similar to that of Hogg and Frank (1992; see above), who contend that dysfunctional family systems may result in either offspring codependency (expressed in either the Enabler or the Hero role) or offspring contradependency (expressed in the Scapegoat role).

The Critical Backlash

Most of the criticisms of the codependency concept surfaced before reports of empirical studies began to appear. For the most part, however, they are nonetheless telling and are relatively easy to sort into three overlapping categories. One category challenges the concept for its lack of clear (or even unclear) empirical evidence, with critics noting that assertions and generalizations concerning codependency are based on clinical impressions and anecdotes, and that they are supported by few or no systematic data (Gierymski & Williams, 1986; Gomberg, 1989). Such conclusions mesh well with our own previous judgment (Wright & Wright, 1990, 1991). With the appearance of published studies, however, we have tempered somewhat our criticism of the inadequate empirical basis for the concept.

A second category challenges the concept for its lack of reasonable conceptual and definitional boundaries. Critics in this category argue that the term *codependency* has been given connotations exceeding justification, if not expanded far beyond any meaningful contribution to theory or practice (Gierymski & Williams, 1986; Gomberg, 1989; Mannion, 1991; Myer, Peterson, & Stoffel-Rosales, 1991; Wright & Wright, 1990, 1991). A number of these critics, however, propose that codependency is a basically valid and useful concept in need of restoration through careful delimitation and measurement (Mannion, 1991; Myer et al., 1991; Wright & Wright, 1990, 1991).

A third category challenges the concept on interpretive grounds, highlighting the social and cultural assumptions underlying its genesis and applications. Inclan and Hernandez (1992), for example, argue that labeling so-called codependent attitudes and behaviors as maladaptive is based on a dominant cultural value that places individuality and autonomy above interdependence, interpersonal loyalty, and family responsibility. This flies in the face of the high value placed on family responsibility within some cultural subgroups, such as among Hispanics and Asians. This criticism finds support from the relationship field in Gaines's (in press) fresh perspective on the impact of cultural values on personal relationships. Gaines observes that the influence of familial and collectivist values—characteristic, respectively, of Hispanics and blacks—differs from that of the presumably dominant individualistic value. Thus it is probable that in some ethnic groups (e.g., Hispanic, black, Asian) codependency will take on a very different look and value.

A far greater number of critics, however, reject the codependency concept as an unjust indictment of women (Asher & Brissett, 1988; Frank & Golden, 1992; Haaken, 1990; Harper & Capdevila, 1990; Krestan & Bepko, 1990; van Wormer, 1989; Webster, 1990). They propose that the concept is based on a fortuitous interpretation of adaptive and coping efforts that express, in exaggerated form, socialized patterns of self-forgetful caregiving and a concern for maintaining relationships. Because such patterns are characteristic of many women but few men, codependency is a pejorative label attached to women who are merely doing what they have been socialized and expected to do. Moreover, to highlight "enabling" as a key aspect of so-called codependency is effectively to blame women for the continued derelictions of their errant male partners and, consequently, for their own problems with those partners.

Among the foregoing critics, Asher and Brissett (1988) argue that women often identify themselves as "codependent" as a result of experience in codependency counseling or support groups and, having accepted the label, "reconstruct" their lives (past and present) around their presumed codependency. Thus Asher and Brissett, along with other like-minded critics, are opposed to codependency treatment and support groups, claiming that such programs reinforce the myth of female blame and responsibility and encourage women to maintain stultifying and damaging relationships.

In contrast to this view, our own understanding of codependency treatment is that it fosters the codependent's awareness that he or she is not responsible for either the existence or the consequences of the "dependent's" destructive attitudes and behaviors. Nor can the codependent correct or control those attitudes and behaviors by coercive or manipulative responses of his or her own. The codependent is, however, encouraged to control his or her own behavior, and to do so in a way that, first, compels the "dependent" to bear the consequences of his or her own actions and, second, promotes the codependent's independent growth and well-being.

Concerning the evolution and status of the codependency concept, our current assessment is that it was, until recently, badly underdocumented and is, to this day, woefully ill defined and overextended. This combination of factors renders the concept and its proponents open to serious criticisms of the kinds we have just reviewed. On the other hand, the research that has accumulated to date, including our own, is consistent with some of the major claims of codependency theorists. Along with this research, our experience with codependents and with codependency counselors leaves us with the conviction that individuals in relationships with alcoholics or similarly troubling partners very often do exhibit distinctively "codependent" attitudes, self-perceptions, and behaviors. We turn now to our own emerging view of codependent relating.

Codependent-Dependent Relating as a Process

We consider it unfortunate that the concept of codependency has become so thoroughly dissociated from its original referents. We do not question the significance of the syndrome specified in the currently dominant "personality" view. We do, however, question both its newness and its adequacy for conceptualizing codependency. Concerning its (lack of) newness, the personality view of codependency is so similar as to be virtually identical to Karen Horney's (1942, 1945) work on the neurotically compliant personality. In fact, Horney (1942) once devoted an entire chapter to the description of a "morbidly dependent" personality that reads much like a section from Norwood's (1985) popular book on codependency, *Women Who Love Too Much*.

Concerning its conceptual (in)adequacy, we find the personality view of codependency lacking in two respects. First, con-

ceptualizing and measuring codependency as a "traitlike characteristic" precludes, by definition, the possibility that codependent relating may be mostly, if not wholly, the codependent's
adaptive responses to the demands of maintaining a relationship
with an addicted or otherwise problematic partner. Second,
whereas counselor-theorists universally identify codependency
as a multivariate phenomenon, advocates of the traitlike view
reduce it to a single personality score. Thus univariate measures
such as the SFCS (Fischer et al., 1991) neither address nor imply
several characteristics of codependent relating that are commonly listed in the foundational literature on codependency.
This, we believe, minimizes both the complexity and the dis-
tinctiveness of the concept.

This is not to say that we consider the personality syndrome
approach irrelevant to the study of codependency. As we shall
show, however, we believe this approach deals with a special
kind of codependency-proneness rather than codependency
itself. We believe further that letting the proneness stand for the
existence of actual behaviors and interaction patterns fosters
errors of observation and interpretation that account for much
of the highly criticized misapplication and overgeneralization
of the codependency concept. A person may, for example, be
inclined to behave toward others in supportive, cooperative,
and sometimes even self-sacrificial ways. Or a person may, out
of a sense of loyalty or responsibility, maintain a less-than-
perfect personal relationship. Is a person who characteristically
does either or both of these things necessarily being "codependent"? Is such an individual necessarily wrong or pathological?
Are there not other reasons for behaving in these ways? In
combination, these ways of behaving may, indeed, make an
individual a candidate for developing codependent-dependent
relationships, but will that person inevitably do so?

Reinstating the Foundational
Meaning of Codependency

In our own studies, we have attempted to reinstate the
original meaning of codependency by conceptualizing the char-

acteristics of codependent relating independent of any assumptions about preexisting dispositions (Wright & Wright, 1990, 1991). We reasoned that if codependent relating were definitively associated with a personality syndrome, this association would eventually be borne out in research. But to establish such an association, it would be crucial to have independent measures of codependent relating and the presumably relevant personality syndrome.

Our approach has been straightforward. We first culled the relevant literature to arrive at a comprehensive list of codependent characteristics. We then defined each of these characteristics in a manner amenable to measurement in the format of the Acquaintance Description Form (ADF; P. H. Wright, 1985), a self-report technique designed to obtain a subject's assessment of the strength and quality of his or her relationship with a specified partner. We constructed a specialized version of the ADF by adding the provisional codependency measures to the standard scales. Our ongoing studies, utilizing samples of nonstudent adults involved in serious heterosexual relationships, have culminated in a fourth version of the codependent ADF (the ADF-C4). Our samples have included both noncodependent and codependent subjects, the latter being identified on the basis of 2 or more years' involvement in a stressful relationship with an alcohol- or drug-abusing partner.

In the interest of brevity, we confine ourselves here to a broad summary of findings from two sets of data collected since our most recent published report (Wright & Wright, 1991). Each set of data included responses from more than 175 women and 170 men. For both sets of data, 13 of the 28 ADF-C4 scales differentiated between subjects—both women and men—who were and were not involved in codependent relationships. Of the 13 differentiating measures, 10 were codependency scales and 3 were standard ADF scales. However, according to factor analyses, these 13 scales did not constitute a single codependency factor. Rather, for each data set, they emerged as Factors II and III following a large first factor indicative of a "solid, rewarding relationship." Factor II included 8 scales that, taken together, were indicative of defensive and overprotective caretaking (e.g., a tendency to control one's partner, a "rescue and change" orientation, an exaggerated sense of responsibility for the partner, denial through externalization of blame for the partner's shortcomings, and a sense of excitement and challenge in the relationship). Factor III included 5 scales that were indicative of enmeshment in the relationship (e.g., exclusiveness, an exaggerated sense of the permanence of the relationship, exaggerated reliance on the partner for a sense of self-worth, and jealousy). Thus a person may show caretaking inclinations without being enmeshed, and vice versa. Our hypothesis, yet to be fully confirmed with adequately controlled data, is that a codependent is a person who scores high on both factors, that is, an enmeshed caretaker.

A Process View of Codependent-Dependent Relating

Our recent data, plus a spectrum of clinical observations, bring us to the following working definition: A codependent is a person enmeshed in a relationship with an exploitative, irresponsible, or destructive partner to whom he or she responds with overprotective and defensive caretaking. Codependency, then, develops within a particular kind of relationship. Becoming codependent does not necessarily imply an underlying personality syndrome or pathology. It could happen to anyone strongly committed to a skillfully manipulative partner. It is, however, more likely to happen to some types of people than to others, such as "nice, normal" people whose socialization has emphasized loyalty and commitment to maintaining relationships and a deep personal concern for the well-being of partners and family members. This would especially include, in our society, many women and perhaps members of some ethnic subgroups (e.g., Hispanics, Asians). Most vulnerable, however, would be individuals whom we have described elsewhere (Wright & Wright, 1991) as "endogenous" codependents, that is, persons from dysfunctional family backgrounds whose experiences have left them with distorted views of what close relationships can and should be, along with narrow and largely negative self-perceptions. It is here that we see the personality approach as relevant to the study of codependency.

At present, we are concentrating on putting the finishing touches on the ADF-C5—the final (we hope) codependent version of the ADF. In the meantime, we are thinking ahead to substantive work on codependent relating. In an earlier analysis, we suggested that symbolic interactionism provides a useful framework for analyzing exogenous (reactive), but not endogenous (chronic), codependency (Wright & Wright, 1991). Although we are not ready to abandon the exogenous/endogenous distinction entirely, we are now inclined to view symbolic interactionism, appropriately augmented, as descriptive of the process of codependent relating in general. We have been encouraged in this view by Wiseman's (1991) symbolic interactionist approach to a longitudinal study of wives of alcoholics in the United States and Finland.

Our thinking at this point, which is necessarily broad and tentative, is this: What we observe as codependent relating is the enactment of a situated identity (Alexander & Wiley, 1981; J. M. Jackson, 1988), that is, a highly personalized role that the codependent acquires vis-à-vis a complementary situated identity assumed by the relational partner. This situated identity constitutes an important aspect of the codependent's definition of the relational situation, a definition that emerges from the partners' ongoing interaction. Such a definition begins with culturally defined roles and values (see Gaines, in press) in combination with the individual's generalized conceptions of self and relationships (see Putallaz, Costanzo, & Klein, 1993). These factors channel interaction toward the development of "dependent" and "codependent" roles. As the definition of the situation becomes more individualized and relationship specific, the partners implicitly negotiate situated identities through their reciprocated self-presentation and altercasting (see, e.g., McCall & Simmons, 1978), a process that eventuates —for the codependent—in a set of behaviors, attitudes, and self-perceptions adding up to enmeshed caretaking. Codependent relating, then, is not likely to surface apart from an appropriate mix of situational and personal influences. In fact, codepen-

dency as behavioral patterns and codependents as persons who
respond in patterned ways to (an)other(s) are, by definition,
relational concepts. It is impossible to be a codependent in
isolation, that is, apart from a relationship with a dependent.
Thus it is impossible to engage in codependency on one's own.

In all probability, the most common "appropriate mix" of
situational and personal influences that promotes codependency comes about when two people from dysfunctional families of origin "find" each other and form a "codependent-
dependent" relationship based on shared mental models and
complementary attitudes and self-perceptions. A different kind
of mix may occur when a person socialized to express coopera-
tiveness, compassion, and concern in close relationships becomes involved with a troubled and troubling partner who is
skilled at manipulative altercasting. There are undoubtedly
others. We believe that this approach focuses on codependency
as a relational process in a manner that gives due recognition to
the "personality" view without according that view such weight
that it obscures the relational processes involved. As our work
continues, we hope to demonstrate the validity and usefulness
of this approach through both basic research and clinical applications. In so doing, our intent, consistent with that of this
volume and series, is to promote greater awareness of the extent to which relational processes influence individuals' self-
definitions and conduct in interpersonal contexts.

6

Understanding How the Dynamics of Ideology Influence Violence Between Intimates

James T. West

Jenni told me this story of how, after being beaten by her husband, she turned to her church and family for help, but everyone encouraged her to act out the role of the long-suffering wife. She described how her priest instructed her to return to her husband:

> And I said, "I can't. What am I supposed to do if he's cheating on me and hits me?" He [the priest] said, "You should forgive him." And I said, "What if he continues to do it?" Then he said, "You should pray that he'll stop" [sarcastic laughter]. I said, "I'm sorry, I'm sorry, I've waited for a long time for him to stop and he hasn't and I'm not going back." Then he told me that I was very selfish and all I cared about was myself and what I was doing. You know, so it was really hard. The priest was mad, my parents were mad, my brother [who was best friends with her husband] didn't talk to me for a long time, I mean he would say, "Hi, how's it going?" Once in a while, he would make rude comments. I mean here I was brought up believing, I mean my parents always said you come from a

large family, you work together, there's no one like your family, only your
family does things for you, you know, really ingrained, the family, the
family, the family, and all of a sudden to have part of my family not just
pissed but totally sided with my ex was tough.

Jenni is one of 80 people I interviewed during a 7-year study
of violent relational processes (West, 1992). Her emphasis on
how she experienced ideological pressure to remain in her
violent relationship was the most common theme to emerge
from the research. It is a theme that cuts across economic,
educational, and racial demographics. For example, whereas
Jenni comes from a middle-class Mexican American family,
Barbara is a professor from a wealthy Caucasian family whose
members are part of the elite of the Mormon church. Barbara
told me:

There is a lot of ideological pressure to stay in the marriage, you have to
stay married. My parents applied it, and my husband said, "You can't
leave, you are breaking your covenant." That argument is, of course,
fallacious. By hitting me, I could argue that he broke his covenants, but
there was all that pressure and just people wanting us to stay married.
They didn't want to see another relationship crumble, but I realize there
was nothing real, there is no material support for doing that. There hasn't
been any material support since I've been single and raising the five kids
by myself. There is no material help, it's really all ideological. No one
really helps out. They just don't want you to upset the apples. I think I
felt that as a real heavy burden that I needed not to blow my marriage. I
had to keep up the picture even though mine was in pieces.

Although Jenni resisted the ideological pressures of church
and family and did not return to her husband, many women
such as Barbara spend years in their violent marriages before
breaking through the institutional pressures that tell them to
stay in their relationships. The fact that many women stay in
violent marriages illustrates why researchers must be aware of
the (re)production of relations of power in which some women
submit to continual subordination and endure violence.

Following the theme of this book series, **Understanding Relationship Processes,** my focus in this chapter is on how we can
gain a better understanding of relational processes by realizing
that ideology influences all relationship forms and all research

about relationships. Specifically, I will show how research on ideology adds valuable insights to relational research through its capacity to unearth how relationships are contextualized within issues of power/knowledge that urge individuals to articulate a system of meaning that privileges institutional interests over other interests (Mumby, 1987, p. 114). All relationships are influenced by ideological forces, and nowhere are these forces more transparent than in violent relationships. Individuals in violent relationships are often so afflicted by ideological pressure to stay in their marriages that they feel they have no means of escape except finally to kill or maim their violent partners. Lorena Bobbitt's case is one highly publicized example of how women feel they must stay in their relationships despite abuse.

Although tragic, these types of violent relationships are pervasive in American society. We need to learn how to both understand and help couples whose relational patterns have become violent. This book series on relationships, and this volume of the series in particular, provides an important opportunity for us to gain a deeper understanding of the cultural and ideological dynamics that influence relational processes.

My purposes in this chapter are (a) to examine theoretical frameworks of scholarship on ideology to disclose how all relationships are shaped by ideology, (b) to provide a brief overview of previous research on violent relationships, (c) to demonstrate that narratives of violence between intimates complicate conventional understandings of relational processes through the significance they place on ideological constraints as a source of the problem, and (d) to suggest productive ways to focus future research.

Understanding the Dynamics of Ideology and How to Use It to Analyze Relationships

The researchers who have contributed chapters to this book describe the relationships they have studied and re-present these relationships to us and construct them in certain ways. Researchers, of course, study a wide diversity of relationships, but they need to recognize that although many relationships are not overtly concerned with power as an issue of control, *all* relationships are enacted within relations of power (West, 1993). A crucial question then becomes: Do researchers (re)present relationships as one-dimensional, devoid of power issues and having only one fixed meaning, or do they show how relationships are dynamic, always in process, contextualized by issues of power and open to multiple interpretations? Unfortunately, many of the past and present research studies concerning relationships have taken a structuralist approach that attaches meaning to relationships based on the personalities or pathological traits of the individuals in the relationships. A structuralist approach centers, or structures, the meaning of relationships on one factor, usually the individual, in an ill-fated attempt to reduce relationships to a behavioristic determination of binary oppositions: cause or effect, hereditary or environment, normal or pathological. The structuralist focus on microindividual factors has pushed macropractices and other cultural meanings of relationships to the margins.

Dissatisfied with the limitations and biases of the structuralist approach, scholars from many disciplines have created a number of new approaches for studying relationships that have come to be known collectively as *poststructuralism*. One vein of the poststructuralist movement is the study of ideology. Ideology is a complex and dynamic concept that I define as the interwoven and inseparable nexus of (a) the production of knowledge, (b) relations of power, and (c) institutional practices.

Using this nexus as its core, research on ideology brings a three-pronged strategy to the understanding of a research topic, in this case, relationships, by triangulating the three dynamics that compose ideology. First, it deconstructs—that is to say, opens up—the ways in which institutions and institutional authorities produce what counts as knowledge in a particular society. This deconstruction examines the multiple meanings and voices that have been silenced by the singular, linear, cause-effect, and fixed meaning that an institution attempts to have the public reproduce and "know" about an event or topic.

It shows how all relationships are dynamic, in process, inherently multidimensional, and open to various interpretations. Second, an ideological approach examines the relations of power in which all relationships are embedded. Third, it does a close self-reflexive reading of how researchers use institutional practices to establish their authority and power to produce knowledge about relationships. This usually includes, but is not limited to, examining the way the researcher positions him- or herself in the relationship with the research subjects and how much authority and voice the researcher gives to the research subjects to speak for themselves instead of being spoken for, reduced to a set of faceless numbers in a chart, or completely silenced.

Beginning with the production of knowledge, I will briefly clarify and describe each of these three prongs in a study of ideology, show how they are interconnected, and show how ideology influences all relational processes. In the first prong of its examination, research on ideology deconstructs how institutions, and the individuals who are in positions of authority to speak for institutions, are involved in the production of knowledge. It questions how institutional authorities structure knowledge in ways that reflect most favorably on their institutions' points of view. It opens up how they use their resources to tell others how to think (know) about relationships in one way and not in other ways.

For example, what were some of the common patterns in relational processes between men who were U.S. combat soldiers in the Vietnam War? How, if at all, did interracial relationships define and explain the meaning of the Vietnam War? Did these relationships reflect an unjust war or a war of racial hatred that the United States lost? Or were relationships harmonious and united in a noble battle to help fight for democracy and to stop the so-called domino effect of communism? The first wave of movies about the Vietnam War sanctioned the latter position; these films were often produced in conjunction with military authorities. However, when men who had been actual Vietnam combat soldiers, such as Oliver Stone, began making movies about the war, their images deconstructed the institutionalized and "noble" versions of the war. For instance, notice how the relationships of the soldiers in Francis Ford Coppola's *Apocalypse Now* provide a very different meaning about the war from that shown in John Wayne's relationships with his infantrymen in the movie *The Green Berets. Apocalypse Now* shows relationships and war as selfish, chaotic, insane, racist, and murderous. *The Green Berets* portrays the Vietnam War as a noble battle of all-American boys working together to stop the "yellow" communist hordes.

The first prong of the ideological approach deconstructs how institutional authorities produce self-enhancing and structured meanings regarding a topic; the second examines how the production of knowledge is inextricably connected to relations of power. As Foucault (1980) points out, the production of knowledge always involves power; he refers to this inseparable combination as "power/knowledge." He goes on to establish that all forms of communication are caught up in the production and (re)presentation of power/knowledge. By producing a singular meaning to an event or topic, institutions communicate to their audiences the "correct" manner in which relations of power should be ordered.

Institutions maintain relations of power and the production of knowledge through what Foucault (1972) calls "discursive fields," sets of institutional practices that prescribe who may speak (or write) in specific locations and how they may speak under different types of conditions. Foss, Foss, and Trapp (1985) describe how discursive fields

> impose conditions on the individuals who speak so that only those deemed qualified by satisfying these conditions may engage in discourse on a specific subject. Among these conditions are legal requirements that give the right to speak in certain ways; lawyers, for example, must pass the bar examination in order to practice law. . . . For example, we listen to medical doctors speak about issues involving health because our society attributes competence to them in this area. (pp. 196-197)

Institutions create and maintain discursive fields as "strategies" (de Certeau, 1984) to maintain the centripetal force of their institutional practices. Through discursive fields, institutions regulate relations of power and the production of knowledge for anyone who comes in contact with them. This allows institutions to form an ideology that tells individuals how to order their relationships with other people.

For example, the psychological community maintains a discursive field that produces specific ways of classifying and objectifying individuals. The discourses of this community guide how psychologists establish relations of power by telling individuals how to transform themselves according to specific modes of subjectivity. However, discursive fields are not stagnant or completely unified; they change along with societal changes in order to try to maintain their power. For instance, the epistemological formulations of psychological practice have changed and been repeatedly reformulated since Freud discursively established them (Foucault, 1973; Rieff, 1987). Religious institutions had for many centuries been the primary sites of confessional power, and one of Freud's political ventures was to move confessional practices away from institutionalized religions and toward a group of medical practitioners (Rieff, 1987).

As decades have gone by, psychology's relations of power have moved away from Freudian confessional practices that focus on parent-child sexuality (i.e., an Oedipus or Electra complex) and toward relationships of the psychologist-as-parent and the patient-as-child. The psychological community's management of the relations of power has focused more and more on providing the proper discursive classification of the conduct of individuals. The number of classifications has proliferated over the past several decades. Currently, the specific classifications of individual pathologies are listed in the third edition of the *Diagnostic and Statistical Manual of Mental Disorders* (*DSM-III*; American Psychiatric Association, 1987). This book organizes the discursive field of the psychological community and thus defines what are and are not considered mental disorders at this particular moment in Western cultural life.

After using the first prong of the study of ideology to examine the production of knowledge and the second prong to analyze how this production of knowledge establishes relations of power, the third prong illustrates how institutions maintain

their authority and power/knowledge through four interconnected techniques that I refer to collectively as *institutional
practices:* monopolizing, normalizing, constituting, and repre-
senting. Institutional practices constitute and normalize the way
we think of our relationships by monopolizing our view of the
world to one "correct" representation. For example, when we
first go to school around age 4, we are not given a menu. We
do not emerge from the school bus and request to learn how to
speak Tagalog and worship as Hindus. Our experience is mo-
nopolized and normalized so that we speak the language of our
parents and of the school, eat what they eat, pray as they pray,
and reproduce knowledge in the way they tell us. Our history
is constituted and represented in one way and not in other ways.
For instance, generations of schoolchildren in the United States
have been taught that October 10 is a national holiday because
Columbus "discovered" America. They were not taught that he
landed in Jamaica and never saw what is now the United States,
or that he murdered and enslaved the people already living there
because they would not worship his Pope's god. Children have
not been taught to question this institutionalized holiday, but to
celebrate it and reproduce a "false" consciousness about its
meaning (Althusser, 1976). They have been taught that Western
European people are superior to "primitive" indigenous peo-
ples. Institutional practices produce knowledge that establishes
the relationships between groups of people in one way and not
in other ways.

Overview of Previous
Research on Violent Relationships

To illustrate further how ideology influences all relationships
and research studies about relationships, and how an ideological
approach can enhance our studies of relational processes, I will
focus specifically on one general type of relationships, namely,
violent relationships. The history of the study of violent relationships gives insight because it exemplifies how the study of
relationships has been tied to the prevailing relations of power

between researcher and research subjects as they changed over the past several decades. Most of the early studies of violent relationships were done by psychologists who tried to link "the cause" of the problem to certain types of personalities (Ball, 1977; Elbow, 1977; Faulk, 1977; Hamberger & Hastings, 1986; Rosenbaum & O'Leary, 1981; Shainess, 1977). However, these attempts to correlate relational violence to personality types without examining other factors was soon recognized as problematic by other researchers. Gelles and Cornell (1985) note:

> The earliest publications on the subject of wife abuse took a distinctively psychiatric view of both offender and victim. Women who were abused were believed to suffer from psychological disorders as did the men who abused them. Research conducted in the 1970s and 1980s found this view of wife battery too simplistic. There are a number of individual, demographic, relational, and situational factors related to violence toward wives. These factors are probably all interrelated. (p. 71)

Recognizing the limitations of a research approach that mirrored the psychological institution's focus on the individual, interpersonal communication researchers, as well as marriage and family counseling researchers, began a series of research studies that attempted to capture the relational factors associated with family violence. These studies highlighted the interactional patterns of couples as the locus of the problem (Berk, Berk, Loseke, & Rauma, 1983; Foss, 1980; Gulotta & Neuberger, 1983; Hotaling & Sugarman, 1986; Rogers & Millar, 1988; Weitzman & Dreen, 1982). They used a pragmatic approach that focused on the couple as a system in which the husband and wife were constantly defining and redefining the relationship (Courtright, Millar, & Rogers, 1979; Giles-Sims, 1983; Manderscheid, Rae, McCarrick, & Silbergeld, 1982; Watzlawick, Beavin, & Jackson, 1967). The couple negotiated the relational pattern through their interaction. The pragmatic perspective outlined how an abusive relationship may be either symmetrical or complementary. Either of these patterns may lead the relationship to become violent if one or both people in the relationship demand constant control of the relational patterns.

The central methodological concern for this type of research became whether violence within an intimate relationship was reflected in a series of redundant patterns within the couples' conversations. As Millar and Rogers (1981) remark, "The concept of redundancy is of primary importance in the clinical literature where it is posited that overly redundant or rigid interaction patterns are related to various individual and family pathologies" (p. 16).

While family, marriage, and communication researchers were concentrating on relational patterns, psychological and sociological researchers turned their attention to measuring the frequency of physical violence in marriages (Dutton, 1988; Huggins & Straus, 1980; Straus, 1979; Straus & Gelles, 1986). In order for researchers to obtain funding for various projects examining violence between intimates, they had to first prove that this problem was occurring more frequently than previously thought. The results of the earliest frequency studies varied greatly. Some suggested that violence between intimates occurred in only 5% of married households, whereas other studies suggested a rate as high as 45%. However, the accuracy of statistical studies and the implications that can be drawn from these results have been disputed. One of the unfortunate consequences of the preoccupation and debate over the frequency of violence in the home was that violence between intimates was "discussed as if all battered women were similar and all battering relationships were alike" (Follingstad, Laughlin, Polek, Rutledge, & Hause, 1991, p. 187). Follingstad et al. (1991) argue, "Recognizing the variability among these women begins to reduce stereotypes and forces researchers to abandon the idea that one cause produces battered victims" (p. 200).

As frequency studies, psychological trait studies, and causal models have increasingly been seen as problematic, one of the most significant developments in the study of relational violence has been a shift toward feminist research and research on ideology. Bersani and Chen (1988) argue:

> For this perspective, the core principle in accounting for pervasive spouse violence is that the traditional family reflects an arrangement of domina-

tion by males. The social structure supports gender inequality, and this inequality is rooted in the history and in the traditions of Western societies. Marriage is viewed as the central element of a patriarchal society. (p. 73)

Gelles and Straus (1988) believe that the attempts to end intimate violence over the past 2 decades have been directly tied to the feminist movement. The patriarchal system created barriers that prevented women from obtaining political positions that would allow them to change their status as second-class citizens and as subjects of abuse (Yllö, 1984). In her research, Yllö (1984, 1988) has viewed relational violence as being immersed in both societal and interpersonal sexist practices that saturate and constitute women's experiences. Gelles and Straus (1988) also describe sexism as a primary contributor to violence in the family:

> Examination of family violence over the years has consistently found that socially structured inequality is a prime contributor to violence in the home. We cannot overemphasize the preventative value of promoting sexual equality and eliminating sexism. (p. 203)

Sexism is not only a contributing factor to violence in the family, but it also permeates the manner in which researchers construct women as research subjects. Psychological literature on intimate violence has sometimes depicted women as being unwilling to help themselves. As Spitzack and Carter (1987) explain:

> Simply pointing to woman as a disadvantaged other falsely implies that women are passive victims, trapped in sex-typed communication constraints with no hope of escape, when in fact they can be viewed as active agents. Valid investigations of female communication behavior require a noncomparative approach which, by implication, not only questions the normative power of male experience, but views women as self-conscious actors, as co-producers of their communicative climates. (p. 410)

Feminist and ideological critiques add a valuable poststructuralist turn to the research on violent relational processes by highlighting the discursive and cultural systems in which the violence is subsumed. For instance, Pahl (1985) describes how

the rhetorical choice of the term *domestic violence* indicates that
violence against a woman "by a husband within their family
home, is somehow seen as a different sort of crime from
violence against a stranger in a public place" (p. 13). As narratives of violence between intimates illustrate, no one should
minimize the violence in a private home as "domestic." This
term, applied to violence in a home, provides an image of the
violence in a family as somehow less severe than violence
between strangers. It also implies relations of power that are
suggestive of a slaveholder hitting a domestic servant. Consequently, many researchers now refer to the problem as *intimate
violence* and emphasize in their research that violence in an
intimate relationship is as brutal and debilitating as any other
form of violence, perhaps more so.

Feminist research and ideological scholarship have slowly
begun to move the focus of the problem away from a violent
"pathological" individual who hits a "victim" and toward the
complex relational and ideological processes that constitute
violent practices. However, most research on violence between
intimates continues to be reported almost exclusively in an 8-
to 15-page journal research format. This dominant format
greatly curtails and marginalizes the subject's ability to speak
about the problem for her- or himself. Even though a poststructuralist view of relational processes is beginning to find a place
in an academic world still dominated by structuralist views,
researchers from both viewpoints rarely allow their subjects to
have direct voice in the research document. Just as abused
women are marginalized to shelters, their voices have been
marginalized and silenced by the way researchers report their
findings within the standard journal format.

The Reproduction
of Violent Relationships

My purpose in this section is to expand on the framework of
the previous two sections by offering a description of how the
narratives of violence between intimates complicate conven-

tional understandings of relational processes by the significance they place on ideological constraints as a source of the problem. In conventional research studies of relational processes, individuals in a relationship are viewed as an autonomous dyad, almost completely independent of forces outside this relationship. However, ideology afflicts all relationship forms; nowhere is this more transparent than in violence between intimates.

Women and men in violent relationships do not describe themselves as being part of an autonomous unit, but as being part of a much broader interconnective cultural system with complex ideological forces. Of the 80 people interviewed for my study of violence between intimates, almost all said that they were encouraged to stay in the violent relationship by both family members and institutional authorities, such as judges, prosecutors, and family counselors. In cases where people followed this advice, they often ended up being severely injured or, in a few cases, killed. Such injuries and deaths could be prevented if family members and institutional authorities would stop encouraging women to stay in violent relationships. For instance, in describing why she stayed in her violent marriage for 8 years, Pat told me:

> His grandmother told me, "Be patient. He'll change." See, I was Catholic then and his family were strong Catholic and they said if I ever got married again it would be adultery, you know, and all this stuff. And I was just naive to it. And I figured it wouldn't be fair for our daughter not to have her father. And so I hung around and took it.

As in Pat's story, many individuals learn that speaking about the problem to other family members or to community authorities does little to help. Barbara described how her attempt to obtain help from various authorities was marginalized by sexist practices:

> A lot of times he would use physical force to make me do something. And a lot of times . . . he would use his economic clout to keep me from doing things. When I think back on it now, this Mormon psychologist, who is really a brilliant man, was just so amazingly arrogant. They never said, "Has anything like this ever happened before? What brought it on?" I

don't think they even asked very many questions about it. They just told me it wouldn't happen again. Like they didn't even interview Ty [her husband] and say, "Will you promise never to do it again?" They were sure it wouldn't. Apparently the stake president called this therapist, which was probably a violation of confidentiality, but he called him and said, "Do you know what is going on here?" because he knew he had counseled us. "Do you know what is going on, is this going to be okay?" And they reassured him that it would be okay. I think that is a collusion, not that anybody was trying to hurt me. I don't think they thought I was at risk. It wasn't that, it was just more their male way of thinking. They didn't think about my safety as an issue and that they saw it as somebody under stress. Just the fact that they didn't look at all the other issues, the issue of safety, issue of controlling, why is he doing this? They didn't go into it very deeply. Even in the therapy they were always focusing on me. I went into therapy originally to say that my husband doesn't love me and he makes me feel sort of insecure. What should we do? It was never that they trusted my judgment and say, oh, she thinks that, I wonder why she thinks that. It was oh, she's wrong so how can we help her quit thinking like this. It was never trusting my judgment. I mean I think that was that male collusion, just trusting more in their male instinct and the male voices and feeling more familiar with Ty's voice, Ty's explanation, than mine. So I was always dealing with men. But I don't see it as a conscious collusion, the conspiracy fear, them sitting around smoking cigars saying how can we keep these women down. It was just a lack of knowing, a lack of interest.

Barbara's statements about how her voice was silenced depict some of the ideological and sexist practices interwoven within the problem of violence between intimates. This silencing process was reiterated by other women, who spoke about the nonsupportive and sexist environment they encountered when they sought help. Yllö (1984, 1988) has given special attention to issues relating to the ideological and sexist practices women encounter inside and outside the family, as has Gordon (1989).

Cultural and institutional practices that are reinforced in many organizational settings often work against women's attempts to communicate their needs. For instance, a director of one of the counseling centers where I did my ethnographic fieldwork described how professional counselors sometimes keep women within the violent relational process:

Realistically, I mean one of the worst offenders, of keeping those women coming back [to the abusive relationship] are people from my own profession. Because there are many people from my profession that are willing to see a couple cojointly. And what they do is they are literally setting the woman up, because frequently what a perpetrator will do is that they will say to the woman is that, "If you weren't so crazy, if you weren't so sick, I wouldn't have to beat you. I wouldn't have to hurt you. I wouldn't have to show you the right way to behave." And so what they do is, it's frequently the abuser who will say, "Well then, let's go see a marital therapist. Let's go see somebody." Or sometimes the victim will say, "Let's go see a marital therapist." But they get into that therapy room and they realize that if they open up and tell the therapist what is really going on, that they are being hurt by their partner, that he is going to beat her up as soon as she gets out of that room. So instead what the therapist sees is this very—they don't see that the perpetrator is manipulative, but instead what they see is this person who is very congenial, very willing to tell the therapist what he sees is wrong with the relationship. Well, the victim sits there and doesn't talk, doesn't say anything, is very sullen, withdrawn, and quiet. The therapist takes the perpetrator aside and says, "I'm really concerned about the signs of depression that I'm seeing in your wife. So what I would like to do is see your wife for a while individually before I see you as a couple." They leave and the husband says, "See, I told you. He thinks you are crazy too." And he's just been given a clear bill of health never to come back again. There are many therapists out there who still carry that on. That are still willing to see families, to see couples cojointly before they get a clear picture of what they are dealing with. The message that that gives the victim at that point is that it is useless. She might as well just stay. The same message that she gets from the police.

When the reproduction and retrenchment of institutional practices is seen as a major stumbling block to women being able to leave their violent relationships, this casts a spotlight on how relational violence is entrenched within a set of ideological practices. Viewing the problem as complex and as connected to ideological systems points to institutions as sometimes being part of the problem and not part of the solution. This sense of institutions sometimes being unhelpful was articulated in numerous narratives among the women I interviewed. For instance, Lilia left her apartment the first time the man she was living with became violent. When she went to press charges against this man, everyone tried to persuade her to forget it:

The city prosecutors would never explain anything to me. I would go in there and virtually cry because I didn't know what was happening, no one would talk with me, they were very rude to me. Many times I heard, "Oh, she's just a spouse abuse." And they would send me out the door until one day I made a big scene, told them I was going to tear apart the office if they did not come and speak to me. And they sent me this lawyer who was very rude to me from the beginning and when he would talk to me, he would point his finger at me and he would tell me, "Oh, 75% of you women just drop charges. You are just going to do the same thing. You are probably already talking to him, this is already a honeymoon stage, you are just doing this because you are pissed off."

Clearly, the most significant finding to be drawn from these narratives is that when women attempt to leave violent relationships and/or seek justice, their efforts are often thwarted by the ideological practices of their families and institutions. Gordon's (1989) historical investigation of family violence in Boston from 1880 to 1960 implicates the American family as having a long history of violence, and institutional authorities as having an equally long history of reinforcing the violence. Also, Gelles and Straus (1988) have shown that discussions of the family as a violent social unit struggle against institutional and media myths that represent the family as the embodiment of all that is good about life in the United States:

> We want to believe that the family is a safe, nurturant environment. We also do not want to see our own behavior, the behavior of our friends, neighbors, and relatives as improper. Thus, most people want to envision family violence as terrible acts, committed by horrible people against innocents. This allows us to construct a problem that is carried out by "people other than us." (p. 42)

Deferring violence to a position where it occurs to people other than us helps perpetuate the complex set of family and relational processes that create an atmosphere in which the violence can take place. Women's narratives about this problem acknowledge that one of the primary reasons the violence continues is because they are ashamed to tell anyone that they are trapped within violent homes. Added to this sense of shame is their terror of the actual physical brutality and repeated threats that they will be killed if they tell anyone.

In conjunction with these factors, the reproduction of the violence also continues because U.S. cultural traditions position the family as a sacred institution. This tradition is reinforced in rhetorical practices on numerous levels within our society and is especially clear in the way individuals' narratives position the institution of family as so important that even numerous violent incidents are not enough to force them to leave their relationships. They describe leaving a relationship as literally an unthinkable act.

Understanding How Ideology Affects Relational Processes: Suggestions for Future Research

In this chapter I have described the fundamental techniques used in conducting research on ideology, how this type of scholarship helps us critique all forms of relational processes, and how ideology affects violent relationships. I have also shown how violent relationships are a significant site for gaining a clear understanding of the link between ideology and relational processes. The narratives of the individuals who have been in violent relationships dramatize how violence is often enacted within scripted roles where ideologies dominate decisions. These complex ideological practices tend to limit severely the ways people think about their violent relationships. These ideological forces also limit the ways institutional authorities and researchers make sense of the problem. Consequently, it becomes important for researchers of relational processes to understand the ideological forces that ask people to give their active consent to forms of sense making of the problem that actually maintain continual subordination.

The way that individuals think about their problems in relationships is not just a matter of idiosyncratic cognitive tendencies. Individuals approach relational problems through various levels of cultural production and multiplicities of power. A thorough examination of relational processes requires that these multiple connections be taken into consideration.

Using the problem of violence between intimates as an illustration, we learn that it is not just a relational problem but a
problem embedded in ideological constraints. We learn that
narratives about relationships struggle against public policies
and attitudes that maximize the individual's role and minimize
the role of institutional practices. For example, in informal
conversations, in my ethnographic work with task forces, and
in colloquia where I have talked about my research on violence
between intimates, one of the questions I am most often asked
is: Why don't these women simply leave the abusive relationships? This often-repeated question reveals that many people
reproduce relations of power that follow the cultural practices
of examining a problem by locating its source at the level of a
dysfunctional individual or a dysfunctional couple. Many people locate the problem almost exclusively as a problem of "those
women" or "those marriages"; they want to reduce the problem
to a few misguided individuals, to a group of "others."

What I point out to such people is that their questions miss
the complexity of the problem, do not address dyadic relational
patterns, and avoid examining cultural relations of power. The
question would address the problem of violence between intimates more accurately if it asked: *How* (not why) and under
what set of rhetorical and ideological conditions is it possible
that the majority of individuals involved in violent relationships
see no alternative but to stay in those relationships? The answer
to this question, from my research and that of others (Ferraro
& Johnson, 1983), seems clear at least as far as can be gathered
from the personal experience narratives of many women. What
these women say is that they thought the violence was their
fault, that they deserved it, that they never thought of leaving
or calling the police, and that they could think of nowhere to
go or what they would do if they did go. Women describe how
they are socialized to believe that their primary roles are those
of wife and homemaker. They are taught that marriage and the
family are sacred. To flee from the violence also means to flee
from these roles and these sacred vows. Some women are capable of making immediate transitions; however, most women
say they are not. For women to be able to break the cycle of

violence, they must be given support that shows them that no sacred vows and no institutional and cultural practices require them to tolerate violence.

Can we make a difference in reducing violence and violent relationships? In recent years, new laws, new support centers, and new institutional policies have been making positive changes in the ways violence between intimates is handled. However, it is important to emphasize that these changes are not uniform, and they are not always quick to take hold. They vary greatly from one locale to another. Consequently, the narratives of relational violence take on more importance, for they serve as a gauge to tell us exactly how the new laws are enforced or unenforced, effective or ineffective, and they serve as a reminder about how institutions directly affect the social actions of individuals in violent relationships.

The narratives also give us insights into how ideologies affect all relational processes and how institutions avoid implicating themselves as part of a problem by focusing on a set of "dysfunctional" individuals. It is through this strategy of having the individual as the center of the problem that law enforcement officers, judicial officials, counselors, and other institutional representatives attempt to exempt themselves from any type of self-examination. However, if we listen closely and give voice to the narratives of the individuals with whom we interact in our research, no matter what type of relational problems we may focus on, we will learn how they are greatly affected by the ideological practices of various institutions and how these institutions may be part of the problem.

By listening closely to people's narratives about their relational processes we are able to find the nexus of ideology. We discover the link between discourses about relationships and the institutions that tell individuals, both consciously and unconsciously, how to make sense of those relationships. What I want to underscore, although I do not have the space to examine it adequately here, is that narratives that reveal the nexus of ideology should be analyzed as open texts that show not only how people are repressed, but how they create forms of resistance and thereby can potentially reach a sense of liberation.

In examining how ideology affects the relational processes of violence between intimates, we find mostly a repressive force. However, in other relationship forms we may find the opposite, or a mixture of repression and liberation. And one of the potential benefits of research on ideology in conjunction with relational processes is that we discover how some people are liberated by becoming aware for the first time that they have been unconsciously following a set of ideological practices that is detrimental to their best interests. For example, Barbara described how after the first time her husband beat her she went to the police station and the officers said there was nothing they could do. In retrospect, she was able to understand how she was subsumed within a "patriarchal scheme" and how she slowly liberated herself, but at the time of the violence she could not comprehend the social and ideological forces influencing her life:

> Well, I was still really in the structure. I just said [in response to the police not helping], "Oh, well, I guess that's how the world [is]." I didn't see it as a big patriarchy, or a big collusion against women, I didn't ever think of anything like that. I just thought that's how the system is and it didn't seem fair to me, but I was already sort of getting that life wasn't fair. You know, it's really sort of amazing that it took me so long to come to a feminist consciousness after that experience. I think it was because of my whole way of viewing the world was really based within the patriarchal scheme. I mean it was really important to me that things were like that because I did have five kids by now. And I needed to believe that a man was going to protect me and that I wasn't going to have to work outside the home. I had bought in so far into that, that it was important for those things to keep being true. So I remember even in the therapy, sort of resisting having those basic fundamental beliefs upset because I wanted them to be like that.

Barbara's description of how she had bought in to her role as wife and how this role kept her from leaving her violent marriage provides a good summary of the personal experience narratives of most individuals who have survived violent marriages. Their narratives describe how ideological forces discourage them from leaving their relationships and why intimate violence is the leading cause of death in the United States for women between the ages of 24 and 49 (Browne, 1987).

For future studies of relationships, it is important to understand how the concept of ideology is a constitutive force that suggests to people how they "should" enact their relational processes. Attempts to understand relationships are mediated through ideology. To study relational processes is to study the relations of power that give them form and substance. We can hope that future research will make more use of poststructuralist and ideological approaches that allow us the ability to unearth the structures of power and knowledge that have made the culture of the United States such a violent one.

In learning to focus on relationships as constituted by ideology, relational researchers need to articulate the institutional practices that suggest to individuals how they should "interpellate" themselves or constitute their interactions in accordance with institutional rules (Althusser, 1976; Belsey, 1980). As Williams (1989) argues, researchers must learn to understand hegemonic social forces by analyzing "the central, effective and dominant system of meanings and values, which are not merely abstract but which are organized and lived" (p. 383). This type of analysis focuses on the multidimensional sense making that occurs when people transact relationships. The researcher emphasizes how people reproduce or resist ideologies and how they articulate meanings about their relationships (Conquergood, 1991). With this focus on ideologies—the production of knowledge, relations of power as established through discursive fields, and institutional practices—researchers will be better able to understand relationships and what roles institutions play in defining those relationships and in normalizing specific practices in them. It will open up scholars' thinking to the way they and their subjects are connected and constituted by ideologies such as patriarchy, colonialism, rationalism, and capitalism. Certainly, there are numerous ways to study relationships, and understanding how ideologies contextualize all relationships is fundamental to any full analysis of relational processes.

HIV/AIDS: A Crucible for Understanding the Dark Side of Sexual Interactions

Sheryl Perlmutter Bowen

Paula Michal-Johnson

In 1994, the Centers for Disease Control and Prevention made available to radio and television stations public service announcements that were explicit about the ways in which heterosexuals can protect themselves from contracting human immunodeficiency virus (HIV) infection. Although these landmark ads acknowledge the double-edged sword of sexual liaisons, they do not begin to address the sorts of specific behaviors and relationship dynamics that jeopardize individuals' lives. They do not, for instance, attend to homeless or runaway youths, for whom HIV transmission has skyrocketed; to high-risk crack-addicted men and women who sell their bodies to satisfy their habits; to alcohol-influenced sexual liaisons; or to victims of rape and forced sex.

HIV/AIDS confronts relationship researchers with a host of concerns that are both complex and unfamiliar. Just as the government has not acknowledged this dark side in its public service announcements, relationship researchers have not yet fully grasped how to approach the ways that HIV/AIDS affects personal and sexual relationships. The term *HIV/AIDS* itself reflects the distinction between viral infection and terminal disease (*HIV/AIDS* is currently the preferred term for describing the virus that causes AIDS, or acquired immune deficiency syndrome). The epidemiology of HIV/AIDS includes substance abuse and injection drugs, sexual transmission, and blood-to-blood transmission through high-risk sex and exchange of blood products. The web is further complicated by highly stigmatized forms of sexual expression (homosexual sexual interactions) and illicit behavior (violence and prostitution).

In this chapter we examine three specific high-risk relational situations that militate against protection from HIV/AIDS: those involving alcohol use, drug use, and relationship violence. Our treatment of each of these contexts is consistent with the focus on processes emphasized in the series of which this volume is a part. Specifically, we concentrate on the personal and interpersonal processes that increase or decrease the HIV risk attached to sexual activity. Just as this particular volume challenges many of the assumptions that underlie traditional understandings of relationship goals and behaviors, this chapter asks the reader to consider how HIV risk challenges traditional assumptions about relationship processes.

Although in the 1990s, contraction of HIV/AIDS is a risk for all sexually active individuals, some personal and relationship processes intensify the danger. The jeopardy faced by heterosexual partners in conventional dating relationships has received the greatest attention by researchers, leaving understudied those kinds of relationships or sexual liaisons in which risk is greatest. Specifically, we focus here on three situations that pose particularly high risks: sexual liaisons under the influence of alcohol, trading sex for money to buy drugs, and sexual activity in abusive relationships. These interactions do not, for the most part, take place in idealized, close relationships. Partially because they have been less studied than college dating relationships, the processes that make them especially high risk have not been well mapped. Drawing on our own research and that of others, we will try to clarify how various personal and interpersonal dynamics intersect with sexual activity in ways that affect the likelihood of contracting HIV in these maximal threat conditions. Before proceeding, however, we must lay some groundwork for the discussion. First, we establish the boundaries of what counts as sexual activity and how sexual scripts are influenced by the social processes of drinking, drug use, and physical abuse. We introduce metaphor as a way to illustrate some of the individual and interpersonal lenses that may guide the course of sexual interaction. Second, we trace the evolution of HIV/AIDS interpersonal research to identify where the scholarly dialogue in this sphere has taken place. Third, we explore each of the three types of high-risk sexual liaison by reporting relevant research that charts the territory in which the communicative processes unfold. In each of these problematic scenes, we explore possible metaphors that emerge out of sexual episodes. Finally, we identify barriers to researching these dark-side phenomena and note promising avenues of research that can help us make sense of them.

What Counts as Sexual Activity

Although sexual intimacy is sometimes held out as the pinnacle of relational development, sexual interaction is not a separate, exclusive, or special process for some people, but a relatively ordinary part of life. In some traditional ways of understanding sexuality, biological arousal and social imprints are key elements. Reiss (1989), for instance, views sexuality as "erotic arousal and genital responses resulting from following shared sexual scripts" (p. 6). McKinney and Sprecher (1991) expand this definition to include the "close relationship" and say that sexuality includes "sexual behaviors, arousal and responses, as well as . . . sexual attitudes, desires and communication" (p. 2). Duck (1991) suggests that negotiation and decision making render sexual communication a process that changes over time. The above-noted discussions do not stipulate whether the partners involved are same sex or opposite sex, nor do they consider the age of the partners, both of which are important factors because they affect what is normative for a couple. In these definitions there appear to be tacit assumptions that sex is part of an ongoing relationship, which certainly is not always the case. These definitions may include but do not require oral, anal, or vaginal intercourse, all of which carry HIV risk. Especially in the context of the discussion of HIV risk, low-risk sexual stimulation deserves some consideration; are lower-risk behaviors viable alternatives to intercourse in the three settings we address in this chapter?

To explore HIV/AIDS-relevant episodes, where sexual acts occur in what we may call "troubled" contexts, we are compelled to look at the intersection of the personal, interpersonal, and cultural/societal experiences that shape or constrain different transactions. As Reiss addresses the notion of the "sexual script" of a society, we believe it is important to acknowledge that sexual scripts may be tied to the dynamics of particular social processes. Cultural groupings, whether they be defined ethnically (e.g., African American, Hispanic, or WASP), by sexual orientation (e.g., straight, gay, lesbian, or bisexual), or by social group (e.g., college students, drug communities), offer variations on what is typical and/or acceptable for sexual and relational partners (Blumstein & Schwartz, 1983). These influences matter in our understanding of sexual activity as well as in HIV prevention (Michal-Johnson & Bowen, 1992).

Edgar and Fitzpatrick (1993) report on a series of studies that indicate that young college students are particularly adept at identifying as well as producing typical sequences of events that culminate in sexual intercourse between previously unacquainted individuals. When couples meet in a public setting, they first engage in initial exchanges, verbal and nonverbal, and they proceed to dancing and complimenting, perhaps touching one another in a social way. They continue with a physical contact stage in which intimate touching and kissing occurs. They then initiate leave-taking behavior that moves them from the public to a private setting. The following subscene involves a variety of behaviors that might be labeled foreplay, occurring when they arrive at a private setting (an apartment or room), get comfortable, and decide that intercourse is going to happen (whether or not token resistance occurs). The final sequence of behaviors in the bedroom culminates with an actual act of intercourse.

We suspect that some of these script elements are found in each of the social settings we discuss in this chapter, but the elements may vary depending on the nature of the interaction. For instance, if we consider relationship violence as a frame, sexuality can be linked to a predictable cycle of abuse that shapes or constrains the relationship dynamics. This is further compounded by cultural differences. For example, African American women in shelters for victims of battering sometimes justify the violence of African American men as a function of racism and economic pressures. The gender roles and views of family prescribed in particular cultures also create interpretive frameworks within which sexual activities are negotiated. Often Latinas are raised with male dominance and "machismo" as prevailing familial values. Encouraging HIV prevention, including condom use, among Latinas comes at a cultural price: challenging the right of the male to dictate in the bedroom and the system of traditional Catholic values that prohibits birth control. To understand sex-for-drugs transactions, we must examine the script inherent in addictions. In looking at alcohol as an avenue for seduction among college students, we must examine normative alcohol and sexual scripts for heterosexual college students. These examples show how we must broaden our scope to understand the sexual experience, considering gender, ethnic, cultural, and racial influences. As we explore the three situations discussed in this chapter in terms of risk for HIV/AIDS, we must recognize how those situational influences shape interpersonal dynamics and risk prevention behavior.

Metaphors That Unpack
the Dynamics of Risk Behavior

Whereas the notion of script is one that asks how a scene is played out, the concept of metaphor can help us to understand what personal and interpersonal processes in sexual encounters look like. Metaphors offer insight into the key mind-sets that individuals carry into their encounters. They also help to illustrate the possibilities that different individuals may simultaneously operate out of the same or different metaphors as they engage in sexual interaction. To the extent that the same metaphor is used by both partners, it is easier to talk about how the script plays out. We analyze each of the three backdrops for high-risk sexual encounters using metaphors such as the following:

- *Hunting:* The *hunter* goes out looking for *prey*, uses the proper equipment to disable the target, and takes it home as a trophy.
- *Caveman:* He is big and strong; he claims his woman, she submits. This metaphor comes into play in very traditional, perhaps primitive, sexual stereotypes.
- *Ensnaring:* The *captor* strategically sets a trap for the unwitting or hapless *captive*.
- *The fairy tale:* This metaphor requires traditional stereotypes of the *prince* who rescues and takes care of the *damsel in distress*.
- *The dance:* This may involve learned dance steps, with leaders and followers, or a free-form activity, where individuals respond to the music and enact their own dance.
- *The game:* Established rules govern how players who are *winners* and *losers* take turns attempting to outsmart each other.
- *Going with the flow:* This is a wait-and-see process that presumes that either participant can stop the flow whenever he or she chooses.
- *The barter:* This presumes, as in social exchange theory, that both parties interact as long as they believe they are experiencing rewards and will cease to interact when rewards diminish.

- *Play:* Participants toy with each other in creative ways that allow each player to suspend disbelief of "reality" for a time; each is free to take on roles different from his or her normal persona.
- *Out of my head:* Individuals are assumed to bear no responsibility for their own actions and so are free of guilt; being under the influence of a substance "made them do it."
- *Raging hormones:* This describes the biological drive of the species to reduce the physical tension created by sexual desire and excitement.
- *Tricking:* One of the participants uses his or her superior cunning to outwit the other.

In this way of thinking, we should note, social exchange analysis is but one of many ways to interpret a sexual liaison. We do not presume that the metaphors described above are the only relevant ones; we introduce them only to illustrate the complexity of unraveling high-risk behaviors in certain situations and to indicate a potential avenue for future research.

Research on Sexual
Communication Practices and HIV

Traditionally, scholars concerned with interpersonal interaction in the domains of consensual, committed, heterosexual, married, and developing relationships have examined white college student populations. They have not studied ephemeral or sporadic interactions, because these are difficult to gauge and access and because they transgress the bounds of "nice" relationships. In addition, researchers have focused on rational views of relationships, not to mention their bias toward studying healthy, positive relationships. This bias has been challenged by Bochner (1982) and Parks (1982), who argue that lying is important to study. Presuming that participants in relationships are rational social actors who function in situations where clear choices and criteria for them exist limits the study of those problematic episodes in which these criteria do not exist and/or are not applied.

Communication and HIV: Getting Around to Sex

To be sure, we are not throwing stones at those studying in the "traditional" realm of personal relationships. In fact, that is precisely where our work began. Initially, we studied college students as a risk group and described the extent of their relational talk about AIDS with romantic partners (Bowen & Michal-Johnson, 1989). We discovered that most college students in a multicampus study were not openly talking about HIV risk or prevention with partners, possibly because of personal and social taboos that prohibit it (Bowen & Michal-Johnson, 1990). Students attempted to gather information about the perceived risk of partners through third parties and reported avoiding direct talk with partners because of embarrassment or fear of spoiling the heat of the moment. Few of their communicative strategies were adequate or effective for HIV prevention.

We also examined two factors that we thought might influence communication strategies for self-protection. First, we hypothesized that assertiveness would be an important aspect of negotiating safer sex but found that traditional measures of assertiveness did not fit the dynamics of assertiveness in sexual interactions (Michal-Johnson & Bowen, 1988). Second, we attempted to link individual communicator style (Norton, 1983) with reported discussions of safer sex, but this analysis again yielded no relationship (Bowen & Michal-Johnson, 1990). Each of these avenues moved us further down the road to the conclusion that the nature of sexual liaisons includes far more complex dynamics than previous research has suggested. We learned that traditional skills approaches alone, such as assertiveness training, do not apply to sexual encounters, and sexual assertiveness must be studied as a separate phenomenon. Our presumption that being able to talk about AIDS would lead to negotiation of safer sex proved naive.

It is worth noting that only in the past few years have social psychologists and communication scholars begun to publish work on sexual interactions. Cupach and Metts (1991), for instance, have conducted research on sexuality and communication in established couples. The possibility of sexual transmission of HIV/AIDS led others in communication to study how talk functions in sexual liaisons. Adelman in 1988 was beginning to explore the attributes of the sexual experience as a playful and erotic process (Adelman, Moytl, & Downs, 1988; see also Adelman, 1992a, 1992b). Miller and her colleagues have explored scripts for safer-sex negotiations (e.g., Miller, Bettencourt, DeBro, & Hoffman, 1993) among heterosexuals and among gay men (Miller & Burns, in press). Edgar and Fitzpatrick (1988) used a compliance-gaining framework to understand safer-sex practices and since have examined scripts for sexual encounters (Edgar & Fitzpatrick, 1993) and resistance and response to the suggestion of condom use (Edgar, Freimuth, Hammond, McDonald, & Fink, 1992). Cline, Freeman, and Johnson (1990) investigated safer-sex practices and talk about AIDS and found that some people substitute talk about safer sex for the use of condoms. Metts and Fitzpatrick (1992) argue that "knowing your partner," as advised by the U.S. surgeon general, is not sufficient for effective HIV prevention. We have recently worked with AIDS education agencies to understand the highest-risk sexual behavior of members of the African American underclass (Bowen & Michal-Johnson, in press). Although the efforts of this small coterie of communication researchers have sought to map key communication aspects of HIV/AIDS, much systematic study of those at highest risk for HIV/AIDS remains to be done. Much of the work mentioned above has been geared to prevention of HIV transmission. Other valuable arenas for study are relationships between individuals who have the virus and know it, and relationships between those who have AIDS. For example, Serovich and Greene (1993; Serovich, Greene, & Parrott, 1992) have worked on the process and impact of disclosure of HIV status.

For the most part, the study of communication and HIV prevention has focused on presumably rational equal partners. As we enter the environments of alcohol use, drug use, and domestic violence, focusing on HIV risk, we identify the specific risks and describe the individual and interactive processes involved. Our understanding of these processes comes from empirical research that has been conducted within several disciplines. This research has helped us to develop a description of typical episodes in which HIV risk is greatest, and we invoke metaphors that may describe how individuals operate in them. We begin by discussing the most studied group of all time, college students, and their use of alcohol as a risk factor in sexual activities.

College Student Sex, Alcohol, and HIV/AIDS

We know a number of things about college students that are relevant to the issues raised in this chapter. First, we know that college students are at risk for HIV because of their high levels of sexual activity. Second, we know that the majority are not talking about AIDS in their interactions with partners or practicing safer sex, activities that may relate to risk reduction. Finally, we know that drinking alcohol is common among college students. We will support each of these points as we discuss the communication issues that arise from alcohol-influenced sexual interactions among college students.

College Student HIV Risk

College students are at risk for HIV infection given their relatively high levels of sexual experimentation. The Centers for Disease Control published data in 1990 indicating that at that time 1 out of every 500 college students was HIV positive. Current statistics indicate that 6.5% of all cases of AIDS in women and 3.4% of all cases in men occur among people ages 20 to 24 (Centers for Disease Control and Prevention, 1994). Furthermore, it is likely that most cases of AIDS among persons 25 to 35 years old were acquired when the individuals were in their late teens and early 20s (Butcher, Manning, & O'Neal, 1991). In addition, college students tend to base their decisions and activities on unrealistic optimism, which accompanies the perception of invulnerability characteristic of youth (van der

Pligt, Otten, Richard, & van der Velde, 1993). They systematically underestimate the likelihood of HIV infection (Linville, Fischer, & Fischhoff, 1993), regardless of their high levels of sexual activity (Cochran & Mays, 1990; Darling & Davidson, 1986; Spees, 1987; Sprecher & McKinney, 1993). Given the potential for exponential increases in HIV infection in this age group, college students are indeed important to study.

Knowledge and Discussion of HIV

A body of literature is developing that is specifically related to HIV. A number of researchers have reported on AIDS knowledge, attitudes, and behaviors (for example, Butcher et al., 1991; Cochran & Mays, 1990; O'Leary, Goodhart, Jemmott, & Boccher-Lattimore, 1992; Oswalt & Matsen, 1993; Williams et al., 1992). Cline and her colleagues (1990; Cline, Johnson & Freeman, 1992) have studied the extent and nature of talk about AIDS between college students who are dating, as have we (Bowen & Michal-Johnson, 1989, 1990). Unfortunately, the talk is not present in high-risk interactions. Edgar et al. (1992) have explored the use and nonuse of condoms among college students. Miller and her colleagues (1993) have attempted to develop models of safer-sex interactions. Negotiation of safer sex is not easily accomplished, and, in fact, safer sex is practiced by too few students. Oswalt and Matsen (1993) report that 44% of the respondents in their study used condoms only 50% of the times they had sex. As the number of partners increased, condom usage became less frequent. Numerous researchers admit that a variety of issues come into play in the sexual scene—self-esteem, degree of loneliness, peer pressure, and perceptions of how a partner is likely to react, to mention just a few. Alcohol use is another factor that undermines an individual's ability to negotiate safer sex.

Alcohol Use

Drinking seems to be ubiquitous among college students. The common practice of imbibing alcohol—whether beer, wine, or hard liquor—is portrayed by the media and is still in vogue, despite the fact that most students are younger than 21, the legal drinking age in most states. In the communication field, Seibold and Thomas (1992) have documented college students' widespread use and abuse of alcohol. Lederman (1993) uses the expression "beer goggles," which conveys the idea that anyone of the opposite sex looks attractive when one has been drinking, to describe a phenomenon that may link drinking and sexual activity.

Drinking and Safer Sex?

The college student-alcohol-sex triangle operates in a fairly obvious way: Students are more likely to engage in sex when they have been drinking. Given the statistics on condom use noted above, the sex students have may not include protection from HIV transmission. Furthermore, sex after drinking is perceived as typical or expected, although there are some sex differences in the perceptions surrounding alcohol use and sex. Below, we offer a brief overview of some of the literature that clarifies these relationships.

Based on probability, drinking is a pathway to high-risk sexual interaction. Butcher et al. (1991) found that approximately 70% of both men and women in their sample reported having unplanned intercourse because they were intoxicated; 29% of their respondents reported never using condoms under any conditions. In O'Leary et al.'s (1992) New Jersey sample, men reported being more likely than women to have sex while under the influence, and white students were more likely to do so than blacks. Of unmarried, sexually active students in O'Leary et al.'s study, 76% reported engaging in risky behavior. Hingson, Strunin, Berlin, and Heeren (1990) found that among the Massachusetts adolescents they sampled who drink and use drugs, 16% used condoms less often after drinking, and 25% used them less often after drug use. Williams et al. (1992) also note the correspondence between alcohol and sex. These studies provide evidence that students are indeed engaging in risky behaviors, and that the confluence of sex and alcohol is of primary importance. These studies do not, however, distinguish between sexual intercourse in first-time encounters and intercourse in established relationships.

At least one study has explored other factors that correlate with drinking and sexual activity. McEwan, McCallum, Bhopal, and Madhok (1992) found that students who drink and smoke cigarettes are more likely to practice unsafe sexual behaviors: 16.3% of medium drinkers and 27.1% of heavy drinkers in their sample reported having sex with someone they had just met without using a condom. Medium and heavy drinkers also reported having sex with someone they knew had had a lot of sexual partners, at rates of 16.3% and 19.3%, respectively. The data McEwan et al. gathered from a mail survey and from direct interviews with students were relatively consistent.

In this milieu, it is helpful to point out that sex differences play an important role in sexual activity and risk behaviors of college students. Christopher and Cate (1985) found that men and women gave different reasons for deciding on first sexual encounters. Men rated obligation/pressure as more important than did women, and women rated positive affection/communication items as more important than did men. If the couples were only casually dating, however, physical arousal and "circumstantial factors" (such as the influence of alcohol or drugs) were more likely to be reported as reasons for sex. Similar studies reported by Sprecher and McKinney (1993) substantiate a greater reliance of women on affection and love as reasons for sex, whereas physical release or lust more strongly influences men's engagement in sex.

A second area of research that substantiates relationships between alcohol use and behaviors in which individuals might not ordinarily engage concerns the "cognitive expectancies" that surround drinking. Sexual behavior is seen as more likely, even if it incurs risk, when people are drinking. These powerful expectations increase the likelihood of the occurrence of unprotected sex, thus increasing the risk of HIV transmission. A number of researchers have utilized experimental designs in which subjects were asked to respond to scenarios that manipulated drinking and sexual behavior (e.g., Corcoran & Bell, 1990; Corcoran & Thomas, 1991; Leigh, Aramburu, & Norris, 1992). Again, they have found sex differences in the attributions made about the participants in the scenarios. Whereas men were perceived to be more likely to initiate intercourse, both men and women believed that sexual activity was more likely when story characters ingested alcohol rather than soft drinks (Corcoran & Thomas, 1991). Leigh et al. (1992) found sex differences that to some extent reflect traditional sex role stereotypes, in which sexual behavior by males is more typical and includes more casual sexual encounters: "Whereas male subjects thought that both partners were sexiest when both parties were drinking beer, women gave their lowest rating of sexuality in that condition" (p. 354). What we can infer from at least some of these studies is that because women and men have sex for different reasons and under different conditions, they may not necessarily respond to the same intervention strategies for HIV prevention.

The "widely shared belief that alcohol acts as a sexual disinhibitor, i.e., that the effects of alcohol consumption lead people to engage in sexual acts in which they might not otherwise engage" (Reinarman & Leigh, 1987, p. 436), is also known as the *disinhibition hypothesis*. Reinarman and Leigh's (1987) work seems to support the existence of several of the metaphors presented above. For example, the metaphors of going with the flow, raging hormones, play, the dance, and the hunt may all be enacted under the influence of alcohol. The "out of my head" metaphor is used only with the influence of alcohol or some other drug, because it involves accounting for behavior by blaming substance use. These metaphors are enacted in slightly different ways. For instance, college students often report that they can control their actions when drinking, and they believe that they can say no to unwanted sexual activity; thus they may report just "going with the flow" of the evening, seeing where things will lead, never once believing that their actions can jeopardize them. Or they may believe that they have no control at all, because it is a biological drive (raging hormones) that pushes them to sexual action. Men are stereotyped as believing this more than women, supporting Robbins's (1989) claim that males and females use drugs and alcohol differently, for different reasons, and that substance abuse "exerts a greater psychological impact on females but a greater impact on the social functioning of males" (p. 126). Similar in some ways to going with the flow, potential sexual partners may "play" with each other, toying and teasing to see how far things will go sexually. This might be seen with two friends who, under the influence of alcohol, play with the idea of a sexual liaison. Or the music that typically accompanies college student parties or bars provides the backdrop for the dance, the steps and ending of which both parties know—it simply becomes a matter of which variation they will enact (Edgar & Fitzpatrick, 1993). Although Edgar and Fitzpatrick's (1993) research participants reported that alcohol is not necessary in the culmination of sexual intercourse, conversations we have had with our students and our previous research suggest otherwise. In another way, men and women both may prepare themselves for an evening out as if readying for a "hunt." They primp and preen, choosing just the right clothes, displaying just the right mannerisms, in hopes of capturing a sexual partner. Finally, students may report being out of their heads because of the influence of alcohol, and thus not fully responsible for unprotected sex or sex with a virtual stranger whom they have no intention of seeing again. In our AIDS talk research, some students have reported being too drunk to bring up the issue of AIDS or condom use.

Reinarman and Leigh's (1987) literature review provides empirical support of the effects of beliefs surrounding alcohol use. In terms of HIV risk, they note that "ego-defensive attributional strategies may bear upon the relationship between alcohol and AIDS insofar as drinkers may subjectively minimize the likelihood that they will do something sexually risky under the influence" (p. 447). Furthermore, they suggest that future research in this area might "explore whether drinkers use drinking to help themselves deny or suspend their knowledge of sexual risks; whether drinking and/or drunkenness play a part in being sexually 'swept away'; and whether being swept away allows a form of 'time out' in which the risk of unsafe sexual practices increases" (p. 452).

Thus alcohol affects the dynamics of interaction in that it supplies an additional layer of perceptual issues, including the cognitive expectancies and different filters used by men and women. We can see that decision-making and choice-making abilities are altered by alcohol, because people under the influence typically abandon rational screens. Their vigilance goes down. Their ability to refuse unwanted actions also decreases as they feel themselves to be in greater control than they really are. New research questions and different research strategies—ones more cognizant of situational and sex influences on sexual activities—are needed if we are to understand the college student sexual liaisons that occur when students have been drinking. The challenge for scholars is to figure out what influences sexual activity in varying circumstances so that interventions can be targeted. Can researchers and clinicians alter accepted rules of collegiate encounters? Can we change the interpretive rules that college students seem to use in social and sexual interactions? Can we lessen students' engagement in activities that heighten the risk of unsafe sex?

Drug Use and HIV Transmission

Our concern with sexual activity shows that, as with alcohol use, the use of either intravenous (IV) or non-IV drugs may promote high-risk sexual behavior. Intravenous drug use complicates the potential transmission of HIV. Users are at risk if they share needles or other paraphernalia, and unsuspecting sexual partners of intravenous drug users (IVDUs) are at risk for HIV regardless of whether or not they use IV drugs. Complicating this risk picture is the fact that generalizations about drug use and sex are not simple to make, because the "IV drug-using population is heterogeneous with respect to drug use, life-style and risk-associated behaviors" (Turner, Miller, & Moses, 1989, p. 189; see also Booth & Watters, 1992). Although they are often labeled deviant, drug users utilize the same moral beliefs and values as do people in the "dominant culture" (Balshem, Oxman, van Rooyen, & Girod, 1992). Drugs may also be used recreationally within groups by people who otherwise lead what would be called normal lives; that is, they hold jobs, own property, and so on. In other circles, drug users may be addicted, "down and out," living from fix to fix. The disproportionate rates of HIV and other sexually transmitted diseases in African American communities have less to do with ethnic or racial culture than with the politics of poverty experienced by many African Americans (Balshem et al., 1992; Bowser, Fullilove, & Fullilove, 1990; Dalton, 1989; Fullilove, Fullilove, Bowser, & Gross, 1990). It is important to understand that drug use that puts people at risk for HIV/AIDS is not limited to drug-crazed fiends.

Trading sexual favors for drugs, or using money from paid sexual acts to obtain drugs, is increasing, particularly among crack users (Balshem et al., 1992; Inciardi, 1989). Here again is an issue that is not readily addressed by the existing literature on personal relationships. On one hand, such transactions are seen as pure exchange, and so economically based models (such as social exchange theory) should apply. A person has money or drugs that another wants in order to achieve the goal of "getting high." That person is willing to do whatever it takes to reach that goal, even if it means consenting to sexual acts with a relative stranger. This would seem to enact the barter metaphor described above, yet straightforward exchange and the metaphors it invites do not capture all sex-for-drugs interaction. Sometimes the "out of my head" metaphor is invoked, when the drug or the addiction takes over for the individual. On the other hand, issues concerning power and violation raised by this phenomenon are not satisfactorily addressed by economic models (Wood, 1993a). Addicted persons are vulnerable to others who may take advantage of them, as they become the hunted. In their quest to satiate their addictions, they may be abused by others and may engage in behavior (e.g., sex, crime) they would not engage in outside the specter of addiction. Sexual acts performed in such situations are not about sex, but about doing what it takes to get the drug. Users may also invoke the hunting metaphor as they seek prey to get money to pay for their drugs. One informant told us that when she turned tricks to get money, she had no sexual feelings; that is, the sex was simply a means to an end. The drugs and the drive to obtain them substitute for authentic feelings and desires. For such people, condom use for disease prevention is not always foremost in their minds (Kenen & Armstrong, 1992). This reaction flies in the face of traditional definitions of erotic arousal and shared sexual scripts.

What does the sex-for-drugs transaction look like? How does it happen? A female informant, currently in recovery, told us how she actively used crack while raising a family and living with her own parents and siblings. She traded sex for drugs obsessively, disregarding the HIV risk. In another practice, male and female "running buddies" are likely to share injection equipment and to inject each other, according to Turner et al. (1989). These actions appear to have strong sexual connotations. Male running buddies may share needles and the same women in serial sexual relationships, acts rife with HIV risk. In the same vein, Magana (1991) describes a form of sexual behavior among a group of Hispanic migrant workers called "becoming milk brothers," in which several men in rapid succession have sexual intercourse with a single woman. There is an assumption that the woman uses the sex to enable her to get drugs, despite her being a victim or target in an extremely debasing situation.

Several pictures emerge of people engaged in sex-for-drugs interactions. Men may use drugs to accomplish their goals of having sex with women; drugs, especially crack, are associated with power, wealth, and glamour that make a person possessing them seem more attractive. Women who trade sex for drugs, called "crack stars," "strawberries," or "rock stars" (Balshem et al., 1992; Woodhouse, 1989), may meet men in crack houses, cars, or clubs. In crack houses, sex is often purely an economic chit. Women perform fellatio with frequency in order to earn money to gain their high. Thus they engage in barter in which rewards are perceived to outweigh the costs. As we have seen, women may be traded around a group of male users as prey or pieces of meat by "cavemen" who think they have gained the right to take women in this way. In cars, addicted women compete with prostitutes to get the trade. Sex workers on the streets perceive a conflict between themselves as professionals and the rock stars who offer sexual services to the clients of sex workers. Professional sex workers see their actions as their "work"; the others may be using a variety of metaphors to guide their actions, such as barter or the game. In the club scene, it is not only heavy drug users who frequent clubs, but many light users also visit. In fact, one of Balshem et al.'s respondents reported that the exchange of crack is similar in effect to the alcohol-based singles scene, where men and women hook up for the evening. The men may not even be crack users but use the drug only as a sexual bartering tool in their hunt for a sexual target, or to ensnare a sexual partner. The game that many of these people engage in, if seen as a game, is surely one in which the stakes are extremely high.

Drug use or abuse itself can be viewed as either a masking behavior or a predisposition. In either mode, it is initially a tool of personal control. When viewed as a masking behavior, drug use is seen as a way of dulling pain and diverting attention from problems. The metaphor of "out of my head" may be used to account for some behaviors. However, if addiction sets in, the substance dominates and controls, becoming itself a problem. Alternatively, when seen as a predisposition, taking drugs is viewed as a way to meet intense needs for stimulation. So, in accounting for an individual's ability to trade sex for drugs or to resist drug offers, we must acknowledge both the state and stage of the drug addict and its impact on HIV risk reduction.

HIV/AIDS Risks and Violence in Relationships

Whereas alcohol or drug use affects the dynamics of sexual interaction and inhibits safer-sex practices, violent relationships operate in a crucible that often negates options for protection. In a violent relationship, the long-term importance of protection from AIDS is eclipsed by the short-term and immediate threatening interaction, in which a woman's safety or even her life is in danger. In fact, nationally, nearly one third of female homicide victims are killed by their husbands or boyfriends; "a National Institute of Mental Health study estimates that 21% of all women who use emergency room services are battered: and half of all rapes to women over age 30 are related to domestic violence" (Allen, 1993). Although most of the literature on domestic violence focuses on heterosexual partners, violence between same-sex partners is apparent in the experience of practitioners and in limited studies (Schilit, Yong Lie, & Montagne, 1990). The need to examine violent relationships in the context of HIV risk is compelling and introduces circumstances that present perpetrators and victims with somewhat contradictory sets of communicative constraints and options.

Description of the Phenomenon

Violence in intimate relationships is often viewed as a result of the actions of one individual against another; this leads to discussion of victims and victimizers. Adopting this view, researchers have written about traits or predispositions that enable individuals to function as aggressors or as targets. A more accurate conceptualization acknowledges the interactive nature of intimate violence (Whitchurch & Pace, 1993). Focusing just on aggressors is imprudent, because perpetrators are most often not violent in their interactions and relationships outside the family or the relational unit. Stets (1992) suggests that dating aggression has more to do with interaction patterns within a particular relationship than with the violent individual's background characteristics. Sabourin, Infante, and Rudd (1993) view verbal aggression as both a predispositional trait and a relational pattern. Significantly, predisposition alone does not account for violence; instead, the predisposition must be within a relational context that encourages the enactment of violence. Several studies have clarified interpersonal violence as episodes with perpetrators, victims, and mutually violent couples. Felson (1992) and Stets (1992) favor a social interactionist view of aggression that de-emphasizes victimhood. However, as we have explored the literature we have noticed a strong tendency on the part of authors to use language in which the *abuser* is most often depicted as male and the *abused* or the *victim* is female.

Practitioners often refer to a "cycle of abuse" that assumes that individuals who engage in violence use power and control as the primary ways of making sense of relationships (Women Against Abuse, 1992). The cycle model is predicated on data that reveal that 73% of males and 50% of female aggressors experienced family violence in their families of origin (Flynn, 1987, p. 298). The cycle is best understood as a process kept in motion by prototypical strategies: blaming and shifting responsibility for the abuse, invoking male privilege, exercising economic controls, emotional manipulation and abuse, intimidating, coercing, and threatening, sexual abuse, physical violence, isolating the target, using children as pawns, and minimizing or denying abuse (Allen, 1993). Abusers often attempt to reengage clients of shelters for abused spouses by invoking several "promise strategies" (Michal-Johnson, 1992). Abusers promise to change behavior ("I'll go to church with you"), avow love ("I miss you so much, I'd never do it again"), offer purchases ("I'll get you what you've always wanted"), and promise that things will be different now ("I've learned my lesson").

Depending on the relationship, the abuse process engages partners in a somewhat predictable dance or script that operates on a level at which the relationship itself is not questioned and HIV risk exists throughout. Only when the viability of the relationship is questioned does the option of leaving the violence and the HIV risk become possible. As we are focusing on sexual acts in which HIV risk occurs because of intravenous drug use and/or unprotected extrarelational sex, the risk can occur at any point in the cycle of abuse.

Metaphors that emerge for participants in the sexual acts that take place in violent relationships may differ depending on whether the male is viewed as the abuser and the female as the target. First, for example, a man may see sexual acts as part of his privilege (the caveman mentality—"I have the right to have sex when, where, and how I want it"). This control may include withholding sex as emotional manipulation, particularly if the woman initiates sex, and intimidating, coercing, and threatening the partner with sex as an assault. Second, a woman stuck in the cycle of abuse may use sexual overtures as a sedative to defuse a violent situation (she may use sex as a way to control the man, to "ensnare" him and change the "game" they are playing), as a way of possibly minimizing physical abuse; acts of violence themselves often result in forced sexual activity. One woman interviewed in a shelter for abused women reported that "after sex he goes to sleep, it's like putting the monster to sleep" (Michal-Johnson, 1992). Some victims of abuse may employ the strategy of "tricking" their abusers. For instance, to avoid sex with her abuser, a woman may tell him that she is just too tired at that moment, but if he will wake her up in a couple of hours, she will be ready—her hope is that he will go to sleep and forget about having sex.

Given the delicacy of such tense interactions, negotiating for condom use may actually escalate anger and aggression. One researcher has documented cases in which women's following conventional public health advice to negotiate condom use intensified the violence directed toward them (de la Cancela, 1989). Women in such relationships who want to protect themselves from HIV infection must often work outside the range of typical negotiation strategies; some successfully trick their partners to achieve their goal. Many practitioners encourage abused women to lie to their partners, suggesting that a woman tell her partner she has a yeast infection and that he must wear a condom so he will not contract the disease (Linda Carter, personal communication, 1994). Such strategies may work when couples engage in sex to "make up," but when a woman uses sex to divert an abuser from violence, she cannot predictably plan for an act of intercourse. The use of sex as a sedative places women at increased risk for HIV, because violent episodes may occur at any time.

Typically in abuse situations, women give their abusers multiple chances and find excuses for their behavior, hoping that things will change (and the fairy tale will have a happy ending). Male abusers sometimes cite raging hormones and being "out of their heads" as excuses for their behavior.

Relationships Vulnerable
to Violence and HIV Risk

Violence in interpersonal relationships occurs between dating, cohabiting, and married individuals. Billingham (1987), for instance, notes that violence occurs in dating relationships with varying degrees of emotional commitment. This topic was first studied by Makepeace (1981) and was further investigated by Bird, Stith, and Schladale (1991), who found that between 39% and 54% of participants in dating violence maintain ongoing relationships despite physical abuse. Flynn (1990) cites Straus, Gelles, and Steinmetz's (1980) finding that nearly half (49.5%) of dating violence is mutually abusive violence.

Some researchers suspect that courtship violence serves as a training ground for marital violence. In an often-cited study, Dobash and Dobash (1979, cited in Flynn, 1987) found that 23% of the women in their sample who were in abusive relationships indicated they had been abused by their partners prior to marriage. Although dating violence tends to result in far less physical damage than does violence between cohabiting couples or marital partners, it may be an early phase in a process that escalates in intensity or danger. This can complicate the HIV risk reduction efficacy of partners because the pattern of the relationship has existed over a long period of time. It may also be the case that there is far more dating violence than we know about in so-called normal relationships.

Kilpatrick, Edmunds, and Seymour (1992) remind us that women with alcohol and drug abuse problems have often been victims of sexual violence and family violence, so that we see a self-perpetuating spiral in terms of substance abuse and violence. Rosenfeld and Lewis (1993) suggest that individuals who have experienced childhood sexual abuse are "less likely to set personal boundaries and [more likely to] have diminished senses of entitlement to health and well-being" (p. 159). Their findings have a bearing on abused women in that the ability to negotiate HIV protection is bound up in the ability to establish personal boundaries where a partner is involved. Women are more vulnerable in a way that lessens their ability to protect themselves and therefore increases the risk of HIV transmission. Current wisdom suggests that persons with low self-esteem are especially at risk of being targets of dating violence (Comins, 1984). However, recent work by Burke, Stets, and Pirog-Good (1989) qualifies the role of self-esteem in violent relationships, suggesting it only influences the willingness of an individual to accept aggression as a means of conflict resolution.

Communicative Strategies
in Dating and Spousal Violence

Bird et al. (1991, p. 48) identify four behaviors that intensify dating violence for victims: withdrawing, disagreeing, insulting, and swearing. Furthermore, they note that partners involved in violent episodes are more likely to use indirect/unilateral negotiation styles, which suggests that they are generally less satisfied with the relationship and more prone to disagreement and violence. For married partners, Wiggins (1983) comments on the three factors that Dobash and Dobash (1979) list as eliciting physical aggression: (a) the wife's not acceding to spousal demands concerning contact with other males, housekeeping, money management, childbearing, and sexual and other personal needs; (b) the wife's making demands of the spouse, questioning his behavior or opinion; and (c) a third party's interference in the husband's beating of the wife. Compliance with the aggressor's demands usually decreases the violence. Counteraggression and "frequently, even her confessions of noncompliance or indications of suffering (e.g., crying) intensified rather than diminished the hostility" (Wiggins, 1983, p. 111). Any of these behaviors might trigger an episode that becomes sexual, placing either or both partners at risk for HIV infection.

Interpretations of Violence

As we have noted, sex occurs at various points within the cycle of abuse, and, as with the sex, the violence is perceived in different ways depending on when it happens. Sex differences appear to exist in perceptions of the motives of assaulters (Follingstad, Wright, Lloyd, & Sebastian, 1991). Whereas females view male aggressors as controlling and retaliative, males view female aggressors as wanting to show how angry they are and as retaliating for emotional hurt or mistreatment. Flynn (1987) explains how interpretations of violence may actually encourage its continuation: "Anger and confusion are the two most frequently reported responses" (p. 296; see also Cate, Henton, Koval, Christopher, & Lloyd, 1982; Henton & Cate, 1983). Most individuals report perceiving acts of violence as unplanned and spontaneous, and nearly one third interpret violent acts as expressions of love (Flynn, 1987). Males and females differ in their reasons for violent behavior. Lenore Walker (1984) notes that women tend to use violence in self-defense, or as an end result of total loss of control—that is, the breaking point (Campbell, 1993). Men, on the other hand, see violence as a means of control (Campbell, 1993). Makepeace (1986) asserts that intimidation of the partner is the preeminent male motive for violence. Not surprisingly, men who are violent inflict more severe physical damage than do women who are violent (Steinmetz, 1977; cited in Flynn, 1990). In looking at these different interpretations, it is easy to see why HIV prevention often is not easily engaged in the dynamics of a process where retribution and self-defense are the dominant attributions of men and women in the abuse cycle.

Substance Abuse as a Variable

There is little debate about the prevalence of alcohol and substance abuse in violent interactions. Although causal conclusions cannot yet be drawn, alcohol and drug use are clearly present in many instances of relationship violence (Martin, 1992; Norton & Morgan, 1989). Berenson, Stiglich, Wilkinson, and Anderson (1991), Leonard, Bromet, Parkinson, Day, and Ryan (1985), and Schilit et al. (1990) all reaffirm that the risk of abuse increases when alcohol and/or other substances are used by one or both partners. Women Against Abuse (1992) describes substance abuse as an enabler or a trigger to violence: Men who batter often use substance abuse as an excuse for assault (the "out of my head" excuse). Protection orders are less effective with abusers who are under the influence of alcohol or drugs, and assaults that occur under the influence are likely to be severe, causing serious injury to the victim. Furthermore, substance-abusing battered women seem to use drugs to cope with abuse. This, however, puts the victim at greater risk, because she is more likely to fight back than to flee. Because counterattack tends to escalate violence, women who fight back are the most and worst injured of battered women in shelters. Finally, substance abuse may cause women to experience higher degrees of helplessness and dependency on their partners (which fits into the rescue component of the fairy tale metaphor).

A number of communication processes deserve attention. First, we must better understand how partners conceptualize abusive relationships and interpret them in light of HIV/AIDS. When does the female become an apologist, excusing a partner's violence because of his difficult life, for example, and in a sense excusing her risk of exposure to HIV? When does she take on the role of the accommodator? What behaviors tend to intensify violence, and what behaviors tend to diminish it? Are there, in fact, a series of strategies that men and women use or might use to detoxify violent interactions? Is it possible for partners to work out shared meanings that define their roles and that allow for protection from transmission of HIV, and do not just excuse or justify the violence?

Whether we are talking about alcohol-impaired risk assessment, drug and sex scenes, or abusive relationships, we can identify elements of each that are typical of all relationships, not just those that are walking on the dark side. Nice people become involved in manipulative interactions (not just college students drinking innocently enough at parties), people use others in relationships (not just in sex-for-drugs transactions), and control is a pivotal issue in relationships (even where full-blown violence does not occur).

Barriers to the Investigation of
Sexual Communication and HIV/AIDS

Why have relationship scholars not studied more vigorously the difficult communication challenges involved in the sexual processes of the HIV/AIDS epidemic? The epidemic brings the scholar into foreign territory, where the research enterprise is difficult, risky, and expensive—in terms of both time and money—and obtaining reliable subjects is challenging.

Clearly, the initiation and the procurement of funding for the study of HIV/AIDS risks in sexual interaction requires interdisciplinary cooperation. Scholars of communication processes must join with sociologists who understand structural substance abuse and violence, with social psychologists who have studied sexual issues, and with public health professionals to create interdisciplinary teams that can orchestrate projects to document the dynamics of these hard-to-study interactions. Because poverty marks many of the persons who would be the subjects of such studies, funding is absolutely essential if researchers are to conduct work of sufficient scope and power to address many of these issues. Informants and participants will all need to be paid for their participation. Researchers will also need to be savvy about the use of monetary rewards among the poor.

Gaining access to subjects for study is problematic because addicts, alcoholics, and abused individuals are often unwilling to identify themselves. Relying on agencies requires that researchers contact administrators in advance and convince them that allowing access will benefit them and their clients. In the study of domestic violence, participants' positions in the cycle of abuse affect how subjects can be reached and constrain their responses to researchers. Women still engaged in violent relationships can be studied only in natural outside groups acceptable to their abusing partners. Women in shelters who have sought sanctuary are in different stages of separation and acknowledgment of the violence from those who have not moved out of their abusive relationships. College students also need to be studied in their social environments, outside of classroom settings where they may be coerced into completing self-report questionnaires.

Investigation of both partners' points of view would likely indicate substantial differences in perspectives and meanings. Although it is ideal to study both relational partners, it is often impossible to gain access to both. Partners who took part in alcohol-influenced one-night stands are often not available, and sometimes not known. Nor are the johns who take part in sex-for-drugs transactions. Similar barriers exist for partner violence. For instance, the violent relationship is conducted in private, between partners with patterns of communication that can trigger violent episodes. Studying its mutuality requires both research participants in the violent relationship to cross-validate strategies. Because of the nature of these phenomena, obtaining both parties' stories becomes extremely difficult. Those partners who are available are those who have gone through programs designed to end the violence and are still together. Knowledge of the population is critical in choosing research strategies. In our work with BEBASHI (Blacks Educating Blacks About Sexual Health Issues), we found that it is common among educators to assume that a high percentage of individuals in drug rehabilitation programs also have histories of abuse.

Researchers attempting to document sexual and drug practices rely on several routes of access, such as interviews on the streets, often through outreach efforts (Iguchi et al., 1992), or with people in recovery programs (Balshem et al., 1992; Huebert & James, 1992). Methodological difficulties in surveys of sexual behavior can limit the reliability of data (Turner et al., 1989). Balshem and her colleagues (1992) note that the self-reflexiveness of informants in recovery compared with those still using drugs may account for some real differences in self-report data. Probably because of difficulties in access, much existing research is limited to frequency data of self-reported sexual, drug, and crime practices (see Inciardi, 1989). Other studies have attempted to assess rates of HIV infection based on reports of high-risk behavior (Liebman, Mulia, & McIlvaine, 1992). Despite the findings that people who use and abuse drugs are much like the rest of us, conducting research on IVDU presents challenging barriers (Turner et al., 1989).

Promising Research Directions

Of the research reported above, we highlight in this section research programs that may lead to breakthroughs in the hard-to-access populations described in this chapter. Relationship researchers need to study the communication patterns in sexual scripts that operate in sex-for-drugs transactions, seductions in which alcohol is present, and interpersonal violence. Edgar and Fitzpatrick's (1993) work on sexual scripts of college students offers good initial work that needs to be extended to those relationships most at risk. Far more work has focused on college students' use of alcohol than on either substance abuse or relationship violence. With alcohol use and sometimes with substance abuse, the altered state of consciousness becomes a gateway to sex, or sex becomes a gateway to obtaining an illegal substance. In domestic violence situations, women often use sex to minimize or deflect abuse and men regard sex as a vehicle for demonstrating dominance. In addition, these complicated pro-cesses function simultaneously at multiple levels: the biological/physiological, intrapersonal/perceptual, and interpersonal dimensions bound up in culture and family history. We need to examine how scripts operate in these sorts of interactions with all of the corresponding cultural and personal overlays.

Researchers investigating this area should engage in research that is not predicated on the "rational" model. In the high-risk situations discussed here, the rational processes often assumed by researchers tend to be debilitated or absent. In the case of alcohol, decisions to drink are within the conscious control of the individual, but as the effects of alcohol kick in, an individual's ability to choose consciously or to decide to leave a situation are affected. Lederman (1993) addresses the essential nature of planning and making explicit choices in alcohol-laden environments. We would encourage research that examines how or if planning is activated in dark-side interactions.

In parallel fashion, addiction creates powerful needs that may eclipse rational decision making, and the specter of violence may be so immediate that long-term dangers, even life-threatening ones, may not be salient. Thus the rational process of decision making is derailed. Perhaps Alberts, Miller-Rassulo, and Hecht's (1991) work on drug refusal strategies offers promise for the mapping of communicative behaviors that can be used in training individuals to refuse sexual behavior, as well as drug behavior, successfully. We would encourage research that examines the tendency of individuals to "go with the flow" and allow events to unfold, and that examines the metaphors that may act as indirect guides of behavior.

Studies of high sensation seeking (Donohew, Lorch, & Palmgreen, 1991; Palmgreen et al., 1993) exemplify the sorts of studies that should be pursued when direct intervention is the goal. Are individuals who score high on measures of sensation seeking more likely than others to engage in drug and alcohol abuse and partner violence and to ignore prevention messages about high-risk sexual behavior?

Some questions that deserve our attention are these: What factors in a situation trigger unsafe sexual practices? What aspects of an individual's own orientation toward a social event come into play in particular relational contexts? What verbal and nonverbal cues are salient to social actors in various situations that may signify vulnerability or predatory tendencies? Which communication skills enable individuals to assert themselves in situations where status differences, personal needs (such as those for acceptance, inclusion, and affection), and a heightened desire for pleasure interact? And—especially important—we need to know much more about the meanings individuals create around sex, drugs, and violence, both as separate and combined phenomena. We must better understand the role of metaphors in the minds of those who place themselves at risk through the pathways we have addressed in this chapter.

As we consider the implications of studying dark-side interactions in relationships, we suggest that by looking at such interactions we can learn something about how interactions occur in more mainstream relationships. First, we suggest that it is possible to view relationship behavior as a process that is "larger than" the bounds of social exchange theory, as we have illustrated through the use of multiple metaphors. Second, there is an "arational" nature to relationship behavior in which

individuals flounder into liaisons with little conscious awareness; they engage certain social forces that pull them into
dangerous liaisons. We would argue that this also occurs in
"normal" relationships as people pursue goals of relationship
maintenance. In the relationships that we call deviant, it is easier
to see our aghast, "Oh, my God" reactions to behavior that is
clearly outside the range of polite society. Nonetheless, we
would argue that most, if not all, personal relationships carry
with them notions of deviance or excess, particularly where sex
is concerned. Many of the metaphors we have discussed above
are equally applicable in nonabusive and substance-abuse-free
relationships. We urge our readers to consider the discussions
of the three troubled settings we engage in this chapter and test
their understanding of how "standard" relationship frames
incorporate many of these processes.

Conclusion

A common thread uniting the difficult dark-side situations
described above is that they confirm how extremely complex
and interactive sexual processes become when they are subjected to mind-altering substances and violence. Sex, as an HIV
risk factor, in combination with any one or more of the three
behavior sets described in this chapter, creates permutations of
interaction that become harder and harder for AIDS prevention
programs to target successfully. The personal and interpersonal
influences on sexual processes in high-risk situations constitute
not only an important and timely topic for relationship research, but also, without question, a pressing international
health concern.

8

Painting a New Face on Relationships: Relationship Remodeling in Response to Chronic Illness

Renee F. Lyons

Darlene Meade

A couple buys a new house. It's new for them, but it's actually 50 years old. After residing there for 2 years, they decide that certain things about the house need changing. The kitchen requires upgrading, as do the bathrooms. Most rooms need painting and new flooring. A nursery is required. So the couple agree to remodel, because they are basically happy with the house and do not wish the expense or disruption of moving.

In home remodeling, it is obvious that people are engaged in a conscious effort to adapt their physical environment: to keep a home and to reshape it for the better, or to suit new circumstances. Applying the notion of remodeling to personal relationships, relationship remodeling could be defined as actions taken by individuals, dyads, or families (or other social groupings) to maintain their personal relationships satisfactorily.

Relationship remodeling is observed around dissatisfactions with relationship functioning by one or both partners or the acknowledgment that aspects of relationship functioning are no longer possible. Whereas relationship remodeling may be a useful concept for understanding relationship processes, such as preventive maintenance, repair, and adaptation, it is of particular value in examining circumstances where external threats challenge the satisfactory maintenance of relationships. Events may change relationships, but what do people do with what happens to them? When faced with significant and continuous life stressors, what adaptational or remodeling strategies do people draw from in the service of their relationships?

One particular challenge that evokes relationship remodeling is the occurrence of a serious health problem, such as cancer or multiple sclerosis, in one of the parties to the relationship. Previous research has addressed the prevalence of serious chronic health problems and their intrusiveness in relationships (Lyons, Sullivan, & Ritvo, 1994; Rolland, 1988). In this chapter, we discuss chronic illness and the challenges it brings to the maintenance and quality of relationships. We expand on the notion of relationship remodeling by providing sample accounts that illustrate how illness stressors are appraised and how relationship remodeling strategies are devised by women with multiple sclerosis. We conclude with both an examination of four dialectical tensions that may influence relationship remodeling efforts in the face of illness and some ideas for further research.

Our focus on illness in this chapter is consistent with the emphasis in this book series on relationship processes because the methods that partners use to manage the stress of chronic illness change over time in response to health challenges. Our attention to how relationships adapt to chronic illness is also supportive of the goal of this particular volume, which seeks to call attention to the processes attached to challenges in relationships.

Recent work has given welcome attention to ways in which people maintain relationships in normal working order. This emphasis, although important, has so far been restricted to relationships in which partners are not experiencing serious health problems. Yet many participants in relationships are encumbered by medical problems, and we need to consider how relationships that include health issues are maintained. In this chapter we attend specifically to situations in which chronic illness affects one partner in an established personal relationship. Understanding how continuous medical constraints contour relational dynamics has potential to enlarge our insight not only into relationships in which illness is a constant, but also into those in which it is not. The study of previously under-investigated relationship issues exposes gaps in existing knowledge. It has theoretical import for the overall conceptualization of relationships that guides research and social services.

The Relevance of Examining
Relationships and Chronic Illness

Chronic illnesses are health problems that typically result in challenges to physical and psychosocial functioning and to the performance of social roles around work, leisure, family, and friendships. The word *chronic* signifies a long-term condition encompassing a course that may be stable, unpredictable, or progressive. Examples of familiar chronic medical conditions include AIDS, arthritis, cancer, diabetes, heart disease, multiple sclerosis, and stroke. Epidemiological data indicate that such chronic health problems have become North America's dominant health issue (Eisenberg, 1977). For example, more than two out of three families are affected by cancer alone (American Cancer Society, 1978).

Average life expectancy in the United States has increased from 49 years in 1900 to more than 75 years today, and the proportion of the population 55 years and older has more than doubled in the same period (National Center for Health Statistics, 1984). Chronic health problems such as cardiovascular disease, cancer, and stroke have now largely replaced infectious diseases as the leading causes of death (Satariano & Syme,

1981). Consequently, people are living longer, but lengthened life spans are often accompanied by physical disabilities and/or chronic health problems (Coyne & Fiske, 1992). Estimates are that up to 50% of the North American population will at some time experience chronic health problems such as cancer, stroke, and cardiovascular disease (Cole, 1974). People over the age of 65 often experience multiple disabling health problems, for example, arthritis, hypertension, heart disease, stroke, and/or vision and hearing impairment. Almost every health problem has a specific body of literature on personal relationships and social support; however, there may be some notable similarities in the effects of a wide range of medical problems on relationships.

Interest in the relationship challenges of illness has developed on two fronts: personal relationships research and coping research. On the relationships side, there has been growing interest in understanding how life events such as illness affect relationships (e.g., Blaxter, 1976; French, 1984; Lyons, 1991; Morgan & March, 1992; Russell, 1985). In understanding the social effects of illness, there is much that the study of illness in the social context can teach us about how people adapt relationships to significant life change. People with health problems, and their significant others, are often experienced remodelers. They are usually pressed into making substantial lifestyle adaptations owing to illness. From a process perspective, chronicity and illness unpredictability (as seen in such conditions as arthritis, cancer, heart disease, and multiple sclerosis) usually create the need for *chronic adaptational activity*.

Many researchers who study coping processes have also realized the parallel contribution of relationships to the illness experience. This has obviously occurred for those who study social support processes (e.g., Berkman, 1986; Berkman & Syme, 1979; Hammer, 1983); however, there is growing recognition that relationships not only provide support in coping with illness, but may also be major illness stressors (Blaxter, 1976; Charmaz, 1991; Dunkel-Schetter & Wortman, 1982; Fiore, Becker, & Coppell, 1983; French, 1984). Relationship maintenance has been identified as a key adaptive task in coping with illness (Moos & Tsu, 1977). There is also a growing recognition that illness is an issue not only for the individual with the condition, but for family members, particularly caregivers, and friends.

From their research on couples coping with cardiovascular disease, Coyne, Ellard, and Smith (1990) suggest that individual models of stress and coping do not accommodate the relationship-focused coping strategies they observed in couples and families dealing with health problems. As Coyne noted in a recent interview:

> People in enduring relationships know that they cannot simply be concerned about the stressor at hand, but need to take into account the actions of the partner, the relational implications of what they themselves do and the need to preserve the quality and resourcefulness of the relationship. (quoted in Lyons, 1993b, p. 12)

The role of relationship-focused coping (or adjustment in relationships) has also been emphasized by Gottlieb in his work on couples with chronically ill children and on couples coping with Alzheimer's disease. He suggests that the seeking of social support may act as a relationship maintenance and remodeling strategy:

> I began to realize that coping is determined in part by the need to maintain relationships with others—not to alienate them by one's way of coping. The reason for drawing on relationships for support is to shore those relationships up, and the reason for coping in certain ways is to keep important people involved with you or at least to believe that this is the case. (quoted in Lyons, 1993b, p. 11)

Relationship Challenges of Chronic Illness

What are the special relationship challenges of chronic illness, and how do people deal with them? Although there may be some consistency in the ways in which people address all types of external threats to their relationships, Baxter (1990) and Rawlins (1994) posit different transformational methods for different sorts of relational tensions. Each tension or issue contains its own personalized set of potential strategies. This problem-focused approach to relationship adaptation/remodeling parallels the findings of researchers concerned with coping, who have found that particular stressors are responded to with different types of coping strategies. We can conceive of the process of relationship remodeling as similar to coping processes, which involve stress appraisal, identification of adaptive tasks (what needs doing) and coping resources (constraints and opportunities), and the design of coping strategies (Lazarus & Folkman, 1984). Of course, the examination of the process of coping and adaptation in relationships is more complex than the examination of coping in individuals. In the first place, relationships are composed of at least two people and one relationship, let alone contextual factors such as their embeddedness in a network of other relationships. Second, one or both members may initiate relationship change, but both are directly affected by it. Third, one or both members may resist or be threatened by change, or there may be considerable conflict around the necessity for or the mode of change. Cost and power issues in the relationship may be exacerbated.

Despite noble intentions, competencies for maintaining relationships without chronic illness are often beyond people's grasp. Superimpose the additional complexities of illness, and people must navigate carefully over particularly strange and foreboding relational terrain. Illness may bring with it threats to social identity, performance of roles, and hopes for the future. It may require people to modify conditions and behaviors so that they and their relationships can accommodate illness. This is done to counter the social intrusiveness of the illness, which can overwhelm individuals in their relationships (Charmaz, 1991). When illness enters, each party in the relationship asks, What will life be like for me in this relationship, and for us?

The threat to a relationship posed by illness may occur in a context where the illness itself (e.g., treatment procedures, pain, fatigue, limited mobility) reduces the physical and psychological resources available for the people involved to deal with relationship challenges. Left unchallenged, illness and its impact on lifestyle can reduce social networks (Janssen, Philipsen, &

Halfens, 1990), increase marital difficulties (Sullivan, Mikail, & Weinshenker, 1992), reduce social contact with valued others, terminate activity-based (work, sport) contacts, and result in dysfunctional relationships in which there is little meaningful companionate activity, support, communication, or intimacy. (For a research review on relationships and illness, see Lyons et al., in press.)

In support of our claims about these relational effects of illness and relationship remodeling strategies, we introduce phenomenological accounts of real-life experience from a qualitative study of mothers with multiple sclerosis (MS). We chose these mothers with MS because the variety of symptoms and the unpredictable course of MS have been shown to be particularly disruptive to relationships (Brooks & Matson, 1982; Burnfield & Burnfield, 1982; Maybury & Brewin, 1984; Miles, 1979), with onset appearing at a critical time in the life cycle for adult relationships (Russell, 1985). MS usually appears between the ages of 20 and 40, often early in marriage and parenthood. Our intent in presenting these accounts is not to generalize about the relationship experiences of people with health problems but to provide detailed insight from in-depth research on a small number of respondents. The following sections on relationship challenges and remodeling strategies may appear to be somewhat of a laundry list, but we believe it is necessary to clarify the types of relationship stressors that may be created by illness in order to understand the construction of problem-focused relationship remodeling strategies. We can then discuss relational processes during the challenge of chronic illness.

Eight women participated in three focus group discussions (Lyons, 1993a) and two personal interviews regarding illness and personal relationships. The focus groups and interviews (2- to 3-hour sessions) were audiotaped, transcribed, and content analyzed. The age range of participants was 26 to 40; all had current partners. Three were employed, and four had "retired" from paid employment because of MS. Duration of MS ranged from 3 to 21 years. The symptoms experienced by the women in the sample included fatigue, numbness, hand tremors, weakness, sensitivity to heat and cold, vision difficulties, pain, bowel and bladder difficulties, and balance and mobility difficulties (requiring use of a cane).

The Relationship Challenges of MS

These women's experience of MS included several salient challenges that involved dealing with symptoms in relationships, shared meanings of the illness in relationships, affects social roles and companionate activity, and social exchange. Along with the direct impact on relationships, these challenges also affected self-esteem and personal resources for coping with MS (as the reader will note in the respondents' talk about the issues).

Dealing With Illness Symptoms in Relationships

Although there were varying experiences with onset, severity, and course of symptoms, two main illness characteristics that intruded on and threatened relationships were *fatigue* and *symptom unpredictability.*

> MS is rude. It just keeps popping up. . . . You know, as soon as you start something, you're exhausted. You have to sit down. And it ruins everything.
>
> A perfect name for MS: Mighty Strange disease. . . . You don't know what's coming next. You see, one day you're fine. The next day you're in a wheelchair. And then you're back to a cane and it's cycle, cycle, cycle. Mighty strange.

Shared Understandings and Meanings of Illness

There were numerous accounts of significant others' not understanding what it is like to have MS, a lack of shared knowledge about the condition.

> But I find that most partners do not really understand what you are going through because they don't have our problem. They can see it, yes. But they're not going through it.

This issue was particularly apparent with respect to invisible symptoms:

> For someone to come along and say, "There's nothing wrong with you," and someone who has been there all along, it's hard. It makes it sometimes harder for you to deal with as well. Because . . . maybe this is all in my mind. Maybe I am crazy, maybe this doesn't exist. . . . Sometimes you wonder.

Because of emotional vulnerability, "confirmational" comments from others such as this threatened self-esteem, perhaps unintentionally.

The women needed to employ relational competence, sensitivity, and tact in clarifying the illness for others, particularly children:

> My son's very good. He explains to people that his mother has sore legs. By the time he was 4, he'd asked me point-blank if I was going to die. "Will sore legs kill you, Mommy? Is it going to make you die?"
> "No, M. Sore legs will never make me die."
> "Okay."

Social Roles and Companionate Activity

In several accounts the respondents indicated that illness widened the gap between their expected roles in personal relationships and their current "performance." Adapting gap theory (Calmen, 1984), relationship satisfaction is the space between the perception of "what is" and "what ought to be" in relationship characteristics that are considered to be important. This may not be simply a "feel-good" notion of satisfaction. Both commitment and satisfaction may involve concern for partner outcomes, relationship investments and alternatives, personal identity tied to relationship identity, cognitive interdependence (shared history, meaning), future goals, and commitment values (Rusbult & Buunk, 1993). In this case, relationship quality/satisfaction was closely tied to a normative view of role performance as mother, wife, friend, coworker.

And I think that's what it boils down to. We're not perfect and we want to be. We want to be the perfect wife, the perfect mother, the perfect housewife, and the perfect friend.

This gap between current and "acceptable" social role performance was of particular concern with respect to relationships with children—the need to be considered a "good" mother:

And I can't act as goofy as some of the other mothers. . . . I don't have the freedom to just sort of . . . move like I want to or do what I want to.

When he starts getting older and he starts comparing me to other mothers, that's going to be hard. I just hope I come out with the right things to say.

My mother said we were a couple that should never have had kids, because of the fact that, with the MS, I can't always pick up and go with the kids. Like we've . . . they've missed out on. . . . If I could drive . . . go take them to the beach, go for walks. Just things that don't cost a lot of money. . . . And like, during the summer when I'm hot and tired . . . and I can't go out for a walk with them and then. . . . It sort of makes it . . . you think, well . . . maybe I shouldn't have.

During exacerbations of the disease, desires for relationship maintenance, socializing, and sexual intimacy were reduced.

When you're having an attack, you just don't want to be around. . . . You don't want to talk to your friends. . . . You just don't make an effort to go and see anybody.

The temptation's there just to bury yourself.

There are times when . . . I remember having a sex life. I mean a real one. Not . . . quickies here and there. Because I'm too tired. . . . So it's certainly been a drain on . . . I feel I'm too young . . . to be losing that part.

There was a hesitation in making commitments for future social activity.

And I find with any programs that I want to get my children involved in, I'm afraid to go and sign them up because you don't know when an attack is going to come. . . . And they'll start to get used to going this place or going and doing something, and then halfway through it, they're going to have to stop because you can't get them there.

Relationships sometimes lost spontaneity and intimacy:

> And I just can't get in a car and drive across the bridge to see [my mother].
> So I think that maybe some of the closeness and the freedom of the
> relationship is gone, because you can only do so much over the phone.
> You always have to have someone else with you.

A further issue related to not working outside of the home
and being at home when others are at work:

> I find it's very hard . . . now to keep . . . relationships. It's not like before
> where maybe you'd have a street of 30 people and you'd have a close
> relationship with a neighbor because they were home and you were home,
> and so you just find yourself more cut off.

Limited energy led to a prioritization of social roles. Energy was
usually allocated first to children, then to partner, then to kin
and friends, and then to neighbors:

> Once you have kids . . . you've made that commitment and . . . I don't
> know . . . I think you owe it to the kids. To provide them with what you
> can and as long as you can.

Social Exchange, Support, and Equity

Perceived social support, reciprocity, and equity became more
salient determinants of relationship quality and of emotional
well-being. In addition to the many practical issues around
household tasks, caregiving, and finances that required attention, support meant having people to depend on for companionship and understanding:

> It's your emotional outlook. . . . If you know you've got somebody that
> you can depend on, . . . you're feeling fitter emotionally and then you can
> handle the physical parts yourself.
>
> I need to have at least one person that . . . they'll know what I need before
> I know what I need. Someone that is fine-tuned . . . that knows you.
>
> Just if . . . I feel like I'm going to cry . . . to know that that person is going
> to understand and not make a big deal about it. That you can be yourself.

Clarifying exactly what was needed from significant others was important; for example, companionship compared with "help," to be seen as a friend or companion versus someone always associated with help:

> So, I think it's . . . having someone that will help you, but not always physically. . . . But it's just that when he . . . you know, maybe I'm trying to do something and I'm depressed . . . maybe he'll call someone and say, "J's having a bad day. Will you come and spend some time?" And I think that's the bigger thing. That . . . they'll encourage relationships with other people. I mean, I had my mother that helped me with chores and things like that. But he'd often say, "Why can't she just come over and visit with you?" Like, I think he knows that's the important part.

Children were a valued source of social support, although the social support literature rarely acknowledges their contribution.

> That there's somebody there, that you can unload on. . . . I mean, I know sometimes it's my son. He seems to know if you're having . . . like, a rough week, or . . . rough day. Yeah. He's still very . . . demonstrative. You know, like, he'll come up and give you a hug and things like that. Or my daughter will do that.
> I was just lying there [on the couch] . . . and he looked at me and he came over and he said, "Mommy tired? Mommy tired?"
> I said, "Mommy's tired."
> "Close your eyes." And he crawled up next to me and laid down with me and he gave me a kiss, he said, "I love you, Mommy."
> . . . your old heart! But they really know.

Along with receipt of support, there was a need for reciprocity and fairness in relationships.

> I still think it's important that . . . your friend can confide in you as well. They can talk to you at some deep level of emotional kind of discussion. I guess not just me spilling my guts, but they feel confident enough to do the same thing back.
> Well, we actually had kind of an interesting couple of weeks. I started another attack—this hand has gone kind of weird on me. And I wasn't quite over my last attack that I was treated for and I was really down. And at the same time, R. [partner] pulled a muscle in his shoulder and . . . he

finally . . . I'm glad he said it. . . . He said, "It seems like your MS is more important than my shoulder." And [I said], "No, that's not the case." But by the time I get in bed at 11 o'clock at night, and he wants me to rub his shoulder, I'm just too tired. . . . And while he understands [that], and he's really very helpful, he was feeling lousy too. . . . But at least he was able to say that. And so, the next night, I made an extra effort. By 8 o'clock, we sat down and actually . . . before I got too tired, and I put some stuff on his shoulder.

Although the exchange and equity research attends to individuals' maximizing or ensuring their own gains, for these women relationship satisfaction was tied not only to the self, but to concerns for partner/friend outcomes and their well-being.

M. had to cancel his sea trip, the whole shebang. Yeah, [my doctor] said there was no way I could be on my own. So . . . it was quite a crisis for us.

It's also hard to deal with when you're talking to a friend . . . a close friend. They ask you how you're doing and you tell them a little bit and you can see them on the verge of tears. . . . "Don't cry, I mean, I'm not dying." . . . You know, it's kind of backward. I want to console them.

In summary, the respondents were able to articulate the impact of illness on their lives and their relationships. They were concerned about its effect on reshaping both objective and subjective aspects of relationships on many levels, including the role of self in relationships, the role of relationships, and the everyday workings of valued relationships. Looking at the four categories of relationship challenges, one can conclude that the general themes/challenges are not unlike those found in other relationships. Satisfactory maintenance relates to (a) the ability to communicate about important issues, (b) common knowledge and meaning about issues, (c) feeling competent in relationship roles, and (d) dealing with issues of exchange, support, and equity. So we may be seeing the sorts of common relationship challenges that are present in the maintenance of relationships, but attempts to meet these challenges may be substantially more difficult for relationships in which one participant has a chronic medical condition.

Relationship Remodeling Strategies

What types of relationship remodeling strategies are devised to address the above challenges? The idea of relationship remodeling suggests that at least one person is committed enough to a relationship to design adaptations to enhance its quality. Reviewing our conceptualization of relational remodeling, the intent is to keep certain relationships and to keep them in forms that are reasonably satisfying. In response to an external threat to the satisfactory maintenance of relationships, there are several possible options: relationship withdrawal or termination, adaptation of the existing relationship, and relationship maintenance that resists changes, with little or no effort to adapt. Herein lie the differences between relationship change strategies (RCSs), relationship maintenance strategies (RMSs), and relationship remodeling strategies (RRSs). The intent of RCSs may not be to maintain a relationship in its current form, but to change it because of dissatisfactions that are not the result of external constraints, or else to redefine it either as ended or as a different type of relationship.

What is the distinction between RMSs and RRSs? Relationship maintenance has been variously defined as keeping relationships in existence, keeping relationships in a specified state or condition, keeping relationships in satisfactory condition, preventing negative outcomes, and keeping relationships in repair (Dindia & Baxter, 1987; Dindia & Canary, 1993; Duck, 1988). RMSs can be used to repair or change relationships or to keep relationships as they are (Baxter & Dindia, 1990). RRSs (perhaps a subset of RMSs) imply adaptation and change, as well as the desire for both maintenance and enhancement. Of course, many changes in relationships are not attributable to RCSs, RMSs, or RRSs. Changes in social network structure, relationship functioning, and relationship quality may be outside of conscious choice and decision making.

As with home remodeling, the job of relationship remodeling can be big or small. Relatively commonplace changes that people make in relationships include instrumental adaptations such as reallocation of household and child-care tasks, spending more time alone or together, taking a vacation, deciding to go out more often, taking more time for intimacy, attending to each other's needs more carefully, or making individual lifestyle changes in work, leisure, or family. Although these everyday activities and adaptations may appear to be relatively minor occurrences in the grand scheme of personal relationships research, they may in fact constitute the structural supports (speaking constructionally) as well as contribute to the overall framework and design of the relationship (Duck, 1986, 1988, 1992).

In the study of mothers with MS, there were numerous examples of relationship remodeling strategies that study participants and/or significant others employed to address the challenges of illness. We have organized these RRSs under three major themes: mental renovations, companionate activity modifications, and network remodeling.

Mental Renovations

Mental renovations include cognitive and emotional strategies to modify expectations of a "normative" self in relationships. B. Wright (1983) has termed this process in individuals *revaluation*—the enlargement and adaptation of one's scope of values. With respect to relationships, this might include changed perspectives about what is important in marriage and friendship. The following are accounts of mental renovations found in the MS study.

Revaluing Self With Relational Asset Values

You see that you're not as flawed as people make you out to be. That you can still be a woman, you can still be a mother. . . . You know, even with the MS, I know that I'm a good mother.

Assuming an Adaptational Cognitive Style

But I think we have to adjust our mind to think, "Okay, I can't do it this way, but how can I do it?"

Positive Thinking

So, it's like, look on the positive side. If tomorrow something happens, you can't get around . . . oh, well, the day after, you will.

Maintaining a Sense of Self-Efficacy

You have to have a fighting spirit. Like, I'm not going to let this control me. I'm going to live, but pace myself. . . . You have your limitations and you understand them.

Focusing Attention on Specific Illness Challenges

Stop worrying about things that you cannot change. . . . And there's other things that you can. . . . If you can change [it], fine, and if you can't, don't dwell on it—you're just wasting energy: energy that we need.

Focusing on the Present

You have to seize . . . especially for a child, the moment. Spend as much time as you can. Because what happens if tomorrow you can't do . . . you can't go for a ride on the swings like you did today, or you could have done today. So you have to make sure you make time for them.

Capitalizing on Illness

MS is not all bad. It's a neat, little, tidy excuse. . . . "I'd like to help any way I can, but . . . I have MS, you know" on the phone to whoever is calling for volunteers and wants you in a meeting at night. It's not all bad, it gets you out of some stuff. It just helps you to keep it all in perspective and helps . . . people lower their expectations.

Downplaying MS as a Constraint

I think it's important not to let MS stand in your way. . . . In making friendships, I think, "Oh, I'm different," and I may hold back. . . . Because if it's going to be a friend, they don't care.

Not Allowing Illness to Assume a
Dominant Place in Life and Relationships

Because you don't have the time to think about yourself. About all what's wrong with you. . . . And that is an asset. Because if I didn't have those two children, I'd be able to sit here all day and think about how my legs are rubbery, or I'm dizzy, or I've got bad hand tremors and how bad I feel. . . . This way I don't have time. . . . I have to get them up. Get them dressed. Make them breakfast and get them to school . . . just do little things for them. And worry about them seeing what was wrong with me so they won't worry.

I think it's really easy to become preoccupied. I mean . . . it's not an easy condition. . . . You can spend a lot of time studying how your foot feels today . . . or how you're walking today in comparison with how you did yesterday and looking for. . . . It's like anything, anybody can get caught up in the state of their health. I think what the big thing is . . . is remembering that there are other people there and that they have needs, too.

Companionate Activity Modifications

Containment of disability effects involves activity adaptations to avoid conflict with disability symptoms, such as weakness and fatigue. This includes the temporal scheduling of events around "healthy" times, or remissions. Modifications include activity adaptation and substitution and changes in the locations, timing, and intensity of companionate activity. Issues of cooperation, task allocation, and support are also salient in many relationships when one of the persons has a chronic health problem. The following are examples of how these changes occurred in our respondents' networks.

Companionate Activity
Adaptations With Children

Instead of going apple picking I baked the apple cake and sent it to school, and went in and did a story time about apples. . . . It just takes a whole lot of thinking to try and feel like you're a good mom. I mean you just can't do it the easy way. You have to think it through and think of how you can. . . . Constantly I feel I'm thinking how I can . . . be a good mom with the limitations I'm faced with.

And I try to take him places that he can run around. Somewhere safe, like a park. And get his energy worn off and [I] stop feeling guilty.

But I don't think that you can say you're not a good mother because you can't do certain things. Because you can do others. You can take them to a concert where you can go and sit down for an hour or so and enjoy the concert. You can be the mother that the kids want to come talk to.

My little one was 4 and [my son] was 6 and you know . . . The next year come Christmas time, I said to the kids, "Look, it's Christmas for me, too, and I want to enjoy Christmas. And you want me there with you." They scrubbed floors. They learned how to do the wash. They learned how to do everything. And it's been nothing but positive.

Companionate Activity Adaptation With Partners

An important aspect was increased investment of a partner's effort on instrumental tasks to free up energy for relationships:

If I'd had to get all the supper ready and everything, I wouldn't have had the energy to go out and socialize last night. So he . . . by him taking care of the supper, it enabled us to go out. . . . So because he helped, I was able to enjoy the evening and not be too tired.

Extended family members could be particularly supportive of relationship maintenance if they lived nearby:

Mom would take the kids and keep them overnight so that I could sleep in and my husband and I had some time together. Because with both of us working and me so tired . . .

Companionate activity adaptations and attitudes of coworkers made a substantive difference at work.

They're very supportive. I think it's because we've been together so long. We're like a family, which is nice.
And they're all really good with it. And they'll watch me and they can tell. Like, at the end of the day my speech really slurs. And they'll come and they go, "Okay, L., you have five minutes to get your sentence out. What do you want to tell me?" And they'll make a joke of it. Because they know it puts me more at ease. But they're good.

Network Remodeling

As noted above, reduced energy for socializing means that time must be carefully allocated around the network. In some cases, relationships may be terminated or reduced in intensity. Reasons the respondents gave for these strategies included decreased physical proximity, others' nonsupportive or stigma tizing reactions to the illness, and the desire to focus on the more valued relationships. Frequently, other persons with MS and support groups became part of the evolving support network. For some, but not all, support groups seemed to provide a relaxed, accepting social environment:

> Every time I go to a meeting—our chapter's not very large, there's about a dozen people there—I feel so calm. You know, there's some in wheelchairs, and some like myself, and I thought, "Well, these people are almost . . . " they become really close, these people understand if you trip over something. Someone that doesn't have MS will kind of look at you and just, you feel so uncomfortable. These people understand.

In addressing the threat of illness to relationships, there are, in a sense, two sets of challenges: One involves the impact of illness on relationships, and the other involves the adaptation or remodeling of relationships in the face of the external threat of illness. As noted earlier, many of the strategies developed by the women in this sample may appear insignificant and very specific to the stressors at hand. However, the quality of their relationships seemed to be tied to perceived competencies in relationship remodeling on a day-to-day basis and the level of perceived commitment to ensuring the satisfactory maintenance of their relationships.

Dialectical Tensions and Relationship Remodeling

The decision to engage in relationship remodeling was affected by a variety of individual, relational, contextual, and situational factors. For instance, gender was a recurring factor. These women tended to believe that women are more competent in managing when they are ill and also in managing the stress of a partner's illness than are men, and that dealing with illness is, in general, more of a women's issue. The women in this study also were of the opinion that women who are ill are more concerned about the well-being of others than are men with the same illness. Women would invest more effort in the construction of remodeling strategies for the benefit of others, and the relationship, versus their own needs. Illness seemed to push women toward more conservative gender roles. However, there are many others factors besides gender in the appraisals of the relational challenges of illness and in constructing RRSs. We present several of these in the form of relationship dialectical tensions.

As with the process of home remodeling, relationship remodeling can be smooth or rough, but even if smooth it likely contains rough spots. On the one hand, change can be exciting. On the other, it invites potential conflict around the need, nature, and extent of change. In couples, relationship remodeling is usually initiated by one partner, followed by possible reactions in the other partner that might range from agreement and enthusiasm to fierce debate or rejection or avoidance of the issue. Those in the relationship have many concerns: Can we agree on what changes to make? Can I/we actually make the changes desired? What are the costs and gains? Is it worth the investment of effort or the disruption of the status quo? One might think of these debates as extensions of the change processes endemic to all relationships.

As we indicated earlier, RRSs, adaptational efforts to reshape relationships to accommodate illness satisfactorily, can be considered a subset of RMSs. Therefore, it is useful to frame remodeling strategies within a context of relationship maintenance. Although the term *relationship maintenance* may imply stability and consistency, relationships are not static. They are a combination of elements of stability and elements of change, as well as the nature of ebb and flow of these processes (Duck, 1994a). Baxter (1994) speaks of relational maintenance dialectically as "the process of coping with the ceaseless change that results from the struggle of contradictory tendencies inherent in relating" (p. 233). Examples of relationship dialectical tensions include autonomy/connection (the most central), predictability/novelty, and openness/closedness. Montgomery (1993) suggests that the essence of social activity is the nature of movement along a time line of developing, experienced, and transformed dialectical dilemmas. Integrating the notions of dialec-

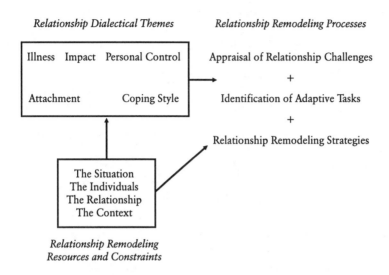

Relationship Dialectical Themes   *Relationship Remodeling Processes*

Illness   Impact   Personal Control   Appraisal of Relationship Challenges

+

Attachment   Coping Style   Identification of Adaptive Tasks

+

Relationship Remodeling Strategies

The Situation
The Individuals
The Relationship
The Context

Relationship Remodeling
Resources and Constraints

Figure 8.1. Factors in External Relationship Challenges and Remodeling

formed dialectical dilemmas. Integrating the notions of dialectics and gaps, relationship maintenance probably has something to do with the degree of dyadic synchrony around dialectics: the harmony, discord, or gap in what each expects to experience in the relationship, and how this changes over time.

The study of relationship dialectics is fairly new and has focused on tensions that seem to be generic to at least those relationships in which dialectics have been studied. We try to build on this base by applying relationship dialectical tensions to the relationship challenges of illness and the resultant design of remodeling strategies. On considering the findings from the mothers study and other research on relationships with persons who have chronic illnesses, we present four dialectical themes that may influence relationship commitment, maintenance, and the engagement in relationship remodeling strategies: illness impact, personal control, attachment, and coping style. The last three might be considered subsets of Baxter's (1990) autonomy/ connection dialectic. These themes are reflected in Figure 8.1 as central factors in coping with the challenges of illness and in relationship remodeling.

Illness Impact: Containing Versus Globalizing Illness

People who are ill and their intimates are chronically in tension with the illness state. How does this joint conflict with illness, which is issue oriented, become personalized and create conflict in relationships? Borrowing from the cognitive reformulation of learned helplessness theory (Abramson, Seligman, & Teasdale, 1978), we propose that conflict escalates to the degree that it becomes seen increasingly as personalized (it is something about you and me that is at the core of this tension), stabilized (resolution or change is unlikely in the near future), and globalized (it is going to affect more and more contexts of living). For example, in the case of a serious illness, the tension could become increasingly personalized if one or both parties are dissatisfied with the way the other is dealing with the issue. The tension could become stabilized if a couple has exhausted all its resources to "fight" the illness, but the medical problem has not gone away. The tension could become globalized as the illness interferes increasingly with the relationship. The implications for relationship remodeling are obvious. A globalized orientation may lead to few attempts to remodel, or it may lead to strategies that include drastic changes. Both may have little chance of success.

Personal Control: Independence Versus Reliance

The perceived ability to exert control over stressful situations is a strategic aspect of coping (Bandura, 1986). Illness is a threat to self-efficacy, and loss of control is a threat to self-identity. For example, an individual's belief that he or she can influence health outcomes will influence the extent to which that person makes an effort to resist the sometimes overwhelming presence of illness. Therefore, maintenance of identity and self-worth are tied to the perceived ability to control the illness and to minimize its intrusiveness. For instance, being forced by decreased mobility to use a wheelchair may be perceived as a defeat. As a respondent in Russell's (1985) study put it, "I just didn't want to give in to this disease" (p. 34). The belief in a just world (Lerner, Miller, & Holmes, 1976) is also tied to self-efficacy.

Another respondent of Russell's expressed the idea that if one pursues a healthy lifestyle, one should feel better: "You try to do everything right; you eat right, you don't smoke, you don't drink, you sleep enough, you have enough rest. And the same things are happening over which you have no control" (p. 31).

The appraisal of illness as acute or chronic may affect self-efficacy, coping strategies, and illness adaptation. For instance, emotional and lifestyle adaptation may be placed on hold until a condition that was perceived as acute and treatable is acknowledged as chronic. Charmaz (1991) suggests that adopting a model of acute care is a coping strategy, a means of resisting the impact of illness on people's lives, their self-efficacy, and their relationships. People who are ill expect symptoms and treatments and learn to plan around them, trying to minimize the intrusiveness of illness on their lives. However, thinking of an illness as chronic—or, worse, accepting that it is degenerative—reduces self-efficacy.

The independence versus reliance dialectic is reflected in the following quotes from the MS mothers study.

The Challenge to Self-Efficacy in Asking for Help

It takes a little pride to ask. These things you used to be able to do, and now, you have to ask. And it just, oooh, that makes you so angry.

Knowing When to Seek Help and Others' Knowing When to Provide It

And there are times when . . . I'm not feeling well . . . I really appreciate having the help. But I don't want the help forced on me when I'm capable of doing it myself. So I guess it's him assuming. . . . That bothers me, that he assumes that I . . . can't do things sometimes, when I really could. So it's . . . I guess he can't read my mind. Can't expect him to.

The Efforts of Others to Maintain and Enhance Self-Efficacy

He won't limit me because he says, "You're a smart enough person, you know what you can and cannot do. But . . . let's not push it." And he'll purposefully plan things [social activities] that he'll know won't stress me.

Striking a Balance Between Self-Efficacy and Support

> If you don't have someone you can ask to do things, then I think what
> happens is . . . you're swamped. Because you're trying to keep a positive
> outlook for the family, for the people that you know. And if you've got
> frustration building up inside you because you can't do things, then that
> frustration vents itself on the people that you don't want to be on the
> other end of it. You want them to see you as someone who can deal with
> things. And I think just having someone help you gives you that strength
> . . . You can actually go ahead and deal with things.

The following account describes changes in children's self-
efficacy as a result of having to deal with illness:

> Like, I find that my kids have . . . grown . . . become more self-sufficient.
> They've learned early on that . . . that they have to take care of themselves
> and that they have to help other people and help the household.

Attachment: Withdrawal Versus Enmeshment

Typically, the situation that close companions face is that one
person has an illness and the other is relatively healthy. The
withdrawal/enmeshment dialectic may be proposed to explain
how experiential differences affect close relationships in such
cases. This dialectic identifies the movement away from relationships or toward relationships. The term *withdrawal* is derived from Russell's (1985) work on the social implications of
illness, in which there is the disengagement of the self from
social roles and responsibilities. At the other end of the dialectic
is *enmeshment,* Minuchin's (1974) term for overly attached
individuals whose identities are too tightly connected to the
relational unit.

The experienced adversity of chronic illness can isolate the
individual from close companions. The person who is ill is
suffering and may manifest suffering in ways painful for companions to behold, and the companions may avoid this pain by
decreasing contact. Reduced functional capacity also isolates,
preventing sharing in ongoing social events. A person who is
fatigued or distracted by symptomatic distress may miss subtle
interpersonal "cues" or shades of meaning that previously, when

shared, contributed to shared intimacy. Disabling health problems may make it impossible for a person to participate in events such as work, sports, or social drinking. This restriction from previously shared contexts of enjoyment and meaning may lead to other types of experiential and consequential outcomes.

At the withdrawal end of the dialectic, these issues are resolved through a reduction in closeness and intimacy. For companions, the relationship becomes progressively less significant and its status of less consequence. For the person with the disability, the separation may be experienced as a negative consequence of illness and disability, a willful decision, or a blow to self-esteem.

At the enmeshment end of the dialectic, individuals become more tightly connected, resulting in overprotectiveness, helplessness, and a lack of individual freedom. A midpoint for explaining relationship effects emerges from the interdependence orientation (Coyne et al., 1990). This perspective emphasizes the needs and goals of both relational partners and the coordination issues in the meeting of needs and goals.

In response, both participants will try to regain the satisfaction levels that preceded the onset of illness. As part of this effort, the aversive disadvantages for the person with the health problem are responded to with acts of companionship and support. Rather than aversive differences being a source of separation, they become cues for compensatory acts of companionship and support that ease the aversiveness of the illness experience. Rather than the illness preventing participation in shared activities, previously shared activities are adapted or new activities are initiated to ensure sustained involvement. This orientation toward interdependence is demonstrated in an account from the MS mothers study in describing her friend's response to MS:

> For a lot of our friends it took a hell of a lot of courage to come and walk into that room. I think that really, I didn't lose any friends out of it and I consider myself quite lucky. Because I can see why people . . . I have seen it happen in other cases where people have been so overwhelmed they back away. . . . And they've been very supportive, even long distance-wise, they've been supportive . . . some of the people we've been closest to.

Coping Style: Individual Versus Communal Coping Orientation (My Problem Versus Our Problem)

Coping has been traditionally conceptualized as the *individual* pursuit of *self-maintenance* through stress; that is, what did I do to deal with the emotional and instrumental stressors of my problem? In varying degrees people not only wish to enhance their own well-being but the well-being of their family and friends, and they wish to decrease the illness burden on them. This orientation may also imply shared responsibility for dealing with illness.

Many aspects of coping and adaptation may be addressed communally, rather than individually. Couples, nuclear or extended family, or close friends may adopt the position that illness is "our problem" rather than "my problem," and so dealing with the emotional (e.g., anger, frustration, disappointment) and instrumental (e.g., income, treatment, child care) aspects of a health problem together substantially changes coping and adaptation processes (Lyons & Meade, 1993a, 1993b).

The following account from the MS mothers study provides an example of the notion of communal coping:

> I phoned up my close family and my close friends and thought I may as well do this all at once. So I sat down with Mother Bell just loving it. I did all the phone calls at once, just one after the other. "The good news is I don't have a brain tumor. The bad news is, I have MS. We'll cope with this. You know, in a couple of weeks, two weeks from now, we'll cope with this."
>
> So it gave everybody sort of that time. Certainly it helped them develop the right perspective although none of them had really been aware of the fact that the brain tumor was another option. . . . And everybody did call back in two weeks. After I'd sort of come to grips with it. But you know, I went home and had a good cry—after I did all those phone calls, I had a cry. My husband went and got our kids from day care and by God, those kids wanted dinner, just the same. And I think by giving the people closest to us this two-week hiatus . . . then they don't feel obliged to say too much right away. And a number of them did say, one of my closest friends: "I just don't know what to say to you." "Don't say anything. It's a bitch . . . but better than a brain tumor."

In this circumstance, the respondent is describing a coping strategy that has little to do with her own well-being directly. She is concerned with the emotional response of her friends to the diagnosis and how they will cope with the news of her illness. She develops a strategy to break the news, intending to facilitate their dealing with it and easing their necessity to say the "right" thing to her. Her language also identifies the issue as "our problem" versus "her problem." She has constructed the illness as a network issue or a relationship challenge rather than isolating herself as the victim. On another note, the explanation of family dinner demands points out the social context within which the illness is being experienced, perhaps reducing the centrality of illness in the face of everyday roles and responsibilities.

In most circumstances where there are close relationships, at least some aspects of coping will be addressed communally. However, the individualistic coping style may be dominant if individuals wish to avoid having others affected by the condition, wish to present a more stoic approach, or feel that others are not capable of providing support or mutual aid. From an equity perspective, the individualistic style removes the necessity of asking for help. Asking for help might be perceived as creating an imbalance in resource exchange. Reciprocity, to regain the balance, might be perceived by a person with a disabling health problem as difficult or undesirable.

Another account describes a couple's attempt at communal coping:

> I remember going to my husband's work. I took him aside and asked him to come into the cafeteria with me. And I said, "I have MS." And I still remember, he hugged me and he said, "We'll deal with it together" and boy, did that mean a lot!

Is this communal coping orientation a common reaction? What personal and cultural factors determine its presence? Is it characteristic of dense social networks or traditional communities, or is it likely to occur in the presence of a supportive extended family? Does it help the person with the health problem to deal with his or her illness? Does it affect the nature of or satisfaction with support provision? Undoubtedly, communal approaches to coping are expected in circumstances such as natural disasters or wars, where it is obvious that there is group suffering. Research needs to examine whether the communal coping perspective would be useful in helping us to understand coping with illness, and how it influences the nature and extent of relationship remodeling.

Summary and Discussion

Using the metaphor of home remodeling, we have introduced the notion of relationship remodeling, conscious efforts to maintain and improve relationships. There are three central elements in relationship remodeling: the commitment to relationship maintenance, the perception that change could contribute to relationship quality, and the identification of specific adaptational strategies that could result in improvements.

We have posited relationship remodeling as an important and useful aspect of relationship research, particularly where significant life changes such as chronic health problems challenge the quality, and possibly the existence, of valued relationships. We have adapted coping theory to examine how people deal with illness in the context of their relationships. To illustrate our discussion, we have provided accounts from a qualitative study of the illness experience of mothers with multiple sclerosis. The relationship stressors of MS include dealing with specific illness symptoms, a lack of shared meaning of the illness between those with the condition and significant others, constraints on social role performance and companionate activity, and difficulty with issues of exchange, support, and equity.

Relationship remodeling strategies include mental renovations, companionate activity modifications, and network remodeling. We have introduced four dialectical themes that may influence how relationships respond to chronic illness and disability: illness impact, personal control, attachment, and coping style. Unquestionably, the conceptual ideas presented in this chapter require further research. The personal accounts provided here allow some phenomenological insights into how individuals, in this case mothers with MS, experience illness in the context of their personal relationships. These accounts do not justify generalization, but they are useful to illustrate focus group methodology and the kinds of issues that might be valuably explored in more extensive research. The benefits of this methodology are not limited to research, however. Participation in this study affected the women themselves, who found it beneficial to share the relationship challenges of illness and their remodeling strategies. Several of the women telephoned the referring clinic to thank the staff for the invitation to participate. From a clinical perspective, the strategies for relationship remodeling should be shared with others who are experiencing similar stressful intrusions in their relationships. Unfortunately, the responsibility for helping family and friends deal with the relationship challenges of illness is not specifically assumed by any of the health professions.

The accounts themselves provide insights into how women experience relationships and illness. They support the notion that women's experience of illness is deeply contextualized by relationships. Motherhood, in particular, contributes substantively to this. Women traditionally have been responsible both for "kinkeeping" (Wellman & Wellman, 1992) and for dealing with illness (Coyne & Fiske, 1992). In general, women's well-being has often been strongly associated with the social context (Gore & Colton, 1991), and illness challenges provide a window through which we may observe this. Are men's experiences of illness as rooted in relationships? Is the issue one of gender role orientation versus gender? We do not as yet have sufficient illness and gender comparisons to address these questions.

The issue of illness's impact on the responsibility to care for children is interesting. On the one hand, parenting implies the need for considerable energy to be devoted to children. On the other hand, however, mothering provides a valued social role that men who retire from work because of illness may not as easily acquire. Child rearing also appears to divert attention from the self-focus that illness often invites.

Numerous studies have been conducted concerning individuals with chronic illness, and considerable work has been done on social support processes; however, we are just beginning to scratch the surface of relationship functioning in illness and realizing that chronic health problems are, in essence, a relationship issue. Research is needed on partner and couple experiences with illness, particularly longitudinal studies of couple, family, and friend relationships. Research is needed also on relationship remodeling motives, strategies, and processes, as well as the types of individual, relational, situational, and contextual factors that influence them.

We have maintained that different events or life changes will result in different sorts of remodeling; however, there are obviously domains with common themes that will be similar across varied life events. Nevertheless, specific items under these domains may vary considerably by such variables as gender, age, the nature of the event, and the relationship under study. Some of the contemporary research on quality of life (e.g., Renwick, 1992) has recognized the need to develop instrumentation with similar domains but considerable item differentiation across populations. This same orientation would be useful in analyzing relationship challenges and remodeling strategies.

Duck (1992, 1994a) argues for the importance of examining the factors that influence the maintenance of relationships, and he urges us not to underrate what may appear to be trivial everyday relationship activities. In our discussion of relationship maintenance and remodeling strategies in the MS mothers study, we have seen not only major changes to relationships but changes to aspects of relationships that constitute their everyday functioning. These are important. As with home remodeling, attention to the "little things" contributes to the success of the renovation.

9

Held Captive by Their Memories: Managing Grief in Relationships

John H. Harvey

Melanie K. Barnes

Heather R. Carlson

Jeffrey Haig

I can't forget him. His memory will always haunt me.

21-year-old woman

They are never gone unless you forget them.

74-year-old widow

The above lines are but a few of the many words that have been written and spoken to express the anguish of loss and the feeling that is experienced by a grieving person who cannot readily escape the image of a departed lover and what might have been. On some occasion, most of us will experience the powerful captivity of memory and unintended thought associated with major losses in our lives. These memories, composed of images, sounds, and other sensory experiences, represent the psychological and emotional continuity that spans different times and places among humans. To a degree, this experience reflects the power of human bonding and represents a healthy memorializing of the lost other and the experience of interaction with the lost other. It also, however, may reflect a type of intrusive, haunting bondage that impedes a grieving person's progress in "getting on with life." In this sense, these memories represent a challenge found in close relationships, just as accounts (Harvey, Weber, & Orbuch, 1990) indicate that other memories can challenge interaction patterns in relationships.

In this chapter, we define and discuss this experience of captivity and provide examples from a recent study of bereavement in which people provided accounts of the deaths of their loved ones and how those deaths have affected them over a period of time. We discuss the idea of "captivity" as both a positive and a negative experience for the survivor. We also consider the following questions: When does captivity of memory occur? Why does it occur, and to whom does it occur most often? What are the contents of these memories?

Another topic of our analysis is how habits connected to past interaction with now-lost loved ones (such as reaching out in the night toward the loved one's side of the bed) may also exert continuing power over the bereaved person. This type of influence may be referred to as the *power of a script that cannot be easily discarded or unlearned* involving a lost other. In this chapter, we use the term *script* to refer to a behavioral pattern or tendency that is routinized and engaged in without much reflection (Schank & Abelson, 1977). In effect, individuals may follow such scripts for some period of time without conscious reflection on their operation.

Although in our analysis we emphasize unintended memory and scripted behavior, it should be recognized that survivors do

AUTHORS' NOTE: We would like to extend our gratitude to Steve Duck and Julia T. Wood for their insightful comments on an earlier draft of this chapter. Requests for information should be sent to the first author at the University of Iowa, Department of Psychology, Iowa City, IA 52242.

on some occasions intentionally search for memories and follow scripts for the express purpose of keeping images and feelings for deceased loved ones alive in their minds. Consider the following such occurrence for a widow experiencing intensive grief:

> In one agonizing ritual after another, Joie White has been trying to hold on to the trappings of a life that was savagely torn apart [in December 1993], when a man who had been confronted by her husband, policeman Jason White, on the steps of a Capitol Hill row house pumped four bullets into his face. . . . "I wear his clothes more than mine . . ." [Her husband's gold wedding band dangles on her ring finger; she also wears a small reproduction of his badge on another finger.] "I will never take any of these off for as long as I live. . . . What I am afraid of is forgetting, forgetting all the wonderful things about Jason." (Kovaleski, *Washington Post,* March 20, 1994, p. B1, © 1994 The Washington Post, reprinted with permission)

The work we present in this chapter has considerable relevance for the theme of this volume. A person who cannot readily put aside memories, thoughts, and behavioral routines connected to a close other has a type of continuing, challenging relationship with that other. This type of challenging relationship may be pleasant to the individual—for example, reminding her or him of the good times shared with someone now dead—or such a continuing relationship in the form of unintended memory may be unpleasant. For example, it may remind the grieving person of all the resources he or she lost with the death of the loved one. Whether pleasant or unpleasant, the memory may challenge the individual by virtue of the surprise nature of its occurrence. Thus the challenges of this type of relationship have their own set of dynamics and may seem quite different from the challenges presented by, for example, an abusive relationship. Both kinds of relationships are challenging, however, in that the individuals involved may be battling for greater control or predictability of their mental experiences and how these affect their behavior, feelings, and general sense of well-being.

This chapter also has commonality with the chapters in this volume dealing with anger, guilt, and other negative feelings. The loss of a close other often produces many negative feelings.

Guilt and anger are common in surviving relationship partners. In fact, such feelings may be part of the dynamic that continues to potentiate the memories and scripts connecting the self to the departed other. Furthermore, the person left often has to wage a mighty battle to convince him- or herself that he or she was not somehow responsible for the other's demise. The well-publicized case of Joan Rivers and her daughter Melissa serves as an illustration. In the June 21, 1993, issue of *People* magazine, Rivers and her daughter told how the suicide of Joan's husband, Edgar, in 1987 had produced in their mother-daughter interaction a period in which blame and guilt were strongly felt, if not expressed. Joan believed that Melissa blamed her for Edgar's death, because Joan and Edgar had separated not long before his suicide. Joan also talked about her own feelings of self-blame for her husband's death. The negative feelings between Joan and Melissa simmered beneath the surface of their relationship until Melissa encountered her own trauma by becoming involved with a man who was physically abusive toward her. She was able to get out of that relationship with the help of her mother, and at that point, the mother and daughter started to renew their bond. They have since become quite close, but, overall, both continue to be affected by their memories of Edgar and how his final deed fits into their individual and collective histories.

This chapter also relates indirectly to Coleman and Ganong's chapter on reconfigured families (Chapter 4). The individual who has lost a close other almost certainly will want to establish a new close relationship and/or to intensify existing ones. Whether or not this new close relationship is intimate or romantic, it is almost axiomatic that most people continue to seek the closeness of others, even after they have suffered grievously through previous losses of relationships. To function well in new romantic relationships, individuals need to recognize the potency of memories and other effects of past loves. In a study described later in this chapter, one widow, age 69, who had remarried a recent widower, made this thoughtful comment about the continued effect of the couple's ex-spouses in the new marriage: "My new husband and I talk about our spouses all the time if we want to. *We both feel it is okay to cry! We lean on each other and understand.*" She went on to say that frequent memories of their deceased partners made both her and her new spouse "cherish the moment" of their current life together.

What Is a Major Loss?

We use the term *major loss* in this chapter to refer to the loss by death of a very close other. There are, of course, many other kinds of major loss, including divorce or dissolution of a relationship, financial ruin, failure in some valued enterprise, and loss of health. In previous work, we have argued that at a more abstract level, a major loss is an event involving a *significant diminution* of one's resources (Harvey, Orbuch, Weber, Merbach, & Alt, 1992). In this case, the reduction in resources is enough to send the individual into a tailspin; expressions such as "the roof caved in," "the bottom fell out," and "my whole world collapsed" are often used by those who have suffered losses to try to depict for others the magnitude of deprivation of self in light of the loss. Such persons often describe the early and quickly altered psychological state of experiencing major loss as being "shocked," "overwhelmed," "numbed," "in despair," and "anguished beyond belief," again, to try to let others know how devastated they were and continue to be.

Levinger (1992) presents a useful commentary on the nature of perceived loss of a close relationship. He notes that the extent to which one indeed feels loss (or a deprivation in personal resources) depends on several factors: How close (involving, interdependent) was the relationship? Did the relationship end suddenly or was the ending more protracted (as in a situation where an individual is dying slowly from a terminal disease)? Levinger posits that when a dying person expresses a clear desire to stop living, it helps his or her loved ones also to accept the demise. Did the loss involve a lengthy period in which partners could withdraw and possibly explore lives not involving the loved one who will soon depart? Levinger suggests that the key difference between loss by death and loss by divorce or dissolution is that loss by death is irreversible and also may have occurred because of physiological reasons that do not involve a person's intention to end the relationship and do not allow for a range of resolutions (i.e., death is unavoidable).

Defining and Analyzing Captivity
by Memory and Behavioral Script

We define *captivity by memory* after a major loss as unintentional memory of a major loss that occurs intermittently over an extended period and that has an impact on a person's life. We define *captivity by behavioral scripts* as behavior that follows routines established with the deceased loved one that is pursued with little thought and over an extended period.

What we are referring to as captivity by one's memory also has been referred to as unintended, involuntary, unconscious, and spontaneous memory (Salaman, 1970; Uleman & Bargh, 1989). At the core of this type of memory is the individual's sense of little personal control over its occurrence. Our position is that, depending on a host of mediating factors, this type of memory may be either positive or negative for the person who regularly experiences it. Based on the account-making conception articulated by Harvey et al. (1990), we believe that one mediator is the extent to which the person who experiences the memory has worked on an account for the loss and achieved a sense of "completion" in the account. Harvey et al. define an account as a storylike construction consisting of interpretive, affective, and descriptive material that focuses on an important event and that usually involves a perceived beginning, middle stage, and end.

We posit that a sense of completion would involve these elements: (a) ultimate acceptance that the loss occurred; (b) understanding of the nature, magnitude, and meaning of the loss for the person developing the account; (c) recognition that major losses are experienced by all people and are a natural part of life; and (d) emphasis on the possible growth in personal strength and potential for contribution to others that may be associated with dealing with major losses. We assume that a diligent process of account making regarding the loss and confiding parts of the account to close others are essential to an individual's arriving at the point of completion and acceptance. We also assume that when an individual has achieved completion to some substantial degree in her or his account, most unintended memories of the lost loved one will have a positive impact, because the remembering person is at peace with the loss and accepts the possibility of encountering memory intrusions that remind her or him of the loved one as a normal occurrence.

As Levinger (1992) suggests, the expected death of a loved one who has been gravely ill for an extended period may moderate a survivor's sense of loss. Such a loss, however, should not necessarily preclude the occurrence of unintended memories and possible related behavioral patterns. But probably the experience most likely to produce later unintended memories is the unexpected death of a loved one. In a later section, we discuss the possible importance of planning to mourn, anticipatory account making, and confiding as helpful to the stimulation of positive unintended memory. When such preparations are not possible, as in the instance of an unexpected death, later unintended memories may be less positive for the survivor. Also, there may remain "unfinished business" that will impair the grieving process and stimulate later unpleasant unexpected memories. One 21-year-old man in our study wrote of a girlfriend who had died suddenly a year earlier, and in so doing he expressed his continuing pain at the memory of her as follows:

> I've tried to forget about her, you know, "put it behind me," but I still have dreams about her, how can you forget about someone if you can't stop thinking about them, and even if I could . . . I'm really not sure I want to.

The Nature of a "Good Adjustment" and Hypothesized Impacts

In her book *Necessary Losses,* Judith Viorst (1986) contends that "the road to human development is paved with renunciation. Throughout life we grow by giving up" (p. 3). In the grief

literature, there is controversy regarding whether "good adjustment" in grieving necessarily involves the breaking of ties
between the bereaved and the dead. For example, Stroebe,
Gergen, Gergen, and Stroebe (1992) interpret Bowlby's (1979)
theory of affectional bonds to suggest that the individual's
well-being in the future and in future close relationships depends on the breaking of affective bonds with the deceased
spouse or lover. Stroebe et al. note that Bowlby's position is that
a short-lived continuation of this bond is appropriate to healthy
mourning, but that long-term continuing presence of the lost
loved one likely would be pathological. Peskin (1993) argues
that Stroebe et al. misrepresent Bowlby in contending that ties
with the deceased need to be severed after a brief period of
mourning. Rather, Peskin suggests, Bowlby asserts that such ties
can continue indefinitely without necessarily being problematic
for the survivor. Peskin also claims that Stroebe et al.'s position
epitomizes Western mythology, which holds that goal direction,
efficiency, and self-reliance require the rupture of emotional
attachments with the deceased.

Our own position on this issue is that some presence of the
lost loved one will exist in the survivor's memory, usually at a
subconscious level, regardless of how diligently he or she tries
to break the bond. We suggest that an effective grieving process
that moves a person along toward recovery does not need to
involve elimination of thoughts and feelings about the lost lover.
Rather, healing is likely to involve the development of a respect
for this presence, along with a full-fledged living in the present.

We believe that each human being has a potential set of
circumstances that could trigger a pattern of captivity of memory that would be difficult to break and substantial in time and
impact. Consider a scenario in which two young people have
been involved for a few years and are progressing steadily
toward marriage. They have made many commitments and
plans for the future. They have anticipated much. They have
laughed and cried together. They already have learned to overcome adversity together. They have discussed in detail the
nature of their future family. They have imagined much. Each
has relied on the other as a primary anchor for emotional

support and as principal confidant regarding dilemmas of living. Then, one of the young people is struck dead in an instant. What does the other do? How does the other cope? Why does the other continue to live?

This scenario is one that has happened many times, and it happened in the life of one of the participants in our study (see the discussion at the end of the chapter). In addition to the sudden occurrence of death, this scenario has variations, such as the instance in which one of the partners leaves the other just before marriage—or at the altar. What will happen to the person who has been left? It would take a quite unusual person in terms of psychological strength not to be crushed by these types of events. It also would take an unusual person not to be bound for some long period to the chain of grieving and wondering what might have been. The first author of this chapter once knew a woman who wore a big diamond engagement ring although she had not been engaged for 5 years. What happened? She was jilted at the altar by someone she really loved and with whom she had expected to spend her life. The rock on her finger was a sign of her present psychological state in maintaining an unrequited love; her frequent mention of this long-departed other was a further indication that her "ball and chain" was of immense symbolic weight.

Being held captive by memories may affect a survivor's daily life as well as how he or she perceives personal relationships in the past, present, and future. It may be simply too painful for an individual to acknowledge and accept the death of a close relational partner immediately. The grief of the young police officer's widow mentioned earlier in this chapter illustrates how some survivors cling to memories of their lost loved ones. In this case, the bereaved person continues to maintain a "phantom" relationship with the deceased, at least for the short term. This behavior, which sometimes includes monologues directed toward the deceased loved one, is a natural part of the healing process. Based on a study of widows and widowers, Bowlby (1980), however, contends that for some bereaved individuals, this type of grieving might go on indefinitely and be helpful to recovery:

In many cases, it seems, the dead spouse is experienced as a companion
who accompanies the bereaved everywhere. . . .
   There is no reason to regard any of these experiences as either unusual
or unfavourable, rather the contrary. . . .
   It seems likely that for many widows and widowers it is precisely
because they are willing for their feelings of attachment to the dead spouse
to persist that their sense of identity is preserved and they become able to
recognize their lives along lines they find meaningful. (pp. 96-100)

Based on our own work, we believe that such behavior is
likely to impede the bereaved person's recovery if continued
indefinitely. As some of the respondents in our own study noted,
if this behavior is continued for long, it may interfere with
present and future close relationships. The people to whom
survivors desire to relate closely may feel that the survivors
cannot treat them in a special way as loved ones because of the
"burden" the survivors have chosen to continue to bear. This
behavior also may stigmatize bereaved persons in the eyes of
casual acquaintances, and it may cause others to avoid bereaved
persons (Neeld, 1990).

Why do some people seem to be "frozen" in their grief and
inability to adopt a new identity after a major loss? Perhaps one
explanation for why it may be difficult to "let go" of a lost other
may be found in analysis of what relationship resources have
been lost to the grieving party. Duck (1994a) has developed a
compelling case for couples' need to find and construct meaning
in their relationships. The meaning they create is produced
largely through daily talks and confiding in one another. When
such talk and the attendant presence, nonverbal support, and
sharing are wrenched from a person's life, he or she may
experience a tremendous void. Many idiosyncratic symbols of
meaning to the relationship and to the survivor's identity are
lost. The empathic experience of sharing another's mind, to a
degree, is gone. If there was great closeness and intimacy in the
relationship, there simply is no ready substitute for the grieving
person. This is the essence of a situation in which a person may
feel a grief that knows no end. The character of that grief is
intrusive and pervasive. When grief is of this profound nature,
the individual may feel that to try consciously to move beyond

the past identity and experiences with the deceased other would be tantamount to giving up on his or her own personal life.

A loss experienced by the first author relates to the significance of losing the sharing of talk about the thoughts and feelings of two minds. He and a close friend of about 1 year frequently shared thoughts about the meaning of death to each of them. Six months later, after the author had moved to another part of the country, he heard that this friend, age 40, was within weeks or even days of death from rapidly spreading lung cancer that had recently been discovered and that had already devastated the friend's body. Gone in a flash was the opportunity to share this experience with his friend. Gone was the opportunity to share other experiences that later would form new memories. Ironically and tragically gone was the opportunity to share the meanings of death.

A derivative of the foregoing logic is that the grieving individual must also release future plans and hopes for interaction with the lost other. As Duck has suggested, relationships by their very nature are future oriented, and individuals are consistently engaging in exchanges that build toward, or at the very least will affect, the future. Savage (1989) suggests a similar point: A powerful factor in grief that endures and impairs is the loss of expected future interaction and the memories that would derive from such interaction.

When Is an Individual
Most Vulnerable to Captivity?

The sudden, unexpected loss of a very close other is one condition most likely to make a person vulnerable to captivity. When death is expected, the opportunity to *plan to mourn* and to begin the processes of account making and confiding may militate against extended, unpleasant memorial intrusion. Planning to mourn, or anticipatory grief (Rosenblatt, 1983), may be just as important as actual mourning, because it probably conveys a sense of some control over how one deals with impending loss.

Another general condition that may influence captivity by memory exists when a grieving person structures her or his environment so as to minimize intrusive cues that the loved one is actually gone. The bereaved person who leaves the lost loved one's room exactly as it was when the loved one died may desire to encounter regularly over an extended period of time cues that remind him or her of the deceased other. We often hear of survivors who pack up and leave residences or locales to try to avoid environmental cues that will continue to remind them of their lost loved ones. It may be assumed that on a random basis, a survivor's living environment will contain some cues that elicit memories of his or her dead loved one.

Photographs and photograph albums have a special status in human lives in their capacity to elicit memories and feelings associated with lost loved ones. Photographs quickly call forth meanings and stories. There undoubtedly is an intriguing study to be done on people's use and display of photographs of lost loved ones and how such photographs enter into their grieving about those losses. We might theorize, for example, that the pervasive display of photographs of a deceased loved one reflects a person's continued bondage to the memories of that person. An index of the person's healing, therefore, may be the decision to put away these photographs (e.g., store them in an album). Furthermore, that act alone may enhance the person's long-term recovery and control over memories of the deceased loved one.

The Whys of Captivity: Who Is Most Vulnerable?

What are the general principles that govern a person's being held captive by memories of a lost other? As implied above in the discussion of future plans, closeness to the lost loved one or the interdependence of the two individuals' lives may affect the nature and magnitude of memory intrusions and the extent to which behavioral scripts related to the deceased person continue after that person's death. We would posit that closeness and interdependence work on memory through the emotional imprinting of experiences with the deceased other. The more compelling these experiences in their impact on a person's sense of self and imputed meanings of life, the more they should be emotionally imprinted. The more they are imprinted, the more unlikely it should be for the memories of a deceased loved one to fade away. In our study, we found that some grieving persons said that practically everything they encountered, every day of their lives, reminded them of deceased loved ones with whom they related for many years.

What categories of people are most susceptible to intrusive memories of lost loved ones? In our grief study, a 58-year-old woman made this remark about her husband, who had died suddenly 5 years before the interview took place:

> I have felt extremely vulnerable and alone—even when surrounded by family and friends. On these occasions, the silence has been deafening. I have kept anticipating that he [her late husband] would return. I have often found myself saving things to share with him.

She indicated many instances of both continued episodic remembering of her dead husband and the type of scripted behavior mentioned in the quote.

This woman is representative of a group of people who appear to be highly vulnerable to being captive to memories of their lost others and hindered from making significant changes in their lives. In their acclaimed analysis of bereavement during the first year, Glick, Weiss, and Parkes (1974) found evidence that the widows and widowers in their sample, who were in midlife (40s and 50s in age) and who had lost their significant others *unexpectedly, with little warning,* exhibited a greater degree of anxiety, self-reproach, and depression than did other groups of mourners who were older and who had had time to prepare for the loss of their significant others. As we have already suggested, sudden loss jolts us from our typical goal-directed behavior and robs us of the opportunity to plan mourning and to engage in such anticipatory activities as account making and confiding. In addition, major loss is less expected at midlife than in later life. Thus, at a very general level, one category of people who are most vulnerable to intrusion is made up of those who unexpectedly experience major loss.

Glick et al. also report on a study that showed parents who had lost adult children in sudden traumatic ways, such as in traffic fatalities, had significantly more problems than did parents who lost children to chronic illnesses, such as cancer. We hasten to note, however, that whether or not death comes suddenly, the loss of a child is a "high grief" type of loss. It usually has many long-term effects on parents, including depression and bouts of anger and self-blame. Writers such as David Morrell (1988) and David Ray (1968) have told stories of their children's lost battles against terminal illnesses, and how the loss of their children still affects them *daily* after many years of grieving. In part, these authors wrote their accounts of these deaths as a way of achieving further healing. Morrell indicates that during a period of 7 years subsequent to his son's death, one of the first thoughts he had each morning on awakening was about his deceased son. He says that he imputed to these thoughts the meaning that he has a deep emotional void in his life that will not soon be filled or easily accepted.

Whether the death of a child occurs quickly or is more drawn out, a parent's capacity for account making and confiding may be reduced by the sheer emotional burden of the loss or impending loss. Morrell suggests that the beginning of his recovery, which involved the start of account making and confiding to readers in the format of his book *Fireflies,* did not commence until about a year after his child's death. At that point, he experienced what he believed was either a spiritual or hallucinogenic episode in which his son seemed to appear to him as a firefly who was beckoning him to help others who also were grieving the deaths of their children.

Given all that we know about grief, it seems likely that parents who lose children will encounter some of the most regular and daunting unexpected memories of these deceased loved ones. Many of us assume that we will bear and raise children, and we expect that in the normal course of events, we will die before they die. A child's death always is a death that is "out of season" for the parent. It shakes the very truths on which she or he has based future hopes and plans. It leaves a void that cannot be filled, even by other children.

The first author has a corresponding friend, now in her 80s, who has written to him for almost 20 consecutive years every Christmas about her son, who was killed while in graduate school in social psychology. She always comments that her son would be such and such age now and speculates on what her fine young son *might* have accomplished in his life and career. In many ways, it is a lonely vigil for the parent, because the deceased person's friends and acquaintances may eventually only infrequently remember the dead loved one. But it is a vigil that the parent may choose to carry on, and one that is perceived as honorable and dignified. Reminding others of the positive nature and accomplishments of the deceased person is a continuing tribute to that person. Such reminders also may be motivated by a desire to persuade others that some deaths did not have to occur when they did (as in the case of a person killed by a drunken driver—which was true for the foregoing mother's story).

There is a strand of evidence emerging from the work of Wortman, Silver, and their colleagues suggesting that at least a minority of parents who have lost children to sudden infant death syndrome may not experience intense distress, show preoccupation with thoughts of the baby's death, or avoid reminders of the baby and his or her death (e.g., Wortman & Silver, 1992). Parents' reactions have been studied as late as 18 months after such infant deaths, with results continuing to show little distress. Hence it is difficult to argue that the parents still are in shock. McIntosh, Silver, and Wortman (1993) argue, and provide data to show, that factors such as religious participation by the parents, the social support they have available, and their ability to find meaning in their baby's death all reduced the parents' distress over the 18-month span studied. From our standpoint, these results are interesting in that they suggest how some parents (but, admittedly, not the majority) show early signs of recovery without the elongated sequence of grieving that our conception and most evidence suggest will be common. For a variety of reasons, however, these mostly young parents still may have been experiencing delays in their grief work. It is conceivable that in the succeeding months or years they too have experienced or will experience some of the sense of overwhelming grief that so many parents experience when such a profound loss occurs. Or, if they do not feel and express such grief, research evidence such as that presented by Pennebaker (1990) suggests that their health may be significantly imperiled.

Another group that research and clinical casework suggest is most vulnerable to captivity consists of young children. Based on their review of the grief literature and their own clinical work, Volkan and Zintl (1993) argue that until a child has completed adolescence, a parent's death is by definition full of unfinished business. During adolescence, the individual often reviews his or her childhood relationship to parents and family and frequently rebels against or relaxes emotional investment in them. This rebellion or curtailing of investment is a natural breaking away and beginning of the formation of allegiance with the larger world. An early adolescent or younger child likely will not have completed this separation and may be particularly affected by the death of a parent. Death means that the process cannot be completed, at least through the assistance or accommodation of the lost parent. Again, we would suggest that these young persons may be so paralyzed by their losses that they may not pursue account making and confiding for many years—perhaps until midlife, when people often try to go back and finish business regarding their relations with their parents that may be impeding their fulfillment.

A last category of mourning people whom we believe are highly vulnerable to captivity is composed of those who have had a series of major losses such that they have not had time to recover from one or more losses when a powerful new loss occurs. Some have said, "When it rains it pours." This maxim applies well to the emotional erosion experienced by people who are hit by multiple losses in a short period of time. In our recent study of grief, one respondent had experienced in a single 6-month period the sudden and unexpected death of her brother, age 24; the termination of a close, romantic relationship; and the dissolution of a business partnership. She withdrew from all people in what she described as the lowest point of her life; she indicated that she began to recover many months later when she suddenly realized that there were reasons to continue living and that she still had a support system. Other respondents had experienced the deaths of more than one very close other within relatively brief spans of time, leaving them totally stunned for months and even years before they could begin to grieve effectively.

Avoidance may be the only way some people can cope with devastating losses. It has been suggested that some Holocaust survivors have "stonewalled" their storytelling, emotional venting, and confiding for many, many years because of the enormity of their losses. Langer's (1991) powerful book *Holocaust Testimonies* provides telling examples of this type of reaction by survivors. For some, avoidance appears to be effective, at least in the short run, because the magnitude of work needed to mourn their losses effectively is staggering.

In less extreme circumstances, a grieving person may have made initial progress in dealing with one loss when another comes along and dashes that progress. This piling up of loss may destroy the person's story-making and confiding activities, or even her or his will to engage in them, and may leave the individual psychologically and physically in a bleak emotional desert for a substantial period. How a person is finally able to crawl out of such a desert is a question for both researchers and counselors.

Content of Recurring, Unintended Memories

As is true with all of the major questions raised in this chapter, we have too little evidence about the content of recurring, unexpected memories of lost loved ones. Based on our own study and informal reports, we suggest that content may lean heavily toward such imagery as the deceased person's face and highly meaningful expressions shown and used by the person. Smiles, tones of voice, how it felt to be touched by the deceased other, and particular verbal expressions that were distinctive for the relationship may also be prominent in the imagery. Similarly, people who have experienced the dissolution of close relationships report memories of entire episodes, such as first sexual experiences with the other, major events such as weddings and births of children, warm feelings associated with celebrations and travels, and major fights, separations, or breakups (Harvey, Flanary, & Morgan, 1986).

Liberating Survivors Who
Do Not Wish to Be Held Captive

> We can never completely "get over" a major loss in the sense that all its effects are negated, that is, "forgotten." Our losses become part of who we are, as precious to us as other aspects of our selves, and so does the transcendence of those losses. (Weenolsen, 1988, p. 57)

Major losses may change us irrevocably and then, if transcended, become positive turning points in our lives. Loss can have positive long-term effects on our lives for several reasons. First, it may humble us, and humility is a critical condition for much human accomplishment. We can learn to confront loss cognitively and emotionally, and to talk about it. Loss may make us stronger in general, so that we can cope with other major losses that likely will come our way. It may also enable us to offer help to others who suffer similar plights (similar to what Erikson, 1963, refers to as "generativity," giving to future generations based on one's own experience). There are many grand examples of work that reveals such generative strength. For example, Elie Wiesel has touched many minds through his telling of the horrors he saw and personally experienced as a teenager in the Nazi death camps of Auschwitz and Buchenwald (see, e.g., Wiesel, 1960). Just as important, he has enhanced the lives of his readers and audiences with the power, art, and hope of his message.

We believe that there is considerable efficacy in a coping approach that involves a person's confronting a loss directly when ready, and not trying to avoid or distract him- or herself from coming to grips with it. As has been shown in related work, confrontation helps move an individual through a sequence of healing steps, whereas long-term avoidance or distraction does not help the person move on (Pennebaker, 1990). The timing of such "readiness" probably is highly idiosyncratic, and there likely is no linear path a person can follow in an attempt to get ready. As for confrontation, our own data suggest that the type of confrontation many people use successfully involves the development of a storylike construction about the whys and wherefores of the loss and how it relates to other events in the person's life (Harvey et al., 1992).

Below, we present excerpts from the accounts of a few survivors we interviewed in a recent study of how people cope with major loss through the death of close others. These individuals described whether and how they have adjusted to their losses. Each had reported a period of significant intrusion of thoughts and feelings about her lost other and recounted how she had found peace with these memories or arrived at a point at which the memories no longer exacted a significant toll on her life. These women's ideas embellish our conception of the role of accounts and confiding in recovery. Each individual quoted below is, in her own way, trying diligently to construct meaning associated with her loss and to transcend the loss. Each also is engaged in the act of confiding, as she tells her story.

The comments of these survivors also help us to understand why thought suppression (i.e., stopping thoughts about a topic, usually by starting to concentrate on something else) may become a common approach to dealing with intrusive memories. As Wegner and Schneider (1989) elaborate, it appears that in the long run, thought suppression is not effective in dealing with intrusion owing to major loss. These researchers advocate that people instead "stop stopping" their thinking about their losses until completion or resolution and emotional venting have occurred.

> I still get emotional and teary thinking about our life together. I finally have learned that I can use his name and tell others what he said without becoming overwhelmed. But I have yet to take off my wedding ring (my

identity!?). I have hope . . . that we will be together again someday. I suspect that I will always be single now. . . . I have recovered by talking to others who have lost spouses. Also, I have played the funeral video and listened to tapes of him singing the Lord's Prayer and his singing at our daughter's wedding. I have a busy life, but I've read grief pamphlets and every book I could find on grieving. (woman, age 68, who lost her husband to cancer 2 years prior to the interview)

I was absolutely devastated by his death. We had been married 42 years and were very close to one another. I couldn't eat or sleep or function normally for a long time. I dwelt on him and what it meant to lose him. . . . I finally decided that *I had to help myself*. . . . I went to a very good grief recovery support group and later became an outreach volunteer working with the newly widowed. . . . You have your precious memories but you have to talk, talk, talk about it and do things for yourself like changing the bedroom around. . . . I talk openly about our former life with my children, friends, and new husband. I often go to the cemetery. I highly recommend getting into a grief support group. You have to work through your grief, and you learn a lot by listening to others. . . . I remarried about two years ago. I met him in my group—he had lost his wife four years ago also. We are very happy and enjoying life again! Life goes on. You're here such a short time. *Live and enjoy family and friends*. (woman, age 63, who lost her husband to an unexpected heart attack, while on vacation, 4 years prior to the interview)

I think about him every minute of every day. I ask myself what he would want me to do. He would want me to be strong. He hated it when I was a "wimp." We had been best friends since high school. We did everything together. . . . I'm getting a little bit better . . . because I have kept busy doing my school work (having reduced the term load from 17 to 9 hours) and my work in the sports information office. . . . His teammates and coaches have been great to me. They talk to me and give me pictures and mementos of him. I have his pictures up all over my room. Before, I didn't have any pictures of him on my walls. I often listen to tapes I made for him and watch a video a friend made of the newscasts of the accident and media interviews with me. This video helps bring me back to reality because I still haven't accepted that he is gone. . . . He went on basketball trips all the time and in the summers and I got used to waiting on him to return. . . . But now I'm trying to accept that he won't return. . . . Some of my close friends have disappointed me. They should be able to see that I want to talk about him and how I feel. . . . They seem afraid to listen. . . . For that reason, I like to be with his family because they are struggling too and show their emotions frequently. . . . I'm trying to get on with my life. . . . But here around all of his friends and even the whole state thought they knew him, it is hard to move on. . . . It is as if I should always be grieving. . . . I've talked to men who have indicated that they would find it difficult to be in a relationship with me because I was his girlfriend and am having such a hard time. . . . I look forward to going away to work this summer because people there will know me as myself and not mainly as his girlfriend, with all those stares and whispers. . . . I've thought a lot about what I lost when he died—it was *our plans.* We planned to marry next year and immediately begin a family. I can't believe that so short a time ago I was planning to start a family soon. I lost everything because we were not married. . . . If we had been married, at least I could have said that I was his wife. . . . I've learned that I can be strong when I have to be and to try to give time to my friends and family because you never know how long you'll have with them. (woman, age 21, a junior in college, who 3 months prior to the interview had lost her boyfriend of 5 years, a nationally recognized college basketball player, in a traffic accident —an accident in which the young woman was a passenger in her boyfriend's car)

We reinterviewed this last woman almost 6 months after the initial interview to investigate her further experience of grief. She had become a senior in college and was 22 at that time. Here are excerpts from the second interview:

It's harder now than in the spring because it has sunk in. Before my friends tried to keep me busy. Now, they are gone. I cry a lot and am depressed. I often cannot sleep until early in the morning. I call people just to have someone to talk to about nothing. . . . I've not been going to classes regularly and have fallen behind in some of them. I don't attend regularly anymore. This summer I wrote letters to him [her late boyfriend] about my experiences in my new job back East. At my job this summer, I met someone and began to date him. I told him about my story on our first date, and he was real understanding. He fell "head over heels" for me. It was a high. When I got back to school, we planned to visit regularly. I went back last week and I didn't feel anything. It's too soon to have those feelings again. There is no rush. I don't want to get upset by discovering that there is no one like him [her late boyfriend]. . . . I just want to be friends with men now. . . . I have an acting class and for an assignment, I acted the part of myself speaking to him at his grave. The class was in tears, but I wasn't moved. I talk to him [her late boyfriend] more now when I am by myself, but I can't bring myself to go to the cemetery. . . . I considered lots of options about two weeks ago, when I was particularly depressed. I even considered suicide, but he would not want me to join him like that [in heaven]. He wants me to be strong. I feel like he is always there with me in the decisions I make. . . . This time last year, I knew exactly what I'd be doing in the future. Now, I don't know. I would like

to leave here [the state where she now lives] when I graduate. I want to
be away from here—I have so many memories. . . . I have to go on with
life, and try to find happiness. Our sixth anniversary is coming up, as is
Thanksgiving and Christmas. I am not looking forward to them. It's going
to be tough. . . . If I had any advice to give others based on my experiences,
it would be to be a lot more open to others' feelings. Try hard not to forget
people who may need you to be *there* for them. You can lose those whom
you love so quickly.

Concluding Remarks

The foregoing excerpts suggest the difficulty of any complete
liberation from unintended memories of a lost other affecting
a survivor's life. Certainly, the young woman who lost her
boyfriend, who also was a larger-than-life hero figure, represents a compelling instance of a person who faces a long-term
challenge to create a new life that is not unduly affected by her
association with her lost loved one. She must deal not only with
normal passages of grieving, but also with the special nature of
the loss and people's frequent linking of her with her departed
companion. The courage displayed by this young woman *only
9 months after the death of her closest and dearest friend and
partner* speaks to the capacity of every human to rise to meet
the challenge of loss. Yet, at this early point in the grieving
process, this woman is struggling mightily, with thoughts of
suicide sometimes occurring.

These excerpts reveal in survivors' own words the importance of their developing stories that attribute meaning for what
happened and of having someone in whom they can confide
those stories on a regular basis. They also reveal the tenacity of
spirit that is necessary to memorialize our departed loved ones
properly, while at the same time trying to live our current and
future lives to the fullest. These survivors help us understand
how we owe it to our departed loved ones to go on with life
and have other close relationships that we cherish and nourish.
As the older respondents in our grief study suggested, it is
crucial that new companions be willing to recognize and accord
significance to the past losses that each has experienced. A type

of graciousness in dealing with loss seems required wherein new companions or lovers are able to tell their stories of lost love freely to one another. And in so doing, they can better nurture and understand one another. A final point we want to make is that after suffering great losses, people are unlikely to find peace without meeting challenges to their minds and hearts. But after engaging in such struggle, they may no longer be "held captive by their memories," but instead, "held gently by their memories."

References

Abramson, L. Y., Seligman, M. E. P., & Teasdale, J. (1978). Learned helplessness in humans: Critique and reformulation. *Journal of Abnormal Psychology, 87*, 49-74.

Acock, A. C., & Demo, D. H. (1994). *Family diversity and well-being.* Thousand Oaks, CA: Sage.

Adelman, M. B. (1992a). Health passions: Safer sex as play. In T. Edgar, M. A. Fitzpatrick, & V. S. Freimuth (Eds.), *AIDS: A communication perspective* (pp. 69-89). Hillsdale, NJ: Lawrence Erlbaum.

Adelman, M. B. (1992b). Sustaining passion: Eroticism and safe-sex talk. *Archives of Sexual Behavior, 5*, 479-484.

Adelman, M. B. (Producer), Moytl, H.D. (Technical Director), & Downs, D. (Acting Director). (1988). *Safe-sex talk* [Video]. Evanston, IL: Northwestern University, Department of Communication Studies.

Ahrons, C. R. (1980). Divorce: A crisis of family transition and change. *Family Relations, 29*, 533-540.

Ahrons, C. R., & Miller, R. B. (1993). The effect of the postdivorce relationship on paternal involvement: A longitudinal analysis. *American Journal of Orthopsychiatry, 63*, 441-450.

Ahrons, C. R., & Rodgers, R. H. (1987). *Divorced families: A multidisciplinary developmental view.* New York: W. W. Norton.

Alberts, J. K., Miller-Rassulo, M. A., & Hecht, M. L. (1991). A typology of drug resistance strategies. *Journal of Applied Communication Research, 19*, 129-151.

Alexander, C. N., & Wiley, M. G. (1981). Situated activity and identity formation. In M. Rosenberg & R. H. Turner (Eds.), *Social psychology: Sociological perspectives*. New York: Basic Books.

Allen, K. (1993). *Physical abuse: A barrier to treatment for some addicted women* [Handout from presentation]. National Institute for Drug Abuse National Conference on Drug Abuse, Research and Practice, Washington, DC.

Althusser, L. (1976). *Essays in self-criticism* (G. Lock, Trans.). London: New Left.

Amato, P. (1993). Children's adjustment to divorce: Theories, hypotheses, and empirical support. *Journal of Marriage and the Family, 55,* 23-38.

Ambert, A. M. (1989). *Ex-spouses and new spouses: A study of relationships*. Greenwich, CT: JAI.

American Cancer Society. (1978). *1978 facts and figures*. New York: Author.

American Psychiatric Association. (1987). *Diagnostic and statistical manual of mental disorders* (3rd ed., rev.). Washington, DC: Author.

Archer, D., & Akert, R. M. (1977). Words and everything else: Verbal and nonverbal cues in social interpretation. *Journal of Personality and Social Psychology, 35,* 443-449.

Arendell, T. (1992). After divorce: Investigations into father absence. *Gender & Society, 6,* 562-586.

Asher, R., & Brissett, D. (1988). Codependency: A view from women married to alcoholics. *International Journal of the Addictions, 23,* 331-350.

Bailey, B. (1988). *From front porch to back seat: Courtship in twentieth-century America*. Baltimore: Johns Hopkins University Press.

Bakan, D. (1966). *The duality of human existence*. Chicago: Rand McNally.

Ball, M. (1977). Issues of violence in family casework. *Social Casework, 58,* 3-12.

Balshem, M., Oxman, G., van Rooyen, D., & Girod, K. (1992). Syphilis, sex and crack cocaine: Images of risk and morality. *Social Science and Medicine, 35,* 147-160.

Bandura, A. (1986). *Social foundations of thought and action: A social cognitive theory*. Englewood Cliffs, NJ: Prentice Hall.

Bartholomew, K. (1993). From childhood to adult relationships: Attachment theory and research. In S. W. Duck (Ed.), *Learning about relationships* (pp. 30-62). Newbury Park, CA: Sage.

Baxter, L. A. (1987). Symbols of relationship identity in relationship cultures. *Journal of Social and Personal Relationships, 4,* 261-279.

Baxter, L. A. (1988). A dialectical perspective on communication strategies in relationship development. In S. W. Duck (Ed.), *Handbook of personal relationships* (pp. 257-273). New York: John Wiley.

Baxter, L. A. (1990). Dialectical contradictions in relationship development. *Journal of Social and Personal Relationships, 7,* 69-88.

Baxter, L. A. (1992). Forms and functions of intimate play in personal relationships. *Human Communication Research, 18,* 336-363.

Baxter, L. A. (1993). The social side of personal relationships: A dialectical perspective. In S. W. Duck (Ed.), *Social context and relationships* (pp. 139-165). Newbury Park, CA: Sage.

Baxter, L. A. (1994). A dialogic approach to relationship maintenance. In D. J. Canary & L. Stafford (Eds.), *Communication and relational maintenance.* New York: Academic Press.

Baxter, L. A., & Dindia, K. (1990). Marital partners' perceptions of marital maintenance strategies. *Journal of Social and Personal Relationships, 7,* 187-208.

Baxter, L. A., & Simon, E. (1993). Relationship maintenance strategies and dialectical contradictions in personal relationships. *Journal of Social and Personal Relationships, 10,* 225-242.

Beer, W. (Ed.). (1988). *Relative strangers: Studies of stepfamily processes.* Totowa, NJ: Rowman & Littlefield.

Belsey, C. (1980). *Critical practice.* New York: Methuen.

Bennett, J. (in press). *The intimate weave: Time and relationships.* New York: Guilford.

Berenson, A., Stiglich, N., Wilkinson, G., & Anderson, G. (1991). Drug abuse and other risk factors for physical abuse in pregnancy among white, non-Hispanic, Black, and Hispanic women. *American Journal of Obstetrics and Gynecology, 164,* 1491-1499.

Berger, C. R., & Bradac, J. (1982). *Language and social knowledge.* London: Arnold.

Bergmann, J. R. (1993). *Discreet indiscretions: The social organization of gossip.* New York: Aldine de Gruyter.

Berk, R., Berk, S., Loseke, D., & Rauma, D. (1983). Mutual combat and other family violence myths. In D. Finkelhor, R. J. Gelles, G. T. Hotaling, & M. A. Straus (Eds.), *The dark side of families: Current family violence research* (pp. 197-212). Beverly Hills, CA: Sage.

Berkman, L. E. (1986). Social networks, support, and health: Taking the next step forward. *American Journal of Epidemiology, 123,* 559-562.

Berkman, L. E., & Syme, S. L. (1979). Social networks, host resistance and mortality: A nine year follow-up of Alameda County residents. *American Journal of Epidemiology, 109,* 186-204.

Bernard, J. (1981). The divorce myth. *Personnel and Guidance Journal, 60,* 67-71.

Bernardes, J. (1993). Responsibilities in studying postmodern families. *Journal of Family Issues, 14,* 35-49.

Bersani, C. A., & Chen, H. (1988). Sociological perspectives in family violence. In V. B. Van Hasselt, R. L. Morrison, A. S. Bellack, & M. Hersen (Eds.), *Handbook of family violence* (pp. 57-86). New York: Plenum.

Billig, M. (1987). *Arguing and thinking: A rhetorical approach to social psychology.* Cambridge: Cambridge University Press.

Billingham, R. (1987). Courtship violence: The patterns of conflict resolution strategies across seven levels of emotional commitment. *Family Relations, 36,* 283-289.

Birchler, G. R., Weiss, R. L., & Vincent, J. P. (1975). Multimethod analysis of social reinforcement exchange between maritally distressed and nondistressed spouse and stranger dyads. *Journal of Personality and Social Psychology, 31,* 349-360.

Bird, G., Stith, S., & Schladale, J. (1991). Psychological resources, coping strategies, and negotiation styles as discriminators of violence in dating relationships. *Family Relations, 40,* 45-50.

Black, C. (1982). *It will never happen to me.* Denver: Medical Administration.

Blaxter, M. (1976). *The meaning of disability.* London: Heinemann.

Block, J. H., Block, J., & Gjerde, P. K. (1988). Parental functioning and the home environment in families of divorce: Prospective and concurrent analysis. *Journal of the American Academy of Child and Adolescent Psychiatry, 27,* 207-213.

Blumer, H. (1936). Social attitudes and nonsymbolic interaction. *Journal of Educational Sociology, 9,* 515-523.

Blumstein, P., & Schwartz, P. (1983). *American couples: Love, sex, and money.* New York: William Morrow.

Bochner, A. P. (1982). On the efficacy of openness in close relationships. In M. Burgoon (Ed.), *Communication yearbook 5* (pp. 109-124). New Brunswick, NJ: Transaction.

Bohannan, P. (1971). *Divorce and after: An analysis of the emotional and social problems of divorce.* Garden City, NY: Anchor.

Booth, R., & Watters, J. K. (1992). A factor analytic approach to modeling AIDS risk behaviors among heterosexual injection drug users. *Journal of Drug Issues, 22,* 807-822.

Boulding, K. (1962). *Conflict and defense: A general theory.* New York: Harper.

Bowen, M. (1978). *Family therapy in clinical practice.* New York: Jason Aronson.

Bowen, S. P., & Michal-Johnson, P. (1989). The crisis of communicating in relationships: Confronting the threat of AIDS. *AIDS and Public Policy, 4,* 10-19.

Bowen, S. P., & Michal-Johnson, P. (1990, November). *Evaluating the validity of college students' strategies for HIV risk assessment with relational partners.* Paper presented at the annual meeting of the Speech Communication Association, Chicago.

Bowen, S. P., & Michal-Johnson, P. (in press). "Telling them for real": A case of culture-specific HIV education for African-Americans in the urban underclass. In L. Fuller & L. Shilling (Eds.), *Communicating about communicable diseases.* Amherst, MA: Human Resources Development.

Bowlby, J. (1963). Pathological mourning and childhood mourning. *Journal of the American Psychoanalytic Association, 11,* 500-541.

Bowlby, J. (1973). *Attachment and loss* (Vol. 2). New York: Basic Books.

Bowlby, J. (1979). *The making and breaking of affectional bonds.* London: Tavistock.

Bowlby, J. (1980). *Attachment and loss: Vol. 3. Loss: Sadness and depression.* London: Hogarth.

Bowlby, J. (1988). *A secure base: Parent-child attachment and healthy human development.* New York: Basic Books.

Bowman, M., & Ahrons, C. (1985). Impact of legal custody status on fathers' parenting postdivorce. *Journal of Marriage and the Family, 47,* 481-488.

Bowser, B. P., Fullilove, M. T., & Fullilove, R. E. (1990). African-American youth and AIDS high-risk behavior. *Youth & Society, 22,* 54-66.

Bradshaw, J. (1988). *Bradshaw on: The family.* Deerfield Beach, FL: Health Communications.

Braver, S. L., Wolchik, S. A., Sandler, I. N., & Sheets, V. L. (1993). A social exchange model of nonresidential parent involvement. In C. Depner & J. Bray (Eds.), *Nonresidential parenting: New vistas in family living* (pp. 87-108). Newbury Park, CA: Sage.

Brody, G. H., Newbaum, E., & Forehand, R. (1988). Serial marriage: A heuristic analysis of an emerging family form. *Psychological Bulletin, 103,* 211-222.

Brooks, N. A., & Matson, R. (1982). Social-psychological adjustment to multiple sclerosis. *Social Science and Medicine, 16,* 2129-2135.

Brown, S. (1988). *Treating adult children of alcoholics: A developmental perspective.* New York: John Wiley.

Browne, A. (1987). *When battered women kill.* New York: Free Press.

Bumpass, L. L. (1990). What's happening to the family? Interactions between demographic and institutional change. *Demography, 27,* 483-498.

Bumpass, L. L., & Sweet, J. A. (1989). National estimates of cohabitation: Cohort levels and union stability. *Demography, 26,* 615-625.

Burgoon, J. K., & Koper, R. J. (1984). Nonverbal and relational communication associated with reticence. *Human Communication Research, 10,* 601-626.

Burke, P., Stets, J., & Pirog-Good, M. (1989). Gender identity, self-esteem, and physical and sexual abuse in dating relationships. In M. Pirog-Good & J. Stets (Eds.), *Violence in dating relationships* (pp. 72-93). New York: Praeger.

Burnfield, A., & Burnfield, P. (1982). Psychosocial aspects of multiple sclerosis. *Physiotherapy, 68,* 149-150.

Butcher, A. H., Manning, D. T., & O'Neal, E. C. (1991). HIV-related sexual behaviors of college students. *Journal of the American College Health Association, 40,* 115-118.

Calmen, K. L. (1984). Quality of life in cancer patients: An hypothesis. *Journal of Medical Ethics, 10,* 124-127.

Campbell, A. (1993). *Men, women, and aggression.* New York: Basic Books.

Canary, D. J., & Stafford, L. (Eds.). (1994). *Communication and relational maintenance.* New York: Academic Press.

Cate, R. M., Henton, J., Koval, J., Christopher, P., & Lloyd, S. (1982). Premarital abuse: A social psychological perspective. *Journal of Family Issues, 3,* 79-90.

Cate, R. M., & Lloyd, S. A. (1992). *Courtship.* Newbury Park, CA: Sage.

Centers for Disease Control and Prevention. (1994). [Data]. *HIV/AIDS Surveillance Report, 5*(4).

Cermak, T. (1986). *Diagnosing and treating co-dependence.* Minneapolis: Johnson Institute.

Chambers, D. L. (1990). Stepparents, biologic parents, and the law's perceptions of "family" after divorce. In S. D. Sugarman & H. H. Kay (Eds.), *Divorce reform at the crossroads* (pp. 102-129). New Haven, CT: Yale University Press.

Charmaz, K. (1991). *Good days, bad days: The self in chronic illness and disability.* New Brunswick, NJ: Rutgers University Press.

Cherlin, A. (1978). Remarriage as an incomplete institution. *American Journal of Sociology, 84,* 634-650.

Christopher, F. S., & Cate, R. M. (1985). Premarital sexual pathways and relationship development. *Journal of Social and Personal Relationships, 2,* 271-288.

Christopher, F. S., Owens, L. A., & Stecker, H. L. (1993). An examination of single men's and women's sexual aggressiveness in dating relationships. *Journal of Social and Personal Relationships, 10,* 511-528.

Cissna, K. N., Cox, D. E., & Bochner, A. P. (1990). The dialectic of marital and parental relationships within the stepfamily. *Communication Monographs, 57,* 44-61.

Cline, R. J., Freeman, K. E., & Johnson, S. J. (1990). Talk among sexual partners about AIDS: Factors differentiating those who talk from those who do not. *Communication Research, 17,* 792-808.

Cline, R. J., Johnson, S. J., & Freeman, K. E. (1992). Talk among sexual partners: Interpersonal communication for risk reduction or risk enhancement. *Health Communication, 4,* 39-56.

Clingempeel, W. G. (1981). Quasi-kin relationships and marital quality. *Journal of Personality and Social Psychology, 41,* 890-901.

Clingempeel, W. G., & Repucci, D. (1982). Joint custody after divorce: Major issues and goals for research. *Psychological Bulletin, 91,* 102-127.

Coale-Lewis, H. C. (1985). Family therapy with stepfamilies. *Journal of Strategic and Systemic Therapies, 4,* 13-23.

Cochran, S. D., & Mays, V. M. (1990). Sex, lies, and HIV. *New England Journal of Medicine, 322,* 774-775.

Cole, P. (1974). Morbidity in the United States. In C. L. Erhardt & J. E. Berlin (Eds.), *Mortality and morbidity in the United States*. Cambridge, MA: Harvard University Press.

Coleman, E. (1988). Chemical dependency and intimacy dysfunction: Inextricably bound. In E. Coleman (Ed.), *Chemical dependency and intimacy dysfunction*. New York: Haworth.

Coleman, J. (1957). *Community conflict*. New York: Free Press.

Coleman, M., & Ganong, L. (1987). The cultural stereotyping of stepfamilies. In K. Pasley & M. Ihinger-Tallman (Eds.), *Remarriage and stepparenting: Current research and theory* (pp. 19-41). New York: Guilford.

Coleman, M., Ganong, L., & Henry, J. (1984a, October/December). Children and stepfamilies. *Leadership,* pp. 6-7.

Coleman, M., Ganong, L., & Henry, J. (1984b). What teachers should know about stepfamilies. *Childhood Education, 60,* 306-309.

Comins, C. (1984). *Courtship violence: A recent study and its implication for future research*. Paper presented at the 2nd National Family Violence Research Conference, University of New Hampshire, Durham.

Conquergood, D. (1991). Rethinking ethnography: Toward a critical cultural politics. *Communication Monographs, 58,* 179-194.

Cooley, C. H. (1970). *Human nature and the social order*. New York: Schocken. (Original work published 1902)

Corazzini, J. G., Williams, K., & Harris, S. (1987). Group therapy for adult children of alcoholics. *Journal for Specialists in Group Work, 12,* 156-161.

Corcoran, K. J., & Bell, B. G. (1990). Opposite sex perceptions of the effects of alcohol consumption on a subsequent sexual activity in a dating situation. *Psychology, 27,* 7-11.

Corcoran, K. J., & Thomas, L. R. (1991). The influence of observed alcohol consumption on perceptions of initiation of sexual activity in a college dating situation. *Journal of Applied Social Psychology, 21,* 500-507.

Coser, L. A. (1956). *The functions of social conflict*. New York: Free Press.

Courtright, J., Millar, F., & Rogers, L. E. (1979). Domineeringness and dominance: Replication and expansion. *Communication Monographs, 46,* 179-192.

Coyne, J. C., Ellard, J. H., & Smith, D. A. (1990). Social support, interdependence, and the dilemmas of helping. In B. R. Sarason, I. G. Sarason, & G. R. Pierce (Eds.), *Social support: An interactional view*. New York: John Wiley.

Coyne, J. C., & Fiske, V. (1992). Couples coping with chronic illness. In T. J. Akamatse, J. C. Crowther, S. C. Hobfoll, & M. A. P. Stevens (Eds.), *Family health psychology*. Washington, DC: Hemisphere.

Crosbie-Burnett, M. (1984). The centrality of the step relationship: A challenge to family theory and practice. *Family Relations, 33,* 459-464.

Cuber, J. F., & Harroff, P. B. (1965). *Sex and the significant Americans*. Baltimore: Pelican.

Cupach, W. R., & Metts, S. (1991). Sexuality and communication in close relationships. In K. McKinney & S. Sprecher (Eds.), *Sexuality in close relationships* (pp. 93-110). Hillsdale, NJ: Lawrence Erlbaum.

Cupach, W. R., & Spitzberg, B. H. (Eds.). (1994). *The dark side of interpersonal communication.* Hillsdale, NJ: Lawrence Erlbaum.

Dalton, H. (1989). AIDS in blackface. *Daedalus, 118,* 205-227.

Darling, C. A., & Davidson, J. D. (1986). Coitally active university students: Sexual behaviors, concerns, and challenges. *Adolescence, 21,* 403-419.

Deal, J., & Wampler, K. S. (1986). Dating violence: The primacy of previous experience. *Journal of Social and Personal Relationships, 3,* 457-471.

de Certeau, M. (1984). *The practice of everyday life* (S. Randall, Trans.). Berkeley: University of California Press.

de la Cancela, V. (1989). Minority AIDS prevention: Moving beyond cultural perspectives towards sociopolitical empowerment. *AIDS Education and Prevention, 1,* 141-153.

Deutsch, M. (1969). Conflicts: Productive and destructive. *Journal of Social Issues, 25,* 7-41.

Dindia, K. (1994). The intrapersonal-interpersonal dialectical process of self-disclosure. In S. W. Duck (Ed.), *Dynamics of relationships* (pp. 27-57). Thousand Oaks, CA: Sage.

Dindia, K., & Baxter, L. A. (1987). Strategies for maintaining and repairing marital relationships. *Journal of Social and Personal Relationships, 4,* 143-158.

Dindia, K., & Canary, D. J. (1993). Definitions and theoretical perspectives on maintaining relationships. *Journal of Social and Personal Relationships, 10,* 163-173.

Dobash, R., & Dobash P. (1979). *Violence against wives.* New York: Free Press.

Donnelly, D., & Finkelhor, D. (1993, November). *Parental relations, socioeconomic status, and father-child contact following divorce.* Paper presented at the annual meeting of the National Council on Family Relations, Baltimore.

Donohew, L., Lorch, E., & Palmgreen, P. (1991). Sensation seeking and targeting of televised anti-drug PSAs. In L. Donohew, H. Sypher, & W. Bukoski (Eds.), *Persuasive communication and drug abuse prevention* (pp. 209-226). Hillsdale, NJ: Lawrence Erlbaum.

Duck, S. W. (1982). A topography of relationship disengagement and dissolution. In S. W. Duck (Ed.), *Personal relationships 4: Dissolving personal relationships.* London: Academic Press.

Duck, S. W. (1984). A perspective on the repair of personal relationships: Repair of what, when? In S. W. Duck (Ed.), *Personal relationships 5: Repairing personal relationships.* London: Academic Press.

Duck, S. W. (1986). *Human relationships.* London: Sage.

Duck, S. W. (1988). *Relating to others.* Monterey: Brooks/Cole.

Duck, S. W. (1990). Relationships as unfinished business: Out of the frying pan and into the 1990s. *Journal of Social and Personal Relationships, 7,* 5-29.

Duck, S. W. (1991). Afterword: Couples and coupling. In K. McKinney & S. Sprecher (Eds.), *Sexuality in close relationships* (pp. 193-205). Hillsdale, NJ: Lawrence Erlbaum.

Duck, S. W. (1992). *Human relationships* (2nd ed.). London: Sage.

Duck, S. W. (1994a). *Meaningful relationships: Talking, sense, and relating.* Thousand Oaks, CA: Sage.

Duck, S. W. (1994b). Steady as (s)he goes: Relational maintenance as a shared meaning system. In D. J. Canary & L. Stafford (Eds.), *Communication and relational maintenance* (pp. 45-60). New York: Academic Press.

Duck, S. W. (1994c). Stratagems, spoils and a serpent's tooth: On the delights and dilemmas of personal relationships. In W. R. Cupach & B. H. Spitzberg (Eds.), *The dark side of interpersonal communication* (pp. 3-24). Hillsdale, NJ: Lawrence Erlbaum.

Dudley, J. R. (1991). Increasing our understanding of divorced fathers who have infrequent contact with their children. *Family Relations, 40,* 279-285.

Dunkel-Schetter, C., & Wortman, C. B. (1982). The interpersonal dynamics of cancer: Problems in social relationships and their impact on the patient. In H. S. Friedman & M. R. DiMatteo (Eds.), *Interpersonal issues in health care* (pp. 69-100). New York: Academic Press.

Durkheim, E. (1966). *Suicide.* New York: Free Press. (Original work published 1851)

Dutton, D. G. (1988). *The domestic assault on women.* Boston: Allyn & Bacon.

Edgar, T., & Fitzpatrick, M. A. (1988). Compliance-gaining in relational interaction: When your life depends on it. *Southern Speech Communication Journal, 53,* 385-405.

Edgar, T., & Fitzpatrick, M. A. (1993). Expectations for sexual interaction: A cognitive test of the sequencing of sexual communication behaviors. *Health Communication, 5,* 239-261.

Edgar, T., Freimuth, V. S., Hammond, S. L., McDonald, D. A., & Fink, E. L. (1992). Strategic sexual communication: Condom use resistance and response. *Health Communication, 4,* 83-104.

Edwards, D., & Potter, J. (1992). *Discursive social psychology.* London: Sage.

Edwards, D., Potter, J., & Middleton, D. (1992). *Social remembering.* London: Sage.

Eisenberg, L. (1977). Disease and illness. *Culture, Medicine, and Psychiatry, 1,* 9-23.

Elbow, M. (1977). Theoretical considerations of violent marriages (personality characteristics of wife abusers). *Social Casework, 58,* 515-526.

Elkin, M. (1987). Joint custody: Affirming that parents and families are forever. *Social Work, 32,* 18-24.

Emmons, R. A. (1992, August). *Revenge: Individual differences and correlates.* Paper presented at the 100th annual meeting of the American Psychological Association, Washington, DC.

Erikson, E. (1963). *Childhood and society* (2nd ed.). New York: W. W. Norton.

Farber, B. (1973). *Family and kinship in modern society.* Glenview, IL: Scott, Foresman.

Farrell, J., & Markman, H. (1986). Individual and interpersonal factors in the etiology of marital distress: The example of remarital couples. In R. Gilmour & S. W. Duck (Eds.), *The emerging field of personal relationships* (pp. 251-263). Hillsdale, NJ: Lawrence Erlbaum.

Faulk, M. (1977, October). Sexual factors in marital violence. *Medical Aspects of Human Sexuality,* pp. 30-43.

Fausel, D. F. (1988). Helping the helper heal: Co-dependency in the helping professions. *Journal of Independent Social Work, 3,* 35-45.

Felmlee, D. (in press). Fatal attractions: Affection and disaffection in intimate relationships. *Journal of Social and Personal Relationships, 12.*

Felson, R. (1992). "Kick 'em when they're down": Explanations of the relationship between stress and interpersonal aggression and violence. *Sociological Quarterly, 33,* 1-16.

Ferraro, K. J., & Johnson, J. (1983). How women experience battering: The process of victimization. *Social Problems, 30,* 325-339.

Fine, M. A., & Fine, D. R. (1992). Recent changes in laws affecting stepfamilies: Suggestions for legal reform. *Family Relations, 41,* 334-340.

Fiore, J., Becker, J., & Coppell, D. B. (1983). Social network interactions: A buffer or a stress? *American Journal of Community Psychology, 11,* 423-440.

Fischer, J. L., & Crawford, D. W. (1992). Codependency and parenting styles. *Journal of Adolescent Research, 7,* 352-363.

Fischer, J. L., Spann, L., & Crawford, D. W. (1991). Measuring codependency. *Alcoholism Treatment Quarterly, 8,* 87-100.

Fischer, J. L., Wampler, R., Lyness, K., & Thomas, E. M. (1992). Offspring codependency: Blocking the impact of family of origin. *Family Dynamics of Addiction Quarterly, 2,* 20-32.

Fitzpatrick, M. A. (1988). *Between husbands and wives: Communication in marriage.* Newbury Park, CA: Sage.

Flynn, C. (1987). Relationship violence: A model for family professionals. *Family Relations, 36,* 295-299.

Flynn, C. (1990). Relationship violence by women: Issues and implications. *Family Relations, 39,* 194-198.

Follingstad, D., Laughlin, J., Polek, D., Rutledge, L., & Hause, E. (1991). Identification of patterns of wife abuse. *Journal of Interpersonal Violence, 6,* 187-204.

Follingstad, D., Wright, S., Lloyd, S., & Sebastian, J. (1991). Sex differences in motivations and effects in dating violence. *Family Relations, 40,* 51-57.

Foss, J. (1980). The paradoxical nature of family relationships and family conflict. In M. A. Straus & G. T. Hotaling (Eds.), *The social causes of husband-wife violence* (pp. 115-135). Minneapolis: University of Minnesota Press.

Foss, S., Foss, K., & Trapp, R. (1985). *Contemporary perspectives on rhetoric.* Prospect Heights, IL: Waveland.

Foucault, M. (1972). *The archaeology of knowledge* (S. Smith, Trans.). New York: Pantheon.

Foucault, M. (1973). *Madness and civilization* (R. Howard, Trans.). New York: Vintage.

Foucault, M. (1980). *Power/knowledge* (C. Gordon, Ed.). New York: Pantheon.

Frank, P. B., & Golden, G. K. (1992). Blaming by naming: Battered women and the epidemic of codependence. *Social Work, 37,* 5-6.

French, R. D. (1984). The long-term relationships of marked people. In E. E. Jones et al. (Eds.), *Social stigma: The psychology of marked relationships* (pp. 255-294). New York: W. H. Freeman.

Freud, S. (1959). Inhibitions, symptoms, and anxiety. In J. Strachey (Ed.), *The standard edition of the complete psychological works of Sigmund Freud* (Vol. 20, pp. 87-172). London: Hogarth. (Original work published 1926)

Fullilove, R. E., Fullilove, M. T., Bowser, B. P., & Gross, S. A. (1990). Risk of sexually transmitted disease among black adolescent crack users in Oakland and San Francisco, Calif. *Journal of the American Medical Association, 263,* 851-855.

Furguson, A. (1792). *Principles of moral and political science.* Edinburgh: W. Chreech.

Furstenberg, F. F. (1987). The new extended family: The experience of parents and children after remarriage. In K. Pasley & M. Ihinger-Tallman (Eds.), *Remarriage and stepparenting: Current research and theory* (pp. 42-61). New York: Guilford.

Furstenberg, F. F., Nord, C. W., Peterson, J. L., & Zill, N. (1983). The life course of children of divorce: Marital disruption and parental conflict. *American Sociological Review, 48,* 656-668.

Gaines, S. O. (in press). Relationships between members of cultural minorities. In J. T. Wood & S. W. Duck (Eds.), *Under-studied relationships: Off the beaten track.* Thousand Oaks, CA: Sage.

Ganong, L. H. (1993). Family diversity in a youth organization: Involvement of single-parents families and stepfamilies in 4-H. *Family Relations, 42,* 286-292.

Ganong, L. H., & Coleman, M. (1989). Preparing for remarriage: Anticipating the issues, seeking solutions. *Family Relations, 38,* 28-33.

Ganong, L. H., & Coleman, M. (1994). *Remarried family relationships.* Thousand Oaks, CA: Sage.

Garfinkel, H. (1956). Conditions of successful degradation. *American Journal of Sociology, 61,* 420-424.

Gelles, R. J., & Cornell, C. P. (1985). *Intimate violence in families.* Beverly Hills, CA: Sage.

Gelles, R. J., & Straus, M. A. (1988). *Intimate violence: The causes and consequences of abuse in the American family.* New York: Simon & Schuster.

Gierymski, T., & Williams, T. (1986). Codependency. *Journal of Psychoactive Drugs, 18,* 7-13.

Giles-Sims, J. (1983). *Wife battering: A systems theory approach.* New York: Guilford.

Glick, I. O., Weiss, R. S., & Parkes, C. M. (1974). *The first year of bereavement.* New York: John Wiley.

Glick, P. C. (1980). Remarriage: Some recent changes and variations. *Journal of Family Issues, 1,* 455-478.

Goetting, A. (1979). The normative integration of the former spouse relationship. *Journal of Divorce, 2,* 395-414.

Goetting, A. (1980). Former spouse-current spouse relationships. *Journal of Family Issues, 1,* 58-80.

Goffman, E. (1959). *Behavior in public places.* Harmondsworth: Penguin.

Goffman, E. (1963). *Stigma: Notes on the management of spoiled identity.* New York: Simon & Schuster.

Goffman, E. (1967). *Interaction ritual: Essays on face-to-face behavior.* Garden City, NY: Anchor.

Goldner, V. (1982). Remarriage family: Structure, system, future. In J. C. Hansen & L. Messenger (Eds.), *Therapy with remarried families* (pp. 187-206). Rockville, MD: Aspen.

Gomberg, E. L. (1989). On terms used and abused: The concept of "codependency." *Drugs and Society, 3,* 113-132.

Gordon, L. (1989). *Heroes of their own lives.* New York: Viking.

Gore, S., & Colton, M. E. (1991). Gender, stress and distress: Social, relational influences. In J. Eckenrode (Ed.), *The social context of coping* (pp. 139-163). New York: Plenum.

Gottman, J. M. (1979). *Marital interaction.* New York: Academic Press.

Gottman, J. M. (1993). *What predicts divorce?* Hillsdale, NJ: Lawrence Erlbaum.

Gottman, J. M., & Levenson, R. (1986). Assessing the role of emotion in marriage. *Behavioral Assessment, 8,* 31-48.

Gottschalk, L. A., Winget, C. N., & Gleser, G. C. (1969). *Manual of instruction for using the Gottschalk-Gleser content analysis scales: Anxiety, hostility, and social alienation-personal disorganization.* Berkeley: University of California Press.

Gulotta, G., & Neuberger, L. (1983). A systemic and attributional approach to victimology. *Victimology, 8,* 5-16.

Haaken, J. (1990). A critical analysis of the codependence construct. *Psychiatry, 53,* 396-406.

Haapanen, R. A. (1977). *Close friendship and individualistic community.* Unpublished doctoral dissertation, University of California, Davis.

Hackstaff, K. B. (1993). The rise of divorce culture and its gendered foundations. *Feminism & Psychology, 3,* 363-368.

Hagestad, G. O., & Smyer, M. A. (1982). Dissolving long-term relationships: Patterns of divorcing in middle age. In S. W. Duck (Ed.), *Personal relationships 4: Dissolving personal relationships*. London: Academic Press.

Hall, F. S. (1991). Dysfunctional managers: The next human resource challenge. *Organizational Dynamics, 20*, 48-57.

Hamberger, L. K., & Hastings, J. E. (1986). Characteristics of spouse abusers: Predictors of treatment acceptance. *Journal of Interpersonal Violence, 1*, 363-373.

Hammer, M. (1983). "Core" and "extended" social networks in relation to health and illness. *Social Science and Medicine, 17*, 405-411.

Hanna, S. L., & Knaub, P. K. (1981). Cohabitation before remarriage: Its relationship to family strengths. *Alternative Lifestyles, 4*, 507-522.

Harman, M. J., & Withers, L. (1992). University students from homes with alcoholic parents: Considerations for therapy groups. *Journal for Specialists in Group Work, 17*, 37-41.

Harper, J., & Capdevila, C. (1990). Codependency: A critique. *Journal of Psychoactive Drugs, 22*, 285-292.

Harré, R. (1977). Friendship as an accomplishment: An ethogenic approach to social relationships. In S. W. Duck (Ed.), *Theory and practice in interpersonal attraction* (pp. 338-354). London: Academic Press.

Harris, L. M., & Sadeghi, A. (1987). Realizing: How facts are created in human interaction. *Journal of Social and Personal Relationships, 4*, 480-495.

Harris, S. A., & MacQuidy, S. (1991). Childhood roles in group therapy: The lost child and the mascot. *Journal for Specialists in Group Work, 16*, 223-229.

Hartley, S. F., & Wiseman, J. P. (1984). *The "ideal" and real components of friendship*. Unpublished manuscript.

Harvey, J. H., Flanary, R., & Morgan, M. (1986). Vivid memories of vivid loves gone by. *Journal of Social and Personal Relationships, 3*, 359-373.

Harvey, J. H., Orbuch, T. L., Weber, A. L., Merbach, N., & Alt, R. (1992). House of pain and hope: Accounts of loss. *Death Studies, 16*, 99-124.

Harvey, J. H., Weber, A. L., & Orbuch, T. L. (1990). *Interpersonal accounts: A social psychological perspective*. Oxford: Basil Blackwell.

Hazan, C., & Shaver, P. R. (1987). Conceptualizing romantic love as an attachment process. *Journal of Personality and Social Psychology, 52*, 511-524.

Hendrick, C., & Hendrick, S. S. (1986). A theory and a method of love. *Journal of Personality and Social Psychology, 50*, 392-402.

Henton, J., & Cate, R. (1983). Romance and violence in dating relationships. *Journal of Family Issues, 4*, 467-482.

Hetherington, E. M., & Clingempeel, W. G. (1992). Coping with marital transitions: A family systems perspective. *Monographs of the Society for Research in Child Development, 57*(2-3, Serial No. 227).

Hetherington, E. M., Cox, M., & Cox, R. (1985). Long-term effects of divorce and remarriage on the adjustment of children. *Journal of the American Academy of Child Psychiatry, 24,* 518-530.

Hill, M. (1992). The role of economic resources and remarriage in financial assistance for children. *Journal of Family Issues, 13,* 158-178.

Hindy, C., Schwartz, J. C., & Brodksy, A. (1989). *If this is love why do I feel so insecure?* New York: Atlantic.

Hingson, R. W., Strunin, L., Berlin, B. M., & Heeren, T. (1990). Beliefs about AIDS, use of alcohol and drugs, and unprotected sex among Massachusetts adolescents. *Journal of American Public Health, 80,* 295-299.

Hoffman, S., & Duncan, G. (1988). What are the economic consequences of divorce? *Demography, 25,* 415-427.

Hogg, J. A., & Frank, M. L. (1992). Toward an interpersonal model of codependence and contradependence. *Journal of Counseling and Development, 70,* 371-375.

Hollander, E. P. (1958). Conformity, status and idiosyncrasy credit. *Psychological Review, 65,* 117-127.

Hopper, J. (1993). The rhetoric of motives in divorce. *Journal of Marriage and the Family, 55,* 801-813.

Horney, K. (1942). *Self analysis.* New York: W. W. Norton.

Horney, K. (1945). *Our inner conflicts.* New York: W. W. Norton.

Hotaling, G. T., & Sugarman, D. B. (1986). An analysis of risk markers in husband to wife violence: The current state of knowledge. *Violence and Victims, 1,* 101-124.

Huebert, K., & James, D. (1992). High-risk behaviors for transmission of HIV among clients in treatment for substance abuse. *Journal of Drug Issues, 22,* 885-901.

Huggins, M., & Straus, M. (1980). Violence and the social structure as reflected in children's books from 1850 to 1970. In M. A. Straus & G. T. Hotaling (Eds.), *The social causes of husband-wife violence* (pp. 51-67). Minneapolis: University of Minnesota Press.

Iguchi, M. Y., Platt, J. J., French, J., Baxter, R. C., Kushner, H., Lidz, V., Bux, D. A., Rosen, M., & Musikoff, H. (1992). Correlates of HIV seropositivity among injection drug users not in treatment. *Journal of Drug Issues, 22,* 849-866.

Ihinger-Tallman, M., Pasley, K., & Buehler, C. (1993). Developing a middle-range theory of father involvement postdivorce. *Journal of Family Issues, 14,* 550-571.

Inciardi, J. A. (1989). Trading sex for crack among juvenile drug users: A research note. *Contemporary Drug Problems, 16,* 689-700.

Inclan, J., & Hernandez, M. (1992). Cross-cultural perspectives on codependence: The case of poor Hispanics. *American Journal of Orthopsychiatry, 62,* 245-255.

Jackson, D. D. (1965). Family rules: Marital quid pro quo. *Archives of General Psychiatry, 12,* 589-594.

Jackson, J. M. (1988). *Social psychology, past and present.* Hillsdale, NJ: Lawrence Erlbaum.

Jacobson, N. S. (1977). Problem solving and contingency in the treatment of marital discord. *Journal of Clinical and Consulting Psychology, 45,* 92-100.

James, W. (1910). *Psychology.* New York: Henry Holt.

Janas, C. (1986). *M*A*S*H 4077:* An analog of an "alcoholic family"? *Journal of the American Academy of Medical Hypnoanalysts, 1,* 47-57.

Janssen, M., Philipsen, H., & Halfens, R. (1990, July 15-20). *Personal networks of chronically ill people.* Paper presented at the Fifth International Conference on Personal Relationships, Oxford.

Johnston, J., & Campbell, L. (1988). *Impasses in divorce.* New York: Free Press.

Johnston, J. R. (1993). Family transitions and children's functioning: The case of parental conflict and divorce. In P. A. Cowan, D. Field, D. A. Hansen, A. Skolnick, & G. Swanson (Eds.), *Family, self, and society: Toward a new agenda for family research* (pp. 197-234). Hillsdale, NJ: Lawrence Erlbaum.

Jones, W. H., & Burdette, M. P. (1994). Betrayal in close relationships. In A. L. Weber & J. H. Harvey (Eds.), *Perspectives on close relationships* (pp. 243-261). New York: Allyn & Bacon.

Katz, J. (1988). *Seductions to crime.* New York: Basic Books.

Kelley, H. H., Berscheid, E., Christensen, A., Harvey, J. H., Huston, T., Levinger, G., Peplau, L., & Peterson, D. (1983). *Close relationships.* New York: W. H. Freeman.

Kelvin, P. (1977). Predictability, power and vulnerability in interpersonal attraction. In S. W. Duck (Ed.), *Theory and practice in interpersonal attraction* (pp. 355-378). London: Academic Press.

Kenen, R. H., & Armstrong, K. (1992). The why, when and whether of condom use among female and male drug users. *Journal of Community Health, 17,* 303-317.

Kilpatrick, D., Edmunds, C., & Seymour, A. (1992). *Rape in America: A report to the nation.* Arlington, VA: National Victim Center.

Kitchens, J. A. (1991). *Understanding and treating codependence.* Englewood Cliffs, NJ: Prentice Hall.

Klein, R., & Milardo, R. M. (1993). Third-party influence on the management of personal relationships. In S. W. Duck (Ed.), *Social context and relationships* (pp. 55-77). Newbury Park, CA: Sage.

Klinger, E. (1977). *Meaning and void: Inner experience and the incentives in people's lives.* Minneapolis: University of Minnesota Press.

Koch, M. A. P., & Lowery, C. R. (1984). Visitation and the noncustodial father. *Journal of Divorce, 8,* 47-65.

Kohut, H. E. (1971). Thoughts on narcissism and narcissistic rage. In H. E. Kohut, *The search for the self.* New York: International University Press.

Kovecses, Z. (1991). A linguist's quest for love. *Journal of Social and Personal Relationships, 8*, 77-98.

Kreisberg, L. (1973). *The sociology of social conflicts.* Englewood Cliffs, NJ: Prentice Hall.

Krestan, J., & Bepko, C. (1990). Codependency: The social reconstruction of female experience. *Smith College Studies in Social Work, 60*, 216-232.

Kruk, E. (1993). Promoting co-operative parenting after separation: A therapeutic/interventionist model of family mediation. *Journal of Family Therapy, 15*, 235-261.

Kvanli, J. A., & Jennings, G. (1987). Recoupling: Development and establishment of the spousal subsystem in remarriage. *Journal of Divorce, 10*, 189-203.

Labov, W., & Fanshel, D. (1977). *Therapeutic discourse.* New York: Academic Press.

La Gaipa, J. J. (1982). Rules and rituals in disengaging from relationships. In S. W. Duck (Ed.), *Personal relationships 4: Dissolving personal relationships* (pp. 189-209). London: Academic Press.

La Gaipa, J. J. (1990). The negative effects of informal support systems. In S. W. Duck (Ed.), with R. C. Silver, *Personal relationships and social support.* London: Sage.

Langer, L. L. (1991). *Holocaust testimonies.* New Haven, CT: Yale University Press.

Lansky, M. (1987). Shame and domestic violence. In D. Nathanson (Ed.), *The many faces of shame.* New York: Guilford.

Lazarus, R. S., & Folkman, S. (1984). *Stress, appraisal, and coping.* New York: Springer.

Lea, M., & Spears, R. (in press). Love at first byte. In J. T. Wood & S. W. Duck (Eds.), *Under-studied relationships: Off the beaten track.* Thousand Oaks, CA: Sage.

Lederman, L. C. (1993). "Friends don't let friends beer goggle": The use and abuse of alcohol among college students. In E. B. Ray (Ed.), *Case studies in health communication* (pp. 161-174). Hillsdale, NJ: Lawrence Erlbaum.

Leigh, B. C., Aramburu, B., & Norris, J. (1992). The morning after: Gender difference in attributions about alcohol-related sexual encounters. *Journal of Applied Social Psychology, 22*, 343-357.

Lemert, E. M. (1967). Paranoia and the dynamics of exclusion. In E. M. Lemert, *Human deviance, social problems and social control* (pp. 197-211). Englewood Cliffs, NJ: Prentice Hall.

Leonard, K., Bromet, E., Parkinson, D., Day, N., & Ryan, C. (1985). Patterns of alcohol use and physically aggressive behavior in men. *Journal of Studies on Alcohol, 46*, 279-282.

Lerner, M. J., Miller, D. T., & Holmes, J. (1976). Deserving and the emergence of forms of justice. In L. Berkowitz & E. Walster (Eds.), *Advances in experimental social psychology* (Vol. 10, pp. 134-162). New York: Academic Press.

Levin, I. (1993). Family as mapped realities. *Journal of Family Issues, 14,* 82-91.

Levinger, G. (1992). Close relationship loss as a set of inkblots. In T. L. Orbuch (Ed.), *Close relationship loss* (pp. 213-221). New York: Springer-Verlag.

Lewis, H. B. (1971). *Shame and guilt in neurosis.* New York: International University Press.

Lewis, H. B. (1976). *Psychic war in men and women.* New York: New York University Press.

Lewis, H. B. (1981). *Freud and modern psychology: Vol. 1. The emotional basis of mental illness.* New York: Plenum.

Lewis, H. B. (1985). *Some thoughts on the moral emotions of shame and guilt.* In L. Cirillo, B. Kaplin, & S. Wapner (Eds.), *Emotions in ideal human development.* Hillsdale, NJ: Lawrence Erlbaum.

Lewis, R. A., & McAvoy, P. (1984). Improving the quality of relationships: Therapeutic intervention with opiate-abusing couples. In S. W. Duck (Ed.), *Personal relationships 5: Repairing personal relationships* (pp. 89-102). London: Academic Press.

Liebman, J., Mulia, N., & McIlvaine, D. (1992). Risk behavior for HIV infection of intravenous drug users and their sexual partners recruited from street settings in Philadelphia. *Journal of Drug Issues, 22,* 867-884.

Linville, P. W., Fischer, G. W., & Fischhoff, B. (1993). AIDS risk perceptions and decision biases. In J. B. Pryor & G. D. Reeder (Eds.), *The social psychology of HIV infection* (pp. 5-38). Hillsdale, NJ: Lawrence Erlbaum.

Lloyd, S. A., & Cate, R. M. (1985). The developmental course of conflict in dissolution of premarital relationships. *Journal of Social and Personal Relationships, 2,* 179-194.

Longley, J., & Pruitt, D. (1980). Groupthink: A critique of Janis's theory. *Review of Personality and Social Psychology, 1,* 74-93.

Loughead, T. A. (1991). Addictions as a process: Commonalities or codependence. *Contemporary Family Therapy, 13,* 455-470.

Lyon, D., & Greenberg, J. (1991). Evidence of codependency in women with an alcoholic parent: Helping out Mr. Wrong. *Journal of Personality and Social Psychology, 61,* 435-439.

Lyons, R. (1991). The effects of acquired illness and disability on friendships. In D. Perlman & W. Jones (Eds.), *Advances in personal relationships* (Vol. 3, pp. 223-277). London: J. Kingsley.

Lyons, R. (1993a). The energy crunch: Relationship and support experiences of mothers with chronic illness. In *Studying human lived experience: Symbolic and ethnographic research '93.* Waterloo, ON: University of Waterloo.

Lyons, R. (1993b). Research on relationships coping with stressful life events: An interview with Ben Gottlieb and James Coyne. *ISSPR Bulletin, 10,* 11-14.

Lyons, R., & Meade, D. (1993a). *Coping and support as communal processes.* Paper presented at the Fourth Conference of the International Network on Personal Relationships, Milwaukee, WI.

Lyons, R., & Meade, D. (1993b). The energy crisis: Mothers with chronic illness. *Canadian Woman Studies, 13*(4), 34-37.

Lyons, R., Sullivan, M., & Ritvo, P. (1994). *Close relationships and chronic health problems.* Thousand Oaks, CA: Sage.

Mace, D. R. (1976). Marital intimacy and the deadly love-anger cycle. *Journal of Marriage and Family Counseling, 2,* 131-137.

Machiavelli, N. (1947). *The prince* (T. G. Bergin, Trans.). New York: Appleton-Century-Crofts. (Original work published 1532)

Magana, J. R. (1991). Sex, drugs and HIV: An ethnographic approach. *Social Science and Medicine, 33,* 5-9.

Makepeace, J. M. (1981). Courtship violence among college students. *Family Relations, 30,* 97-102.

Makepeace, J. M. (1986). Gender differences in courtship violence victimization. *Family Relations, 35,* 383-388.

Manderscheid, R., Rae, D., McCarrick, A., & Silbergeld, S. (1982). A stochastic model of relational control in dyadic interaction. *American Sociological Review, 47,* 62-75.

Mannion, L. (1991). Co-dependency: A case of inflation. *Employee Assistance Quarterly, 7,* 67-81.

Margolin, G., & Wampold, B. E. (1981). A sequential analysis of conflict and accord in distressed and non-distressed marital partners. *Journal of Consulting and Clinical Psychology, 49,* 554-567.

Markman, H. (1981). The prediction of marital distress: A five-year follow-up. *Journal of Consulting and Clinical Psychology, 49,* 760-762.

Martin, S. (1992). The epidemiology of alcohol-related interpersonal violence. *Health and Research World, 16,* 230-237.

Marx, K. (1964). *Economic and philosophic manuscripts of 1844.* New York: International. (Original work published 1844)

Masters, W., & Johnson, V. (1979). *Homosexuality in perspective.* Boston: Little, Brown.

Maybury, C. P., & Brewin, C. R. (1984). Social relationships, knowledge, and adjustment to multiple sclerosis. *Journal of Neurology, Neurosurgery and Psychology, 47,* 372-276.

McCall, G. J. (1982). Becoming unrelated: The management of bond dissolution. In S. W. Duck (Ed.), *Personal relationships 4: Dissolving personal relationships.* (pp. 211-232). London: Academic Press.

McCall, G. J., & Simmons, J. L. (1978). *Interactions and identities* (rev. ed.). New York: Free Press.

McDougall, W. (1908). *An introduction to social psychology.* New York: University Paperbacks.

McEwan, R. T., McCallum, A., Bhopal, R. S., & Madhok, R. (1992). Sex and the risk of HIV infection: The role of alcohol. *British Journal of Addiction, 87,* 577-584.

McGoldrick, M., & Carter, E. A. (1989). Forming a remarried family. In E. A. Carter & M. McGoldrick (Eds.), *The family cycle: A framework for family therapy* (pp. 399-429). New York: Gardner.

McIntosh, D. N., Silver, R. C., & Wortman, C. B. (1993). Religion's role in adjustment to a negative life event: Coping with the loss of a child. *Journal of Personality and Social Psychology, 65,* 812-821.

McKinney, K., & Sprecher, S. (1991). Introduction. In K. McKinney & S. Sprecher (Eds.), *Sexuality in close relationships.* Hillsdale, NJ: Lawrence Erlbaum.

Mead, G. H. (1934). *Mind, self and society: From the standpoint of a social behaviorist.* Chicago: University of Chicago Press.

Mehrabian, A. (1972). *Non-verbal communication.* New York: Aldine.

Mendenhall, W. (1989a). Co-dependency definition and dynamics. *Alcoholism Treatment Quarterly, 6,* 3-17.

Mendenhall, W. (1989b). Codependency treatment. *Alcoholism Treatment Quarterly, 6,* 75-86.

Metts, S., & Fitzpatrick, M. A. (1992). Thinking about safer sex: The risky business of "know your partner" advice. In T. Edgar, M. A. Fitzpatrick, & V. S. Freimuth (Eds.), *AIDS: A communication perspective* (pp. 1-19). Hillsdale, NJ: Lawrence Erlbaum.

Michal-Johnson, P. (1992). *On defining myself: Conversations with abused women of color.* Paper presented at the 78th annual meeting of the Speech Communication Association, Chicago.

Michal-Johnson, P., & Bowen, S. P. (1988, November). *Interpreting AIDS discourse in the romantic relationships of college students.* Paper presented at the annual meeting of the Speech Communication Association, New Orleans, LA.

Michal-Johnson, P., & Bowen, S. P. (1992). The place of culture in HIV education. In T. Edgar, M. A. Fitzpatrick, & V. S. Freimuth (Eds.), *AIDS: A communication perspective* (pp. 147-172). Hillsdale, NJ: Lawrence Erlbaum.

Miell, D. E. (1984). *Cognitive and communicative strategies in developing relationships.* Unpublished doctoral thesis, University of Lancaster.

Miell, D. E. (1987). Remembering relationship development: Constructing a context for interactions. In R. Burnett, P. McGhee, & D. Clarke (Eds.), *Accounting for relationships* (pp. 60-73). London: Methuen.

Miles, A. (1979). Some psycho-social consequences of multiple sclerosis: Problems of social interaction and group identity. *British Journal of Medical Psychology, 52,* 321-331.

Millar, F. E., & Rogers, L. E. (1981, May). *A pragmatic approach to relational communication: A case study.* Paper presented at the annual meeting of the International Communication Association, Minneapolis, MN.

Miller, J. B. (1993). Learning from early relationship experience. In S. W. Duck (Ed.), *Learning about relationships* (pp. 1-29). Newbury Park, CA: Sage.

Miller, L. C., Bettencourt, B. A., DeBro, S. C., & Hoffman, V. (1993). Negotiating safer sex: Interpersonal dynamics. In J. B. Pryor & G. D. Reeder (Eds.), *The social psychology of HIV infection* (pp. 85-123). Hillsdale, NJ: Lawrence Erlbaum.

Miller, L. C., & Burns, D. (in press). Risking disease: On the coherence of gay men's mental models of unsafe sex. In M. McLaughlin & L. C. Miller (Eds.), *Intimate decisions: Accounting for risk-taking in sexual behavior and courtship*. Hillsdale, NJ: Lawrence Erlbaum.

Mills, D. (1984). A model for stepfamily development. *Family Relations, 33,* 365-372.

Minuchin, S. (1974). *Families and family therapy*. Cambridge, MA: Harvard University Press.

Mitchell, C. E. (1989). Psychosocial redevelopment of codependents: A framework for therapeutic assistance. *Family Therapy, 16,* 161-170.

Montgomery, B. (1993). Relationship maintenance versus relationship change: A dialectical dilemma. *Journal of Social and Personal Relationships, 10,* 205-223.

Montgomery, M. J., Anderson, E. R., Hetherington, E. M., & Clingempeel, W. G. (1992). Patterns of courtship for remarriage: Implications for child adjustment and parent-child relationships. *Journal of Marriage and the Family, 54,* 686-698.

Moos, R. H., & Tsu, V. D. (1977). The crisis of physical illness. In R. H. Moos (Ed.), *Coping with physical illness*. New York: Plenum.

Morgan, D., & March, G. H. (1992). The impact of life events on networks of personal relationships: A comparison of widowhood and caring for a spouse with Alzheimer's disease. *Journal of Social and Personal Relationships, 9,* 563-584.

Morgan, L. A. (1988). Outcomes of marital separation: A longitudinal test of predictors. *Journal of Marriage and the Family, 50,* 493-498.

Morrell, D. (1988). *Fireflies*. New York: Dutton.

Mott, F. L. (1990). When is a father really gone? Paternal-child contact in father-absent homes. *Demography, 27,* 499-517.

Mumby, D. (1987). The political function of narrative in organizations. *Communication Monographs, 54,* 113-127.

Myer, R. A., Peterson, S. E., & Stoffel-Rosales, M. (1991). Co-dependency: An examination of underlying assumptions. *Journal of Mental Health Counseling, 13,* 449-458.

National Center for Health Statistics. (1984). *Health, United States, 1984* (DHHS Publication No. PHS 85-1232). Washington, DC: Government Printing Office.

National Center for Health Statistics. (1993). *1988 marriages: Number of the marriage of bride by groom* [Computer program]. Washington, DC: NCHS Computer Center.

Neeld, E. (1990). *Seven choices: Taking the steps to a new life after losing someone you love.* New York: Delta.

Nelson, W. P., & Levant, R. F. (1991). An evaluation of a skills training program for parents in stepfamilies. *Family Relations, 40,* 291-296.

Neuhauser, P. (1988). *Tribal warfare in organizations.* Cambridge, MA: Ballinger.

Noller, P. (1984). *Nonverbal communication and marital interaction.* New York: Pergamon.

Norton, R. (1983). *Communicator style.* Beverly Hills, CA: Sage.

Norton, R., & Morgan, M. (1989). The role of alcohol in mortality and morbidity from interpersonal violence. *Alcohol & Alcoholism, 24,* 565-576.

Norwood, R. (1985). *Women who love too much.* New York: Pocket Books.

Notarius, C., & Markman, H. (1981). The couples interaction scoring system. In E. E. Filsinger & R. A. Lewis (Eds.), *Observing marriages: New behavioral approaches.* Beverly Hills, CA: Sage.

Oh, S. (1986). Remarried men and remarried women: How are they different? *Journal of Divorce, 9,* 107-113.

Okin, S. M. (1989). *Gender, justice, and the family.* New York: HarperCollins.

O'Leary, A., Goodhart, F., Jemmott, L. S., & Boccher-Lattimore, D. (1992). Predictors of safer sex on the college campus: A social cognitive theory analysis. *Journal of the American College Health Association, 40,* 254-263.

Olson, D. (1986). Circumplex model VII: Validation studies and FACES III. *Family Process, 25,* 337-351.

Olson, D., Lavee, Y., & Cubbin, H. (1988). Types of families and family response to stress across the life cycle. In D. Klein & J. Aldous (Eds.), *Social stress and family development* (pp. 16-43). New York: Guilford.

Orbuch, T. L. (Ed.). (1992). *Relationship loss.* New York: Springer-Verlag.

Oswalt, R., & Matsen, K. (1993). Sex, AIDS, and the use of condoms: A survey of compliance in college students. *Psychological Reports, 72,* 764-766.

Pahl, J. (Ed.). (1985). *Private violence and public policy.* London: Routledge & Kegan Paul.

Palmgreen, P., Lorch, E. P., Donohew, L., Harrington, N. G., Dsilva, M., & Helm, D. (1993, May). *Reaching at-risk populations in a mass media drug abuse prevention campaign: Sensation seeking as a targeting variable.* Paper presented at the annual meeting of the International Communication Association, Washington, DC.

Papernow, P. (1993). *Becoming a stepfamily: Patterns of development in remarried families.* New York: Gardner.

Parks, M. R. (1982). Ideology in interpersonal communication: Off the couch and into the world. In M. Burgoon (Ed.), *Communication yearbook 5* (pp. 79-107). New Brunswick, NJ: Transaction.

Parsons, T. (1949). *The structure of social action.* New York: Free Press.

Patterson, G. (1982). *Coercive family process.* Eugene, OR: Castalia.

Pennebaker, J. (1990). *Opening up.* New York: William Morrow.

Peskin, H. (1993). Neither broken hearts nor broken bonds. *American Psychologist, 48,* 990-991.

Peterson, D. R. (1979). Assessing interpersonal relationships by means of interaction records. *Behavioral Assessment, 1,* 221-236.

Planalp, S. (1993). Friends' and acquaintances' conversations II: Coded differences. *Journal of Social and Personal Relationships, 10,* 339-354.

Planalp, S., & Benson, A. (1992). Friends' and acquaintances' conversations I: Observed differences. *Journal of Social and Personal Relationships, 9,* 483-506.

Planalp, S., & Garvin-Doxas, K. (1994). Using mutual knowledge in conversation: Friends as experts in each other. In S. W. Duck (Ed.), *Dynamics of relationships* (pp. 1-26). Thousand Oaks, CA: Sage.

Popenoe, D. (1993). American family decline, 1960-1990. *Journal of Marriage and the Family, 55,* 527-541.

Porseth, R. (1986). Alcohol and the writer: Some biographical and critical issues. *Contemporary Drug Problems, 13,* 361-386.

Price, S. J., & McKenry, P. C. (1988). *Divorce.* Newbury Park, CA: Sage.

Pruitt, D. G., & Rubin, J. Z. (1986). *Social conflict.* New York: Random House.

Prusank, D. T., Duran, R. L., & DeLillo, D. A. (1993). Interpersonal relationships in women's magazines: Dating and relating in the 1970s and 1980s. *Journal of Social and Personal Relationships, 10,* 307-320.

Putallaz, M., Costanzo, P. R., & Klein, T. P. (1993). Parental childhood social experiences and their effects on children's relationships. In S. W. Duck (Ed.), *Learning about relationships* (pp. 63-97). Newbury Park, CA: Sage.

Radecki-Bush, C., Bush, J. P., & Jennings, J. (1988). Effects of jealousy threats on relationship perceptions and emotions. *Journal of Social and Personal Relationships, 5,* 285-303.

Radecki-Bush, C., Farrell, A. D., & Bush, J. P. (1993). Predicting jealous responses: The influence of adult attachment and depression in threat appraisal. *Journal of Social and Personal Relationships, 10,* 569-588.

Raush, H., Barry, W., Hertel, R., & Swain, M. (1974). *Communication, conflict and marriage.* San Francisco: Jossey-Bass.

Rawlins, W. (1992). *Friendship matters.* New York: Aldine de Gruyter.

Rawlins, W. (1994). Being there and growing apart: Sustaining friendships during adulthood. In D. J. Canary & L. Stafford (Eds.), *Communication and relational maintenance.* New York: Academic Press.

Ray, D. (1968). *Sam's book.* Middletown, CT: Wesleyan University Press.

Reinarman, C., & Leigh, B. C. (1987). Culture, cognition, and disinhibition: Notes on sexuality and alcohol in the age of AIDS. *Contemporary Drug Problems, 14,* 335-360.

Reiss, I. (1989). Society and sexuality: A sociological theory. In K. McKinney & S. Sprecher (Eds.), *Human sexuality: The societal and interpersonal context* (pp. 3-29). Norwood, NJ: Ablex.

Renwick, R. (1992). *Quality of Life Project: Phase 1.* Toronto: University of Toronto, Centre for Health Promotion.

Retzinger, S. M. (1985). The resentment process: Videotape studies. *Psychoanalytic Psychology, 2,* 129-151.

Retzinger, S. M. (1987). Resentment and laughter: Video studies of the shame-rage spiral. In H. B. Lewis (Ed.), *The role of shame in symptom formation* (pp. 151-182). Hillsdale, NJ: Lawrence Erlbaum.

Retzinger, S. M. (1989). A theory of mental illness: Integrating social and emotional aspects. *Psychiatry, 52,* 325-335.

Retzinger, S. M. (1991). *Violent emotions: Shame and rage in marital quarrels.* Newbury Park, CA: Sage.

Rieff, P. (1987). *The triumph of the therapeutic.* Chicago: University of Chicago Press.

Robbins, C. (1989). Sex differences in psychosocial consequences of alcohol and drug use. *Journal of Health and Social Behavior, 30,* 117-130.

Rodgers, R. H. (1987). Postmarital family reorganization: A propositional theory. In D. Perlman & S. W. Duck (Eds.), *Intimate relationships: Development, dynamics, and deterioration* (pp. 239-268). Newbury Park, CA: Sage.

Rodin, M. (1982). Nonengagement, failure to engage and disengagement. In S. W. Duck (Ed.), *Personal relationships 4: Dissolving personal relationships* (pp. 31-50). London: Academic Press.

Rogers, L. E., & Millar, F. E. (1988). Relational communication. In S. W. Duck (Ed.), *Handbook of personal relationships* (pp. 289-306). New York: John Wiley.

Rolland, J. S. (1988). A conceptual model of chronic and life-threatening illness and its impact on families. In C. S. Chilman, E. W. Nunnally, & F. M. Cox (Eds.), *Chronic illness and disability* (pp. 17-68). Newbury Park, CA: Sage.

Rosenbaum, A., & O'Leary, K. (1981). Marital violence: Characteristics of abusive couples. *Journal of Consulting and Clinical Psychology, 49,* 63-71.

Rosenblatt, P. (1983). *Bitter, bitter tears.* Minneapolis: University of Minnesota Press.

Rosenfeld, S., & Lewis, D. (1993). The hidden effect of childhood sexual abuse on adolescent and young adult HIV prevention. *AIDS and Public Policy, 8,* 158-163.

Rosenstock, F., & Kutner, B. (1967). Alienation and family crisis. *Sociological Quarterly, 8,* 397-405.

Rossi, A., & Rossi, P. (1990). *Of human bonding: Parent-child relations across the life course.* New York: Aldine de Gruyter.

Rothman, E. (1984). *Hands and hearts: A history of courtship in America.* New York: Basic Books.

Rubin, L. (1983). *Intimate strangers: Men and women together.* New York: Harper.

Ruesch, J., & Bateson, G. (1951). *Communication: The social matrix of psychiatry*. New York: W. W. Norton.

Rusbult, C. E. (1987). Responses to dissatisfaction in close relationships: The exit-voice-loyalty-neglect model. In D. Perlman & S. W. Duck (Eds.), *Intimate relationships: Development, dynamics, and deterioration* (pp. 209-238). Newbury Park, CA: Sage.

Rusbult, C. E., & Buunk, A. P. (1993). Commitment processes in close relationships: An interdependence analysis. *Journal of Social and Personal Relationships, 10,* 175-203.

Russell, S. (1985). *Social implications of multiple sclerosis* (Final report of a formulation apart from the National Health Research and Development Program). Ottawa: Department of Health and Welfare Canada.

Sabourin, T., Infante, D., & Rudd, J. (1993). Verbal aggression in marriages: A comparison of violent, distressed, nonviolent, and nondistressed couples. *Human Communication Research, 20,* 245-267.

Salaman, E. (1970). *A collection of moments: A study of involuntary memories.* New York: St. Martin's.

Saposnek, D. (1983). *Mediating child custody disputes.* San Francisco: Jossey-Bass.

Sarch, A. (1993). Making the connection: Single women's use of the telephone in dating relationships with men. *Journal of Communication, 43,* 128-144.

Satariano, W. A., & Syme, S. L. (1981). Life changes and disease in elderly populations: Coping with change. In G. H. March (Ed.), *Aging: Biology and behavior* (pp. 311-328). New York: Academic Press.

Savage, J. A. (1989). *Mourning unlived lives: A psychological study of child-bearing loss.* Wilmette, IL: Chiron.

Schaef, A. W. (1986). *Codependence: Misdiagnosed—mistreated.* San Francisco: Harper & Row.

Schank, R., & Abelson, R. (1977). *Scripts, plans, goals, and understanding.* Hillsdale, NJ: Lawrence Erlbaum.

Scheff, T. J. (1987). The shame-rage spiral: A case study of an interminable quarrel. In H. B. Lewis (Ed.), *The role of shame in symptom formation.* Hillsdale, NJ: Lawrence Erlbaum.

Scheff, T. J. (1988). Shame and conformity: The deference emotion system. *American Journal of Sociology, 53,* 395-406.

Scheff, T. J. (1990). *Microsociology.* Chicago: University of Chicago Press.

Scheff, T. J., & Retzinger, S. M. (1991). *Emotions and violence: Shame-rage in destructive conflicts.* Lexington, MA: Lexington Books.

Schilit, R., Yong Lie, G., & Montagne, M. (1990). Substance use as a correlate of violence in intimate lesbian relationships. *Journal of Homosexuality, 19*(3), 51-65.

Schneider, C. (1977). *Shame, exposure and privacy.* Boston: Beacon.

Scott, M. B., & Lyman, S. M. (1968). Accounts. *American Sociological Review, 33,* 46-62.

Seibold, D. R., & Thomas, R. W. (1992, May). *College students' interpersonal influence processes in alcohol intervention situations: A critical review and reconceptualization.* Paper presented at the annual meeting of the International Communication Association, Miami, FL.

Seltzer, J. A. (1991). Relationships between fathers and children who live apart: The father's role after separation. *Journal of Marriage and the Family, 53,* 79-101.

Serovich, J. M., & Greene, K. (1993). Perceptions of family boundaries: The case of disclosure of HIV testing information. *Family Relations, 42,* 193-197.

Serovich, J. M., Greene, K., & Parrott, R. (1992). Boundaries and AIDS testing: Privacy and the family system. *Family Relations, 41,* 104-109.

Shainess, N. (1977). Psychological aspects of wife battering. In M. Roy (Ed.), *Battered women* (pp. 111-119). New York: Van Nostrand Reinhold.

Shapiro, J. P., Baumeister, R. F., & Kessler, J. W. (1991). A three-component model of children's teasing: Aggression, humor, and ambiguity. *Journal of Social and Clinical Psychology, 10,* 459-472.

Shoenewolf, G. (1991). *The art of hating.* New York: Random House.

Shotter, J. (1992). What is a "personal relationship"? A rhetorical-responsive account of "unfinished business." In J. H. Harvey, T. L. Orbuch, & A. L. Weber (Eds.), *Attributions, accounts and close relationships* (pp. 19-39). New York: Springer-Verlag.

Sillars, A. L., & Weisberg, J. (1987). Conflict as a social skill. In M. E. Roloff & G. R. Miller (Eds.), *Interpersonal processes: New directions in communication research* (pp. 140-171). Newbury Park, CA: Sage.

Simmel, G. (1950). *The sociology of Georg Simmel* (K. Wolff, Trans.). New York: Free Press.

Simmel, G. (1955). *Conflict and the web of group-affiliations.* New York: Free Press.

Smith, P. K., Bowers, L., Binney, V., & Cowie, H. (1993). Relationships of children involved in bully/victim problems at school. In S. W. Duck (Ed.), *Learning about relationships* (pp. 184-212). Newbury Park, CA: Sage.

Spann, L., & Fischer, J. L. (1990). Identifying codependency. *The Counselor, 8,* 27.

Spees, E. R. (1987). College students' sexual attitudes and behaviors, 1974-1985: A review of the literature. *Journal of College Student Personnel, 28,* 135-140.

Spitzack, C., & Carter, K. (1987). Women in communication studies: A typology for revision. *Quarterly Journal of Speech, 73,* 401-423.

Sprecher, S., & McKinney, K. (1993). *Sexuality.* Newbury Park, CA: Sage.

Stein, C. H. (1993). Felt obligation in adult family relationships. In S. W. Duck (Ed.), *Social context and relationships* (pp. 78-99). Newbury Park, CA: Sage.

Steinmetz, S. K. (1977). *The cycle of violence: Assertive, aggressive, and abusive family interaction.* New York: Praeger.

Stets, J. (1992). Interactive processes in dating aggression: A national study. *Journal of Marriage and the Family, 54,* 165-177.

Straus, M. A. (1979). Measuring intrafamily conflict and violence: The Conflict Tactics (CT) Scale. *Journal of Marriage and the Family, 41,* 75-88.

Straus, M. A., & Gelles, R. J. (1986). Societal change and change in family violence from 1975 to 1985 as revealed by two national surveys. *Journal of Marriage and Family, 48,* 465-479.

Straus, M. A., Gelles, R. J., & Steinmetz, S. K. (1980). *Behind closed doors: Violence in the American family.* Garden City, NY: Anchor/Doubleday.

Stroebe, M., Gergen, M., Gergen, K., & Stroebe, W. (1992). Broken hearts or broken bonds: Love and death in historical perspective. *American Psychologist, 47,* 1205-1212.

Stuart, R. B., & Braver, J. (1973). *Positive and negative exchanges between spouses and strangers.* Unpublished manuscript.

Sullivan, M. J. L., Mikail, S., & Weinshenker, B. (1992, October). *Marital dysfunction, depression, and multiple sclerosis.* Paper presented at the annual meeting of the Atlantic Rehabilitation Association, Halifax.

Sumner, W. (1906). *Folkways.* New York: Ginn.

Surra, C. A. (1987). Reasons for changes in commitment: Variations by courtship style. *Journal of Social and Personal Relationships, 4,* 17-33.

Tenenbaum, J. D. (1991). Legislation for stepfamilies: The Family Law Section Standing Committee report. *Family Law Quarterly, 25*(10), 137.

Tinsley, B., & Parke, R. (1987). Grandparents as interactive and social support agents for families with young infants. *International Journal of Aging and Human Development, 25,* 261-279.

Turner, C. F., Miller, H. G., & Moses, L. E. (1989). *AIDS: Sexual behavior and intravenous drug use.* Washington, DC: National Academy Press.

Uleman, J. S., & Bargh, J. A. (Eds.). (1989). *Unintended thought.* New York: Guilford.

Umberson, D., & Williams, C. L. (1993). Divorced fathers: Parental role strain and psychological distress. *Journal of Family Issues, 14,* 378-400.

van der Pligt, J., Otten, W., Richard, R., & van der Velde, F. (1993). Perceived risk of AIDS: Unrealistic optimism and self-protective action. In J. B. Pryor & G. D. Reeder (Eds.), *The social psychology of HIV infection* (pp. 39-58). Hillsdale, NJ: Lawrence Erlbaum.

van Wormer, K. (1989). Co-dependency: Implications for women and therapy. *Women and Therapy, 8,* 51-63.

Viorst, J. (1986). *Necessary losses.* New York: Fawcett.

Visher, E. B., & Visher, J. S. (1988). *Old loyalties, new ties: Therapeutic strategies with stepfamilies.* New York: Brunner/Mazel.

Volkan, V. D., & Zintl, E. (1993). *Life after loss.* New York: Scribner.

Walfish, S., Stenmark, D. E., Shealy, S. E., & Krone, A. M. (1992). MMPI profiles of women in codependency treatment. *Journal of Personality Assessment, 58*, 211-214.

Walker, L. E. A. (1984). *The battered woman syndrome*. New York: Springer.

Walker, M. C. (1992). Co-dependency and probation. *Federal Probation, 65*, 16-18.

Watzlawick, P., Beavin, J., & Jackson, D. (1967). *Pragmatics of human communication: A study of interaction patterns, pathologies, and paradoxes*. New York: W. W. Norton.

Weber, A. (1983, May). *The breakdown of relationships*. Paper presented at the Social Interaction and Relationships Conference, Nags Head, NC.

Webster, D. (1990). Women and depression (alias codependency). *Family and Community Health, 13*, 58-66.

Weenolsen, P. (1988). *Transcendence of loss over the life span*. New York: Hemisphere.

Wegner, D. M., & Schneider, D. J. (1989). Mental control: The war of the ghosts in the machine. In J. S. Uleman & J. A. Bargh (Eds.), *Unintended thought* (pp. 287-305). New York: Guilford.

Wegscheider, S. (1981). *Another chance: Hope and health for the alcoholic family*. Palo Alto, CA: Science & Behavior.

Weitzman, J., & Dreen, K. (1982). Wife beating: A view of the marital dyad. *Social Casework, 63*, 11-18.

Wellman, B., & Wellman, B. (1992). Domestic affairs and network relations. *Journal of Social and Personal Relationships, 9*, 385-409.

West, J. (1992). *Discursive practices and relations of power: A qualitative study of intimate violence*. Unpublished doctoral dissertation, University of Utah.

West, J. (1993). Ethnography and ideology: The politics of cultural representation. *Western Journal of Communication, 57*, 209-214.

Whitchurch, G., & Pace, J. (1993). Communication skills training and interspousal violence. *Journal of Applied Communication Research, 21*, 98-102.

Whitfield, C. L. (1989). Co-dependence: Our most common addiction. *Alcoholism Treatment Quarterly, 6*, 19-36.

Whitfield, C. L. (1991). *Codependence: Healing the human condition*. Deerfield Beach, FL: Health Communications.

Whitsett, D., & Land, H. (1992). The development of a role strain index for stepparents. *Families in Society, 73*, 14-22.

Wiesel, E. (1960). *Night*. New York: Bantam.

Wiggins, J. (1983). Family violence as a case of interpersonal aggression: A situational analysis. *Social Forces, 62*, 102-123.

Williams, E., Bissell, L., & Sullivan, E. (1991). The effects of codependence on physicians and nurses. *British Journal of Addiction, 86*, 37-42.

Williams, R. (1989). Base and superstructure in Marxist cultural theory. In R. Con Davis & R. Schleifer (Eds.), *Contemporary literary criticism* (pp. 378-390). New York: Longman.

Williams, S. S., Kimble, D. L., Covell, N. H., Weiss, L. H., Newton, K. J., Fisher, J. D., & Fisher, W. A. (1992). College students use implicit personality theory instead of safer sex. *Journal of Applied Social Psychology, 22,* 921-933.

Wiseman, J. P. (1970). *Stations of the lost: The treatment of skid row alcoholics.* Englewood Cliffs, NJ: Prentice Hall.

Wiseman, J. P. (1986). Friendship: Bonds and binds in a voluntary relationship. *Journal of Social and Personal Relationships, 3,* 191-211.

Wiseman, J. P. (1989, May). *Friends and enemies: Are they opposites?* Paper presented at the meeting of the International Network on Personal Relationships, Iowa City.

Wiseman, J. P. (1991). *The other half: Wives of alcoholics and their social-psychological adjustment.* New York: Aldine de Gruyter.

Women Against Abuse. (1992). *Domestic violence: Making the connections* [Fact sheet]. Philadelphia: Author.

Wood, J. T. (1982). Communication and relational culture: Bases for the study of human relationships. *Communication Quarterly, 30,* 75-83.

Wood, J. T. (1993a). Enlarging conceptual boundaries: A critique of research in interpersonal communication. In S. P. Bowen & N. Wyatt (Eds.), *Transforming visions: Feminist critiques in communication studies* (pp. 19-49). Cresskill, NJ: Hampton.

Wood, J. T. (1993b). *Gendered lives: Communication, gender and culture.* Pacific Grove, CA: Wadsworth.

Wood, J. T. (1994). *Who cares? Women, care and culture.* Carbondale: Southern Illinois University Press.

Wood, J. T. (1995a). Feminist scholarship and research on relationships. *Journal of Social and Personal Relationships, 12*(1).

Wood, J. T. (1995b). *Relational communication: Change and continuity in personal relationships.* Belmont, CA: Wadsworth.

Wood, J. T., Dendy, L. L., Dordek, E., Germany, M., & Varallo, S. M. (1994). Dialectic of difference: A thematic analysis of intimates' meanings for difference. In K. Carter & M. Presnell (Eds.), *Interpretive approaches to interpersonal communication* (pp. 115-136). New York: State University of New York Press.

Woodhouse, L. (1989, November 17). *Women with jagged edges: Voices from the culture of substance abuse.* Paper presented at the annual meeting of the American Anthropological Association, Washington, DC.

Wortman, C. B., & Silver, R. C. (1992). Reconsidering assumptions about coping with loss: An overview of current research. In L. Montada, S. Filipp, & M. J. Lerner (Eds.), *Life crises and experiences of loss in adulthood* (pp. 341-365). Hillsdale, NJ: Lawrence Erlbaum.

Wright, B. (1983). *Physical disability: A psycho-social approach.* New York: Harper & Row.

Wright, P. H. (1985). The acquaintance description form. In S. W. Duck & D. Perlman (Eds.), *Understanding personal relationships: An interdisciplinary approach* (pp. 39-62). London: Sage.

Wright, P. H., & Wright, K. D. (1990). Measuring codependents' close relationships: A preliminary study. *Journal of Substance Abuse, 2,* 335-344.

Wright, P. H., & Wright, K. D. (1991). Codependency: Addictive love, adjustive relating, or both? *Contemporary Family Therapy, 13,* 435-454.

Wurmser, L. (1981). *Mask of shame.* Baltimore: Johns Hopkins University Press.

Yllö, K. (1984). The status of women, marital equality and violence against wives. *Journal of Comparative Family Studies, 14,* 67-86.

Yllö, K. (1988). Political and methodological debates in wife abuse research. In K. Yllö & M. Bograd (Eds.), *Feminist perspectives on wife abuse* (pp. 28-50). Newbury Park, CA: Sage.

Zill, N. (1988). Behavior, achievement, and health problems among children in stepfamilies: Findings from a national survey of child health. In E. M. Hetherington & J. Arasteh (Eds.), *The impact of divorce, single parenting, and stepparenting on children* (pp. 325-368). Hillsdale, NJ: Lawrence Erlbaum.

Author Index

Subject Index

About the Contributors

Melanie K. Barnes is Assistant Professor of Communication Studies at DePauw University. She has an M.S. from Illinois State University and is in the process of finishing her doctoral dissertation at the University of Iowa. Her research interests lie in the area of relational communication and include the role of supportive communication in grief and loss, the social construction of close relationships, and language and discourse in everyday contexts.

Sheryl Perlmutter Bowen is Assistant Professor of Communication Arts at Villanova University. She studies sensitive health communication processes, including personal relationships and AIDS discourse, and culturally sensitive HIV education for college students, African Americans, and women. She is coeditor of *Transforming Visions: Feminist Critiques in Communication Studies* (1993).

Heather R. Carlson is a graduate student in the Community Counseling Program at Loyola University and Director of Research for Controlled Resources, Inc., in Chicago. She received a B.A. from the University of Iowa. Her research and counseling activities have focused on grief, eating disorders, and life skills training.

Marilyn Coleman, Ed.D., is Professor and former Chair of Human Development and Family Studies at the University of Missouri. She received an M.S. in child development from the University of Missouri and a doctorate in special education from the University of Missouri. Since 1969, she has been a member of the faculty of the University of Missouri, where she currently teaches courses on marriage and divorce, the changing American family, and remarriage and stepparenting. She is editor of the *Journal of Marriage and the Family* and also serves or has served on the editorial boards of several other journals, including *Family Relations, Journal of Family Issues,* and *Lifestyles: Family and Economic Issues.* She has authored or coauthored three books as well as numerous study guides, book chapters, and journal articles. She has won awards for research and leadership from the American Home Economics Association, and the University of Missouri has honored her with several research and teaching awards. Her research interests are in the areas of remarriage and stepparenting, love, sex roles, and family structure stereotypes.

Steve Duck is currently the Daniel and Amy Starch Research Professor at the University of Iowa, Iowa City. He is the founding editor of the *Journal of Social and Personal Relationships,* and editor or author of more than 25 books on personal relationships. He is the founder of the International Network on Personal Relationships, the professional organization for the field, and has established two series of international conferences on relationships.

Lawrence H. Ganong, Ph.D., is Professor of Nursing and Human Development and Family Studies in the College of Human Environmental Sciences at the University of Missouri in Columbia. He received an M.S. in family studies from Kansas State University, an M.Ed. in counseling psychology from the University of Missouri, and a Ph.D. in family studies from the University of Missouri. He held a faculty position at Central Missouri State University prior to joining the University of Missouri faculty in 1980. He teaches courses in family dynamics and intervention, theories of human development, and research methods, and also regularly teaches a graduate course on remarriage and stepparenting with Marilyn Coleman. He serves or has served on the editorial boards of several professional journals, including the *Journal of Marriage and the Family, Family Relations,* and the *Journal of Family Issues.* He has authored or coauthored two books, a study guide, and approximately 100 articles in professional and popular publications. His two primary research interests are remarriage and stepparenting, and family-related stereotypes, although he has also done research on sex roles, love, and parent education.

Jeffrey Haig received his B.A. from Hobart College and his M.A. from Antioch University in Seattle. He worked as a therapist in Seattle before relocating to Iowa City. His research focus is on grief and loss.

John H. Harvey is a Psychology Professor at the University of Iowa. He is coeditor, with Ickes and Kidd, of the three-volume *New Directions in Attribution Research* (1976, 1978, 1981) and, with Weber, of *Perspectives on Close Relationships* (1994). He is coauthor, with Kelley and associates, of *Close Relationships* (1983) and author of the forthcoming *Odyssey of the Heart: Closeness, Intimacy, and Love.*

Renee F. Lyons, Ph.D., is Associate Professor and Graduate Coordinator in the School of Recreation, Physical and Health Education, at Dalhousie University in Halifax, Nova Scotia. She received her master's degree in counseling psychology from Xavier University in Cincinnati and her doctorate in leisure studies (lifestyle adjustment and disability) from the University of Oregon. Her research interests concern coping and adjustment in chronic illness and disability, particularly the clarification of relational issues and adaptational strategies.

Darlene Meade is a graduate student in health education at Dalhousie University in Halifax, Nova Scotia. She is interested in how women's social relationships influence personal identity and well-being. She is also interested in the use of qualitative, participatory research methods. She and her husband operate a mussel farm in a small seaside village in Nova Scotia.

Paula Michal-Johnson is Associate Professor of Communication Arts at Villanova University. Her research into sensitive health communication processes involves personal relationships and AIDS discourse, culturally sensitive HIV education, and disclosure of HIV in home health care.

Suzanne M. Retzinger, Ph.D., is the author of articles on conflict, mediation, emotions, and mental illnesses. She has worked in the area of conflict and conflict resolution for the past 12 years and is the author of *Violent Emotions: Shame and Rage in Marital Quarrels* (1991) and coauthor, with T. J. Scheff, of *Emotions and Violence: Shame and Rage in Destructive Conflicts* (1991). She is currently a family relations mediator with the superior courts in California.

James T. West teaches classes in the Department of Communication at the University of Hawaii. He received his Ph.D. in communication from the University of Utah in 1992, and his dissertation, on violence between intimates, received the national Speech Communication Association's 1992 Dissertation of the Year Award. He is also President of Quintessential Writing, Inc., which produces interactive CD-ROMs on organizational communication, quality service, and customer satisfaction.

Jacqueline P. Wiseman, Professor Emeritus of Sociology at the University of California, San Diego, has been a Visiting Professor at Yale, Dartmouth, and the University of Helsinki. She won the C. Wright Mills Award from the Society for the Study of Social Problems for her monograph, *Stations of the Lost*. She also was awarded the George Herbert Mead Award by the Society for the Study of Symbolic Interaction for distinguished career research contributions. She has served as a member of the National Academy of Sciences Panel on Alcohol Policies, the governing councils of the American Sociological Association, the Pacific Sociological Association, the National Council on Family Relations, and the Groves Family Conference as well as president of the Society for the Study of Social Problems.

Julia T. Wood is Nelson R. Hairston Distinguished Professor of Communication Studies at the University of North Carolina at Chapel Hill, where she teaches and conducts research on personal relationships and gender, communication, and culture. Within those areas she has written or coauthored eight books, coedited four others, and published more than 60 articles and chapters in books. She is cofounder of the National Conference on Research on Gender and Communication.

Katherine D. Wright, a licensed professional counselor and licensed addiction counselor, maintains a private practice in Grand Forks, North Dakota. She received a Ph.D. in counseling from the University of North Dakota in 1975.

Paul H. Wright, Professor of Psychology at the University of North Dakota, received a Ph.D. in social psychology from the University of Kansas in 1963. His research speciality is personal relationships.